HISTORY OF ISLAMIC EDUCATION IN INDIA AND

NADVAT UL-'ULAMĀ'

Dr. Ghazanfar Ali Khan

KITAB BHAVAN
NEW DELHI-110002 (INDIA)

Kitab Bhavan
Publishers, Distributors, Exporters & Importers
1784, Kalan Mahal, Darya Ganj
New Delhi-110002 (India)

Phone : (91-11) 3277392/93, 3274686
Web Site : www.kitabbhavan.com
E-mail : nasri@vsnl.com
Fax : (91-11) 3263383

Ist Edition : 2004

ISBN : 81-7151-347-6

Laser Typesetting at:
Laser Track
Darya Ganj, New Delhi-2

Published in India by:
Nusrat Ali Nasri for Kitab Bhavan
1784, Kalan Mahal, Darya Ganj
New Delhi-110002 [India]

Printed in India at:
Nice Printing Press
Khureji Khas, Delhi-110051

CONTENTS

Transliteration Table

ا	A, a	ژ	Z , z	ں	Ṇ, ṇ.
ب	B,b	س	S,s	و	W/V,w/v
پ	P,p	ش	SH,sh	ہ	H,h
ت	T,t	ص	Ṣ,ṣ.	ء	ʾ
ٹ	T,t	ض	Ḍ,ḍ.	ی	Y,y
ث	TH,th	ط	Ṭ,ṭ.	بھ	BH,bh
ج	J,j	ظ	Ẓ,ẓ.	پھ	PH,ph
چ	CH,ch	ع	ʿ	تھ	TH,th
ح	Ḥ,ḥ	غ	GH,gh	ٹھ	TH,th
خ	KH,kh	ف	F,f	جھ	JH,jh
د	D,d	ق	Q,q	چھ	CH,ch
ڈ	D,d	ک	K,k	دھ	DH,dh
ذ	DH,dh	گ	G,g	ڈھ	DH,dh.
ر	R,r	ل	L,l	ڑھ	RH,rh
ڑ	Ṛ ,ṛ.	م	M,m	کھ	KH,kh
ز	Ẓ, ẓ	ن	N,n	گھ	GH,gh

Long Vowels

ا	َ	Â, ã
ی	ِ	Î,î
و	ُ	Û,û
و	_	Ô,ô (Ko, Do)
ے	_	E,e (Ke, Se)

Short Vowels

A,a
I,i
U,u

Dipthongs

َ و AU, au Arabic (Maulana)
َ و AW, aw Persian/Urdu (naw, nawkar)
َ ی / ے AI, ai (Shaikh)

ۃ In Pause form-AH, ah (ندوة)
ۃ In Construct form-AT, at (ندوة العلماء)
ال (al) In Construct form = Abu'l (ابوالحسن)

Doubled

ُوّ UWWA, uwwa
ِیّ IYYI,iyyi

Main Gate of Dãr-ul- ‘Ulûm Nadvat-ul- ‘Ulamã’

Main Building of Dãr-ul- ‘Ulûm Nadvat-ul- ‘Ulamã’

Library of Dãr-ul- 'Ulûm Nadvat-ul- 'Ulamã'

Mosque of Dãr-ul- ‘Ulûm Nadvat-ul- ‘Ulamã’

Publication Division of Dãr-ul- 'Ulûm Nadvat-ul- 'Ulamã'

ACKNOWLEDGEMENT

All praise be to Allãh, the Almighty Creator and Sustainer of the worlds, Who made it possible for me to accomplish a task which was quite beyond my ability and powers.

I express my hearty thanks and sincere gratitude to my supervisor *Dr. M.'Azam Qasmi*, Reader, Department of Islamic Studies, A.M.U. Aligarh, for his benevolent guidance, inspiring attitude, sympathetic behaviour, keen interest and devotion throughout the tenure of this work. Without his whole hearted cooperation, it would have been rather impossible to complete the present work.

I am also indebted to Prof. 'Abd ul-'Ali Chairman, Department of Islamic Studies, A.M.U. for his moral and academic encouragements and for providing the necessary facilities. Prof Kabir Aḥmad Jaisi, former Chairman, Department of Islamic Studies, A.M.U. must also be thanked for his invaluable suggestions and encouragements. I am also thankful to Prof. Azdud-Din Khan and Prof. M. Salim Kidwai, both former Chairmen, Department of Islamic Studies, A.M.U. and other teachers of this department especially Dr. Syed Aḥsan, Dr. Ẓafar ul-Isalm, Dr. Ahsan ul-Ḥaq, Dr. Syed Sibte Ḥasan for their kind cooperation and all the helps they extended to me when I was in need of it.

I am also thankful to my friends and fellow scholars,

viz. Dr. Adam Malik Khan, Mr. Tauqir Aḥmad, Dr. Bilal Aḥmad Kutty, Mr. 'Aijaz Aḥmad, Mr. Pervez Ahmad, Mr. Imtiyaz ul-Huda, Mr. Sarfaraz Khan, Mr. Moḥd. Ikram-ullãh Khan, Mr. Mohd Iftikhar, Mr. S.M. 'Arif, Mr. Tariq Anwar, Mr. Muzammil Ḥaq Khan. My special thanks are also due to Mr. Zubair Shadab Khan for writing the name of books in Urdu.

The cooperation of my mother, father, wife-Afsana, brother-Mazhar Ali Khan and Sisters-Zahida and Rashida cannot be overlooked as they made it possible for me to devote to my work with full time and concentration.

The more painstaking part of this research-work has been greatly facilitated by the help and cooperation of the library staff of the Department of Islamic Studies, A.M.U., library of Nadvat ul-'Ulamã, Lucknow and Jamia Millia Islamia, New Delhi. My special thanks are due to Mr. Kabir Aḥmad Khan, Department of Islamic Studies, A.M.U., and Maulana Zahid, Nadvat ul-'Ulamã, both being assistant librarian, who whole-heartedly supplied to me the necessary materials whenever needed.

It is difficult to find the right words with which I can express my indebtedness to the Office-Staff, Department of Islamic Studies, A.M.U., Mr. Zakir 'Ali Beg, Mr. Ubaid ur-Raḥman, Mr. Salim and Mr. Islam for their continuous cooperation.

No less are my thanks due to Mr. Taufiq Aḥmad Khan for his kind help in assiduously typing this thesis, and that too in a short period by dedicating his time till late night hours.

(Ghazanfar 'Ali Khan)
Department of Islamic Studies
Aligarh Muslim Universtity
Aligarh (India)

FOREWORD

1857 was the turning point for the Indians especially for the Muslims. They were enjoying upper hand in the society but now their position was weakened and they suddenly found themselves nowhere. When they came out of the shocks of the time they realised their pitiable condition. The worst was in the field of education. Some very sincere efforts were made in this field by those who knew that with the change of the time and in fastly developing conditions of the world it would not be possible for anyone to stand on his own foot without proper education and modern know how. Those who were very religious in their thoughts considered that the religious education has to be given the utmost priority and religious institutions are to be opened to help improve those detoriating conditions. The others who were minutely observing the changes in all the spheres of life in the world thought that only religious education will not get them any place in the fastly changing world scenario. They were of the opinion that modern education especially the knowledge and learning of English, which has become the need of the time, will the most beneficial way to compete the challenges of the time.

Those belonging to the first category established Darul-uloom Deoband and formulated a syllabus strictly based on religious studies or so-called Darse-Nizamia. They did not include any modern educational system and more so they thought that it will take Muslim society far away from the religion.

The other who were in favour of Modern education and were keeping an eye on the future were strictly of the opinion that modern education is the only remedy of the worsening and decaying conditions of the Muslims. Sir Syed Ahmad Khan who was the pioneer of this thought has already observed the slight of the Muslims. He was very farsighted and had decided to venture in the field of education to upgrade and men. He was of the firm opinion that all the ills among the Muslims are due to lack of education. He was closely following the changing trends of the society and also of the pattern of education while he was close to the English people. He was not against religious education as some Ulama blamed him. But in his view English and modern education was the only way to face the challenges of life and the role of religion in this regard was to check and keep ones faith in religion and religious activities intact. In this opinion there was no conflict between modern education and religion or religious studies. To fulfill his ideas first he opened a school named Madarsatul-uloom which became Mohammadan Anglo Oriental College later on (and Aligarh Muslim University afterwards).

A number of Ulama did not agree with Sir Syed's revolutionary ideas. They feared that if he succeeds the religion may be marginalised in his curriculum. They were also not fully satisfied with the pattern of education at Deoband. They believed that traditional as well as modern education are to be plugged together and should be studies side by side. They agreed upon the need of immediate change in the syllabai of the *madaris* and also resolved to form an institution where the updated curriculum be implemented. Among them were Maulana Mohammad Ali Mongeri, Allama Shibli Nomani, Maulana Shah Sulaiman Phulwarvi, Maulana Mahmud Hasan, Habibur Rehman Khan Sherwani etc. They formally met in Kanpur in 1892 and decided to form an organisation with the name of Nadwatul ulama. The objectives were to make changes in the prevalent system of education and include history, philosophy, economics etc to make it more useful and relevant.

In the beginning efforts were made to introduce the changes, but this could not be done as per needs of the time. The orthodox religious group never allowed the moderate people to introduce much required subjects. But this effort atleast kindled a ray of hope and many people thought that one or the other day Nadwah may fulfill the dreams of the founders.

Though Nadwah did not produce great modern scholars in scientific fields, but it did produce the historians of world repute, the best Urdu writers and scholars and a number of Islamicist who earned name and fame in the world to name a few are Allama Syed Sulaiman Nadvi, Maulana Abdus Salam Nadvi, Maulana Abul Hasanat Nadvi, Shah Moinuddin Nadvi, Maulana Najeeb Ashraf Nadvi, Maulana Riyasat Ali Nadvi, Rais Ahmad Nadvi, Maulana Abdus Salam Kidwai Nadvi, Maulana Imran Khan Nadvi, Maulana Abullaith Nadvi, Maulana Masood Ali etc. Nadwah also produced the greatest religious and literary figure of the modern time Maulana Syed Abul Hasan Ali Nadvi, the gem of Nadwah whose everlasting glow will keep Nadwah shinning. He was unparalleled in his character and achievements. The present Nadwah is the symbol of his love to humanity and learning. His towering personality will always be remembered for his selfless and continued services and endeavours for the development and progress of Nadwah.

Dr. Ghazanfar Ali Khan is a young modern energetic scholar who chose Nadvatululama as his Ph.D. topic. Now he has revised it for the publication in a book form. He has worked hard and tried very successfully to present an authentic document well-equipped references and proofs. I think this is the first time that a critical analysis of the aims, objectives and achievements of Nadwaha are made and presented in English. I hope this will help many people of the world to learn and understand the history of this great institution of Islamic learning.

Prof. M. Salim Kidwai
Ex. Chairman,
Department of Islamic Studies
A.M.U., Aligarh.
Ex. Director,
Institute of Islamic Studies
A.M.U. Aligarh.
Samina Lodge
Sir Sayed Nagar
Aligarh-202001.

1st Feb. 2004

PREFACE

After re-establishing their rule, the Europeans started a policy of persecution against the Indian Muslims because they feared and considered the Muslims as exclusively for what they called the Mutiny of 1857. This policy of continuing persecution by the British ruined the Indian Muslim society, giving rise to a general feeling of helplessness. In this situation of gloom, some farsighted Muslims stood up and took certain steps to restore their self-esteem and preseve their religious identity. Maulana Qãsim Nãnautavi founded Dãr ul-'Ulûm Deoband in 1866 for Islamic education on traditional pattern. Dãr ul-'Ulûm Deoband followed, more or less, *Dars-e Niẓãmi* and did not include modern or Western education in its courses of studies. It was a syllabus meant for the teaching of *Qur'ãn, ḥadîth, tafsîr, fiqh* and *'aqã'id*. Sir Syed Aḥmad Khan, on the other hand, founded M.A.O. College in 1875 at Aligarh and adopted Western arts and sciences. This emphasis on purely religious or totally modern education left between the two educational goals, a widening gap. In fact Nadvat ul-'Ulamã' was established mainly to fill this gap. It aimed at reforming the syllabi of *madãris-e Islãmiya* and striving to lessen the differences among Muslim sects and groups. Soon the fame and reputation of Dãr ul-'Ulûm Nadvat ul-'Ulamã' outshone many Islamic seminaries. It came to be considered next only to Dãr ul-'Ulûm Deoband in the whole of the sub-continent.

The influence of Dãr ul-'Ulûm Nadvat ul-'Ulamã' in the teaching of Arabic language and literature has been very remarkable. The contributions of its graduates particularly in the field of biography and Islamic history are a hallmark of Nadvah. Its scholars are scattered all over the world and have been playing a very conspicuous role in the dissemination of Islamic teachings and values.

The introductory part of this study focuses in detail on the impotance of education in the light of *Qur'ãn* and *ḥadîth* and the history of *madrasãs* and its development with special reference to Saltanat and Mughal period in India. Courses of studies of the *madrasâs* and the reasons of downfall of the *madrasãs* have also been discussed.

In the first chapter, conditions of the Muslim Community in India during 19th century in respect of education have been described at lenght. It highlights the resolutions and policies of the British regarding education. Muslim responses to Western education, social, political, educational and economic condition of the Muslims in the post-1857 period and role of

Maulana Qãsim Nãnautavi, Sir Syed Aḥmad Khan and 'Allãmah Shibli No'mãni in the upliftment of the Muslim Community.

Chapter two is related to the establishment of Dãr ul-'Ulûm Nadvat ul-'Ulamã' and the causes which required the need of urgent attention. The Chapter deals at length with the objectives of Nadvah, outline of the prosposed Dãr ul-'Ulûm, relations between government and Nadvat ul-'Ulamã' and the foundation ceremony of the institution.

In chapter three the first and foremost objective of Nadvah, i.e. to reform and update the subjects and courses of studies has been discussed in detail. The chapter elaborates Shibli's views regarding the curriculum, characteristics of *Dars-e Niẓãmi,* Shãh Wali-ullãh's contirbution to education, Maulana Mongeri's *Musavvedah-e Niṣãb-e `Arabi*, opening of *Darjah-e Takmîl* and the revision and division of the course of stuides.

Chapter four has been divided into two parts. Part first focuses on the lives and contributions of the founders members of Nadvah. Second part highlights the lives and works of the renowned scholars of Nadvah.

INTRODUCTION

1. (A) Qur'ãnic Verses Regarding Dissemination of Education

Iqrã' the first word of the first revelation of the Holy *Qur'ãn*, which means 'Read' or 'Recite' or 'Rehearse' or 'Proclaim aloud' points to the direction, Islam wants for its adherents. It is a direct commandment for the acquisition of knowledge. While writing the commentary of *Surah 'Alaq* (XCVI: 1-5) 'Allãmah Zamakhshri (d. 1144) lays down the importance of education in Islam in the following words:

> "God taught human beings that which they did not know, and this testifieth to the greatness of his beneficence, for He has given to His Servants the knowledge of that which they did not know. And He hath brought them out of darkness of ignorance to the light of knowledge, and made them aware of the inestimable blessings of the knowledge of writing, for great benefits accrue therefrom which God alone compasseth; and

> without the knowledge of writing no other knowledge (*'ulûm*) could be comprehended, nor the sciences placed within bounds, nor the history of the ancients be acquired and their sayings be recorded, nor the revealed books be written; and if that knowledge did not exist, the affairs of religion and the world could not be regulated."[1]

The commandment of *Iqrã'* addresses here not only to the Prophet Muḥammad (S.A.W.) who was un-lettered but also provides a universal direction. The attitude of *Qur'ãn* to knowledge and its acquisition is very positive and emphatic. Time and again, it declares that to acquire knowledge for understanding the Creator's greatness whenever and whatever is possible is a human duty. In the following lines, there are some Qur'ãnic verses which reflect the importance of education;

(i) "My Lord ! Increase me in knowledge." (XX: 114)

(ii) "He hath taught him utterance" (LV: 4).

(iii) "Allãh will exalt those who believe among you, and those who have knowledge to high ranks" (LVIII: 11).

(iv) "Even as We have sent unto you a messenger from among you who reciteth

1. Syed 'Amir 'Ali, *The Spirit of Islam,* Calcutta, 1902, P. 332.

unto you Our revelations and causeth you to grow, and teacheth you the Scripture and wisdom, and teacheth you that which ye knew not." (II:51)

(v) "And Allãh gave him the kindgom and wisdom, and taught him of what which He willeth" (II:251)

Qur'ãn emphasises, as many as 750 times, regarding the acquisition of knowledge directly or indirectly through various words like contemplating, understanding, thinking, reading, writing, being knowledgable, reasoning etc.

(B) Muḥammad's (S.A.W.) Sayings:-

Muḥammad (S.A.W.) himself urged the people to acquire knowledge by all means. His orders, encouragements, inducements and prohibitions reflect the importance of knowledge (*'ilm*). He says,

> "If any one travels on a road in search of knowledge, Allãh will cause him to travel on one of the roads of Paradise, the angels will lower wings form good pleasure with one who seeks knowledge, and the inhabitants of the heavens and the earth and fish in the depth of the water will ask forgiveness for the learned man. The superiority of the learned man over the devout is like that of the moon

on the night when it is full over the rest of the stars. The learned are the heirs of the prophets and prophets leave neither *dinãr* nor *dirhams*, leaving only knowledge, and he who takes it takes an abundant portion."[2]

The Prophet (S.A.W.) directed the believers,

"Acquisition of knowledge is incumbent upon all the faithful, men as well as women.",[3] "Whosoever goes out in search of knowledge is in the path of Allãh till he returns",[4] "Whosoever searches after knowledge it will be expiation for his past sin",[5] "*Ulamã*' are the successors of Prophets",[6] "Acquire knowledge and teach the people"[7] "A learned man is a trust of God on earth."[8]

---

2. *Sunan-e Abu Dãu'd,* Vol. III. Eng. tr. Aḥmad Ḥasan, Al-Madinah Publications, New Delhi. 1985, P. 1034. Also in *Sunan-e Ibn Mãjãh*, Vol. I, Urdu tr. 'Abd ul-Ḥakîm Khan Akhtar Shãhjahanpuri. New Delhi. 2nd ed. 1990. P. 95. And *Jãme' Tirmidhî*, vol.2, Urdu tr. Badî' uz-Zamãn. Delhi. 1983. P. 244.
3. *Sunan-e Ibn Mãjãh*, vol. I, Op. Cit., P. 95.
4. *Jãme' Tirmidhî*. Op. Cit., P. 222.
5. Ibid., P. 222.
6. Ibid., P. 244.
7. *Sunan-e Dãrimi*, Urdu tr. Muḥammad Sa'îd, Matba' Sa'îdî, Karachi, n.d., P. 88.
8. Abu Ḥamîd al-Ghazali, *Iḥyã' 'Ulûm ud-Dîn*, vol. I, Eng. tr. Maulana Fazlul Karim, Kitab Bhavan, New Delhi, 1982, P. 16.

Muḥammad (S.A.W.) says that the seekers of knowledge are placed above the martyrs as well as worshipers;

> "The ink of the learned will be weighed against the blood of martyrs on the Resurrection Day",[9] "The superiority of Prophets over '*ulamā*' are two degree and the superiority of '*ulamā*' over *shuhada* is one degree",[10] "To be present in an assembly of a learned man is better than visiting one thousand sickmen and attending one thousand funerals.",[11] "If a believer hears a good advice and then translate it into action, it is better than his worship for one year",[12] "There are differences of one hundred degrees between a worshiper and a learned man."[13]

Further, the Prophet (S.A.W.) says that best gift for the children (son and daughter) of a guardian is the proper arrangement of good education and training. According to him.

> "No present or gift of a parent, out of all the gifts and presents to a child, is

---

9. Ibid., P. 16.
10. Ibn 'Abd ul-Bar, *al 'Ilm wal 'Ulamā'*, Urdu tr. 'Abd ur-Razzāq Malihābādi, Nadwat ul-Muṣannefin, Delhi, 1953, P. 55
11. Al-Ghazāli, Op. Cit., P. 20.
12. Ibid., P. 23.
13. Ibid., P. 17.

> superior to a good liberal education", "that man gives a liberal education to his child, is better for him than that he gives a large measure of corn in alms."[14]

Not only this, Muḥammad (S.A.W.) forgave the literate captives of the Battle of Badr on the condition that each would teach twelve unlettered Muslims.[15]

(C) *Ṣaḥãbah's* Efforts :-

Besides *Qur'ãn* and *ḥadith, ṣaḥãbah* also encouraged and took interest in the dissemination of education. *Ḥaḍrat* 'Ali about whom Muḥammad (S.A.W.) says, "I am the city of learning, 'Ali is its gate",[16] also emphasized the importance of learning. His ardent love for knowledge is evident from his poetry;

> "Glory is due to none other than to the learned.
> Guided are they and proofs to the seekers of guidence.
> Every body is honoured proportionate to his knowledge.
> But the illeterate and disgraced as enemies of the learned.

14. Mirza Abu'l Faḍl, *Sayings of the Prophet Muḥammad*, Reform Society, Allahabad, 1924, P. 47.
15. Muḥammad Tahir, *Encyclopaedic survey of Islamic Culture*, vol. III, Anmol Publications, New Delhi, 1974, P.94.
16. Syed 'Amir 'Ali, Op. Cit., P. 333. Also in Zafar 'Âlam, *Education in Early Islamic Period*, Markazi Matba' Islami, Delhi, 1991, P.68.

> Acquire knowledge, you will be immortal.
> All men are dead, only the learned are alive."[17]

Once *Ḥaḍrat* 'Ali advised to his student Kãmil as follows:

> "O Kãmil, knowledge is better than wealth. Knowledge guards you but you are guarding wealth. Knowledge dispenses justice while wealth seeks justice. Wealth decreases with expense while knowledge increases with expense."[18]

Ḥaḍrat 'Umar said,

> "Who pray all the nights and fast all the days is lesser calamity than the death of one learned man who is versed in lawful and unlawful things of God"[19]

Ḥaḍrat 'Abd-ullãh ibn 'Abbãs emphasized the value of scholars,

> "If a man teaches good to the people, every thing seeks forgiveness for him, even the fishes of the sea"[20], "to discuss about learning in a portion of night is

---

17. Al-Ghazãli, Op. Cit., P. 18.
18. Ibid., PP. 17-18.
19. Ibid., P. 21.
20. Ibid., P. 24.

dearer to me than to keep up awake throughout the night in prayer"[21]

The same views had been given by *Ḥaḍrat* Abu Hurayrah, *Ḥaḍrat* Abu Dardã, *Ḥaḍrat* 'Abd-ullãh ibn Mas'ûd etc.

(D) Mosques - As *Madrasãh* :-

Qur'ãnic directives, Prophetic sayings and *ṣaḥãhbah's* encouragement to education led the Muslims from the very beginning to take interest in the acquisition and dissemination of learning and education. During the time of Muḥammad (S.A.W.), some *ṣahãbahs* used to stay on a platform, called *ṣuffah*, in the mosque of the Prophet (S.A.W.), in front of the Prophet's (S.A.W.) house, and learnt *Qur'ãn*, *ḥadîth* and their meanings. The mosque was not only a place of worship but also a centre of education. Infact, this mosque of the Prophet (S.A.W.) served as the first model of a mosque-*madrasãh* for later mosques. *Ḥaḍrat* 'Umar sent seventeen teachers of the *Qur'ãn* in every province of Muslim territory and the people attended their lectures in the mosques.[22]

As the time passed, the preachers and teachers were seen scattered all over the conquered lands. So we find that in the third century of *hijrah* all the mosques were firstly the places of worship and

21. Ibid., P. 19.
22. Muḥammad Ṭãhir, Op. Cit., P.1.

secondly the seats of learning. In this regard J. Paderson writes,

> "In the beginning, mosques were an asylum for all branches of Islamic sciences. This was the meeting place of all learned men, the place of devotion and study, of working and discussion."[23]

It is said that Niẓãm ul-Mulk Tûsi (456/1063-480/1087) a Saljûq vizir, was the first who founded an independent *madrasãh*. But this claim was rejected by the historians al-Maqrizi and as-Suyûti on the basis of earlier examples of Muslim Spain. Besides mosques, a separate academy, *Baitul-Hikmah*, was founded by Caliph Mãmûn in 830 AD, at Baghdad with a library, astronomical observatory and hostels for scholars attached to it. Likewise, several other academies were founded later by caliphs, scholars and rich people, e.g. *Khazînat ul-Ḥikmah* of 'Ali bin Yaḥyã (d. 275/888), *Dãr ul-'Ilm* of Musa Jã'far bin Muḥammad (d. 323. 934). *Khazînat ul-Kutub* of Aḍd ud-Daulah (d. 367/977), *Dãr ul- Ḥikmah* of al-Ḥakîm (d.1005), the Fitimid ruler of Egypt etc.[24] These seats of learning were called *madrasãs*.

From the very early time, *madrasãs* were attached to mosques or mosques were being used as *madrasãs*. Usually, the term *madrasãs* is applied where the

---

23. Ibid., P. 4.
24. Ibid., P. 4

teachings of *Qur'ãn* and *ḥadith* are imparted. Apart from mosque, frequently such buildings as *ribãt*, *khãnqãh*, massauleums, *dãirah* etc also fulfilled the purpose of *madrasãs*.[25]

2. *Madrasãs* of India

(A) Saltanat Period

(i) Ghaznavids :- As regard the *madrasãs* of India, Muslim traders and merchants came here long before the Muslim conquest and settled in coastal areas of India. They built mosques and small *maktabs* (for their children) but no record is available for their evidence. In India, Sindh was conquered in 712 AD by Muḥammad bin Qãsim and about three centuries later Punjab was also subjugated by Maḥmûd Ghaznavi who came here in 1001AD. He was much interested in the furtherence of education and patronized scholars and poets. But his seat of rule was Ghaznah (Afghanistan). His son and successor Mas'ûd was too a great patron of learning. Both established many schools and colleges in their Kingdom. The former founded a *madrasãh* at Ghaznah, a big library and a museum were also attached to it where 'Unsûri (a famous Persian poet) had been appointed as a teacher.[26]

---

25. *The Oxford Encyclopaedia of the Modern Islamic World, vol.* III, ed. Jhon. L. Esposito, Oxford University Press. New York. 1995, P. 13.
26. N.N. Law. *Promotion of Learning in India*, Idarah-i Adbiyat-i Delli, Delhi, 1973, P.5. Also in 'Aziz Aḥmad, *An Intellectual History of Islam in India*, Edinburg, 1969, P. 52.

Moreover, the latter constructed many independent buildings for schools and colleges and made arrangements for their expenses and maintenance. As a result of his encouragement to scholarship, many scholars of his period authored books after his name: such as ***Fiqh-e Mas'ûdi*** (فقہ مسعودی) and ***Qãnûn-e Mas'ûdi*** (قانونِ مسعودی) by Qãḍi Abu Muḥammad Naṣḥi and Abu Raiḥãn Khwãrazmi respectively.[27]

(ii) Ghaurids :- Muḥammad Ghauri was the first Muslim ruler of Northern India who also promoted a favourable atmosphere for education in this region. He was found of the company of the learned men and scholars. He founded *madrasãs* at Ajmer for the spread of Islamic learning.[28] His successor Quṭb ud-Dîn Aibak (1206-1210), the founder of slave dynasty in India, was himself a scholar of Arabic and Persian learning and sciences. He founded many *madrasãs* and mosques where both religious and modern learnings were taught.[30] N.N. Law writes that there were hundreds of mosques which like the Churches of Medieval Europe were centre of both religion and learning.[31]

27. Abu'l Ḥasanãt Nadvi, *Hindustãn Ki Qadim Islãmi Darsgãhen*, Matba Ma'arif, Azamgarh, 1936, P. 16.
28. Ibid., P.17 Also is S.M. Jaffar, *Education in Muslim India (1000-1800AC)*, Delhi, 1936, P. 38.
29. Krishnalal Ray, *Education in Medieval India*, B.R.Publishing Corporation, Delhi, 1984, P. 13.
30. S.M. Jaffar. Op. Cit., P. 39.
31. N.N. Law. Op. Cit., P. 19.

(iii) Iltutmish :- Among his successors, Sultan Iltutmish (1211-36) spared no pains to spread education and his court was a meeting place of scholars and intellectuals. Amir Khusrau and Fakhr ul-Mulk 'Uthmãni were attached to his court [32] and Amir Kuhãni (great philosopher) was among those who got their stipends from the state treasury.[33] Iltutmish founded a *madrasãh* at Delhi.[34] It is said that *Madrasãh-e Mu'îzzîyah* was established by him and named after his predecessor Shihãb ud-Dîn Ghauri (whose real name was Mu'iz ud-Dîn Muḥammad Ghauri).[35] Another *madrasãh* of the same name attached to a mosque was erected at Badaun.[36] The other famous *madrasãh* was *Nãṣirîyah.* It is believed that this was also founded by Sultan Iltutmish and named after his eldest son Naṣir ud-Dîn Maḥmûd.[37] The author of ***Tabaqãt-e Nãṣiri,*** Minhãj us-Sirãj was the Principal of the *madrasãh* and superintended its

32. S.M. Jaffar, Op. Cit. P. 40.
33. Ibid., P. 40.
34. Krishnalal Ray. OP. Cit., P. 4.
35. Abu'l Ḥasanãt Nadvi. Op. Cit., P.17. But Syed 'Abd ul-Ḥai writes that it was founded by Sultan Quṭb ud-Dîn Aibak. See in Syed 'Abd ul-Ḥai, *India During Muslim Rule*, Eng. tr. Moḥi ud-Din Aḥmad. Lucknow, 1977. P. 169.
36. Ibid., P. 17.
37. Syed Ṣabãḥ ud-Dîn 'Abd ur-Raḥmãn, *Bazm-i Mamlukiyah,* Matba 'Ma'ãrif, Azamgarh, 1934, P. 236. It is also stated that it was built by Balban when he was Chief Minister. See in *The Encyclopaedia of Islam.* vol. v, new ed., Laiden, 1986, P. 1134.

endowments under Razia Sultana's reign in 1236.[38] Another college *Firozi Madrasãh* at Multan is also said to have been established by him.[39]

(iv) Balban :- Ghiyãth ud-Dîn Balban continued with great vigour and wisdom the policy of his predecessors. Once he advised to his son Prince Muḥammad as quoted by N.N. Law from ***Tãrikh-e Farishta***,

> "Spare no pains to discover men of genius, learning and courage."[40]

Amir Khusrau, Shaikh 'Uthmãn Tirmidhi, Shaikh Badr ud-Dîn 'Ârif, Amir Ḥasan Syed Maula, Shaikh Shakar Ganj, Shaikh Bahã ud-Dîn, Quṭb ud-Dîn Bakhtiyãr Kãki were among those who were highly revered in the Court of Balban.[41] His son Prince Muḥammad was an enlightened patron of literature. His court was open for all scholars. Balban's other son Prince Bughra Khan took more interest in music, dance etc. and perhaps also established a society for it.[42]

(v) Khiljis :- During Khilji dynasty, education, to

---

38. Abu'l Ḥasanãt Nadvi. Op. Cit., P. 18. Also in Syed 'Abd ul-Ḥai, Op. Cit.. P. 169.
39. Muḥammad Akhlãq Aḥmad, *Traditional Education Among Muslims,* Delhi, 1985 P.7.
40. N.N. Law. Op. Cit., P. 27.
41. S.M. Jaffar, Op. CIt., P. 42.
42. Yusuf Ḥusain. *Glimpses of Medieval Indian Culture,* Bombay, 1959, P. 79.

some extent, faced setback. However, Jalãl ud-Dîn, the first ruler of Khilji dynasty was liberal patron of letters. He appointed Amir Khusrau as the librarian of Imperial Library at Delhi. His successor 'Alã ud-Dîn Khilji was uneducated and did not take active interest in education but later he showed some liberal attitude towards the men of letters. He founded a *madrasãh* attached to *Hauḍ-e Khãs*.[43] The inscription of *'Alãi Darwãzã* describes him as,

> "the strengthener of the pulpits of learning and religion and the strengthener of the rules of colleges and places of worship".[44]

(vi) Tughlaqs :- In the Tughlaq dynasty, the first three rulers - viz Ghiyãth ud-Dîn Tughlaq, Muḥammad bin Tughlaq and Firoz Shãh Tughlaq were very well-known for their learning and support to learned people. Their court was resort of men of letters. They constructed magnificent buildings and opened *maktabs* and *madrasãs* in their domain. They made proper arrangements for their maintenance by permanent endowments. Stipends and scholarships were given to the students and skilled teachers had been appointed on regular and good salaries.

Muḥammad bin Tughlaq was himself a man of encyclopaedic knowledge. He was equally

43. Krishnalal Ray. Op. Cit., P. 15
44. S.M. Jaffar, Op. Cit., P. 46.

accomplished in both rational as well as religious sciences and was considered most learned ruler of the Middle Ages.[45] Even critics pay homage to his high intellectual calibre.[46] His zeal for education attracted the scholars from other countries also. During this time, it became customary to establish schools even in small villages. Al-Maqrizi writes that there were as many as one thousand schools in Delhi alone. Education was so common that even slave girls used to be *ḥãfiẓ* of *Qur'ãn* and scholars of Islamic learning.[47] But his idea to shift capital Delhi to Daulatabad greatly hampered the promotion of learning.

His successor Firoz Shah Tughlaq (1351-88) was himself a man of extraordinary learning and integrity. He authored an autobiography known as ***Futuḥãt-e Firozshãhi*** (فتوحاتِ فیروز شاہی). For the dissemination of education, scholars were sent to various parts of his kingdom.[48] He built more than thirty *madrasãs* and scholarships were given to students as well as to teachers. Along with this, many old *madrasãs* were

---

45. Elliot and Dowson, *History of India: As told by its Own Historians,* vol.3, Allahabad, 1964, P. 580.
46. 'Aziz Aḥmad, Op. Cit., P. 53.
47. Syed Mahboob Rizvi, *History of the Dãr ul-'Ulũm Deoband*, Eng. tr., Murtaz Ḥusain F. Qureshi, Deoband, 1980, P. 53.
48. A. Yusuf 'Ali, *Making of India,* London, 1925, P.81.
49. *The Encyclopaedia of Islam,* vol. 5, New, ed., Op. Cit., P. 1135. Also in Elliot and Dowson, Op. Cit., P. 338.

renovated. Residential quarters for both students as well as teachers were attached to some schools.

He paid special attention to the education and training of poor, orphans and slaves and provided them opportunity to acquire relgious education and other arts and crafts. Shams Siraj Afif in ***Tãrikh-e Firoz Shãhi*** (تاریخ فیروز شاہی) writes that there were as many as 1,80,000 slaves who had acquired education and training in different arts, sciences and crafts.[50] He also took special care of the girls' education and established separate schools for them. Ibn Batûta (world traveller) writes that in Hanor (in South India) there were thirteen schools for girls.[51]

Among the *madrasãs* built by him *Madrasãh Firoz Shãhi* was very well-known for its magnificence. Ḍiã' ud-Dîn Barni writes;

> "The *Madrasãh Firoz Shãhi* of Delhi, as regards its grandeur, beauty of building, site and good management and excellence of education has had no parallel. For expenses, royal grants have been fixed. No other building in the capital, Delhi, can match with it in beauty of construction and the suitability of its location. The building of the

50. Syed Mahboob Rizvi. Op. Cit., P. 54.
51. Ibid., P. 54.

> *madrasãh* is very spacious, situated in a garden on the bank of a pond. Hundreds of students, divine doctors and scholars are always present here."[52]

He built *Madrasãh-e Hauḍ Khãs* in Delhi in 1354/755[53] and other *madrasãs* of Delhi known as *Qadam-e Sharîf* or *Qadam-e Rasûl* with a mosque near the tomb of his son Fatḥ Khan (d. 1374)[54] and a *madrasãh* was also built within the Siri Fort.[55]

(vii) Lodhis :- The founder of Lodhi dynasty Bahlol Lodhi did not contribute much in this regard due to his engagement in warfare. But whenever he got time he found company with learned men and poets and gave encouragement to learning. He founded some *madrasãs* for moral and intellectual improvements of his subjects.[56]

His son Sultan Sikandar Lodhi was himself a poet of repute and composed poetry under the pen-name *Gulrukh.*[57] There are eight or nine thousand couplets in his *dîwãn.*[58] His reign was remarkable mainly for three major steps for which his name will always shine in glory-

---

52. Ibid., P. 53.
53. Abu'l Ḥasanãt Nadvi. Op. Cit., P. 19.
54. Syed 'Abd ul-Ḥai. Op. Cit., PP. 169-170. Also in S.M. Jaffar, Op. Cit., P. 52.
55. Ibid., P. 169. Also in Abu'l Ḥasanãt Nadvi, Op. Cit., P.20.
56. Krishnalal Ray. Op. Cit., P. 16.
57. S.M. Jaffar, Op. Cit., P. 54.
58. N.N. Law. Op. Cit., P. 73

(i) He made education compulsory (on certain level) for all his subjects and insisted that all his military officers should be educated.[59]

(ii) He made Persian as a language of lower administration. As a result of which Hindus started to study Persian in such schools as were not attached to mosques.[60] This paved the way for secularization of a stream of education.[61]

(iii) The third characteristics of his educational policy was considerable emphasis on the education of rational sciences (*mã'qulãt*) to the disadvantage of relgious education (*manqûlãt*).[62]

Sikandar Lodhi established several schools in his Kingdom. *Madrasãh Tulanabi* was very famous which was established after the name of Maulana 'Abd-ullãh Tulanabi (Scholar of Persia and Settled at Delhi). He had revised and added some new books on logic and Philosophy.[63] Scholars form different countries came to his court particularly from Arabia, Persia and Central Asia.[64]

59. Ibid., P. 73. Also in S.M. Jaffar. Op. Cit., P. 55, and 'Aziz Aḥmad, Op. Cit., P. 54.
60. Ibid., P.75.
61. 'Aziz Aḥmad Op. Cit., P. 54
62. Ibid., P.54.
63. Syed 'Abd ul-Ḥai. Op. Cit., P. 170.
64. N.N. Law, Op. Cit., P. 77.

He was so interested in education that, he, according to ***Tãrîkh-e Dã'udî*** (تاریخ داؤدی) was accompanied with seventeen accomplished and learned men while in his private apartments.[65]

(B) Mughal Period :- After Lodhi dynasty Mughal rulers also patronised learning and literature widely and established *maktabs* and *madrasãs* and orphanages in their Empire. Ample arrangements were made for free education for the poor. Sufficient stipends and endowments were granted for the students and teachers and for the maintenance and expenses of the *madrasãs*.

(i) Babar :- Babar, the founder of Mughal Empire, was himself a man of scholarly disposition and well-versed in Arabic, Persian and Turkish languages. He was adept both in prose and poetry. He composed poetry of some merit in Turkish. His literary accomplishment is evaluated by Mirza Muḥammad Ḥaider who writes in his book ***Tãrikh-e Rashîdî*** (تاریخ رشیدی)

> "In the composition of Turkish poetry he was second only to Mir 'Ali Shir... He invented a style of verse called *Mubaiyãn* and was the author of a most useful treatise on Jurisprudence....He also wrote on Turkish Prosody"[66]

---

65. S.M. Jaffar, Op. Cit., P. 54.

66. Quoted by N.N. Law. Op. Cit., P. 122

But the greatest of all his works is his ***Memoirs*** which is an index of his intellectual achievements and monument of his memory. S.M. Jaffar writes that he is rightly regarded as the 'Prince of autobiographers'.[67]

He entrusted an additional work, i.e. construction of schools and colleges, to the Public Works Department (*Shuhrat-e Âm*).[68] Since then the promotion of education became the direct concern of state. This also shows Babar's interest in the wide dissemination of education.

(ii) Humayun :- Babar's son and successor, Humayun was a great scholar and was known for his love of learning. He divided the people of his empire into three classes[69] and put the men of letters in the first class called *Ahl-e Sa'ãdat*[70]. Further these three classes were divided into twelve sub-classes of Arrows. The twelfth arrow, made up of purest gold, was for Sultan himself. The eleventh one was for his nearest relatives and tenth one was for the learned and religious person.[71]

Due to his continual engagement in war and other disturbances, he could not concentrate on the promotion of education. His library, however, was

67. S.M. Jaffar, Op. Cit., P. 77.
68. N.N. Law, Op. Cit., PP. 126-127.
69. Three Classes are : (1) *Ahl-e Sa'ãdat,* (2) *Ahl-e Daulat,* (3) *Ahl-e Murãd.*
70. N.N. Law, Op. Cit., P. 129.
71. Ibid., P. 130.

very rich. Lãlã Beg (Beg Bahãdur) was his librarian. During his second reign *Sher Mandal*, the pleasure house of Sher Shãh, was turned into a library.[72] He also constructed an observatory for his personal use. It is to his credit that he invented an astrolabe known as *Usturlãb-e Humãyûnî.*[73] In his period, astronomy and geography made considerable progress. Humayun wrote a treatise on 'Nature of Elements' (*Ṭabãi'-'Anãṣir*).[74]

At Delhi, he founded a *madrasãh* where Shaikh Ḥusain was a teacher. The roof of his tomb was infact a *madrasãh*, where scholars of the day used to teach. The rooms surrounding the tomb were used for residence.[75]

(iii) Akbar :- The reign of Akbar marks an increased secularization of education. Under his educatinal policy, Muslims and Hindus both received education side by side,[76] giving rise to such schools and colleges as were not attached to mosques. Several *maktabs* and *madrasãs*, mosques and *khãnqãhs* were erected in Agra and Fatḫpur Sikri. He built *'Ibãdat Khãnã'* in 1578 in Fatḫpur Sikri in the garden of royal

---

72. Ibid., P. 133. Also in S.M. Jaffar, Op. Cit., P. 78 and Krishnalal Ray, Op. Cit., P. 20.
73. Abu'l Ḥasanãt Nadvi, Op. Cit., P. 21.
74. Ibid., P. 21.
75. Ibid., P. 22.
76. N.N. Law, Op. Cit., P. 160.

palace. There were four big halls, each hall was occupied by Sayyids or the descendants of the Prophet (S.A.W.), learned, *ṣufis* or *shaikhs* and noble officers of the court.[77] In the debating hall, discussions were held by the scholars of different schools of thought. It was used as a platform, from which, religious unity was preached and propagated in the form of his newly devised religion Dîn-e Ilãhi.[78] A big *madrasãh* was also founded at Agra where the scholars from Shiraz were invited and the students from various places came to attend the lectures of renowned scholars.[79]

Akbar made several reforms in the elementary education[80] and laid down some rules by which teaching became more effective.[81] Fatḥ-ullãh Shirãzi, a noted scholar of Arabic literature, theology and rational sciences, to whom Akbar honoured with the title of *'Aḍd ul-Mulk*, assisted in the preparation of Akbar's educational policy.[82] The main feature of Akbar's educational policy was the unification of

77. Ibid., P. 144.
78. S.M. Jaffar. Op. Cit., P. 83.
79. Lãlã Seel Chand, author of ***Tafrih-e 'Imãrãt*** was alive in the Mutiny of 1857, writes that there was a big *madrasãh* where teachers had been called from Shirãz. Abu'l Ḥasanãt Nadvi writes that this *madrasãh* is now distroyed but the locality is still known as *madrasãh* Mohalla. (For detail see Abu'l Ḥasanãt Nadvi. Op. Cit., PP. 28-29)
80. For detail see Akhlãq Aḥmad Op. Cit., P. 12.
81. For detail see Krishnalal Ray Op. Cit., P. 21.
82. 'Aziz Aḥmad. Op. Cit., P. 54.

India-political, social, religious, cultural etc.[83] As regards the subjects which were taught in the schools and *madrasãs* were as follows. After the schooling, where students were trained through Persian language, the higher education included subjects of sciences and arts in the following order: morality, arithmatics, accounts, agriculture, geometry, astronomy, economics, the art of government, physics, logic, abstract mathematics, divinity, history.[84] Apart from these subjects, the works of Dawãni, Mulla Sadra and Mirza Jãn were studied by Muslim students,[85] and the Hindu students used to read *vyãkarna*, *vedãntã* and *pãtãnjali*.[86]

It is noted that during Akbar's reign the nobles of the court also took interest in the cause of education. Mãham Anaga, the foster mother of Akbar, built a *madrasãh* and also a mosque attached to it at Delhi in 1561 known as *Khair ul-Manãzil*.[87] Another wel-known *madrasãh* was *madrasãh-e Khawãjã Mu'în* where Mirza Mufti Samarqandi taught for three years from 1571.[88]

His imperial library was unique in its nature. Books on various subjects had been collected and were

83. S.M. Jaffar. Op. Cit., P. 89.
84. N.N. Law, Op. Cit., PP. 161-162.
85. 'Aziz Aḥmad, Op. Cit., P. 54.
86. N.N. Law, Op. Cit., PP. 162.
87. Abu'l Ḥasanãt Nadvi, Op. Cit., P. 22.
88. N.N. Law, Op. Cit., P. 168.

classified according to language and subject. such as, books in Arabic, Persian, Hindi and Sanskrit were separately classed under sciences and histories.[89] 'Abd ur-Raḥim, son of Bairam Khan, had a library which was open for all.[90] Faizi's personal library consisted of 4600 volumes of books on various subjects.[91] During Akbar's reign, a lot of books were written, compiled and translated on history, philosophy, religion and other sciences.[92]

Narendra Nath Law writes about Akbar's interest towards education and points out that his riegn should also be remembered for the :[93]

(i) Lavish patronage of learned men by stipends and awards.

(ii) Foundation of educational institutions.

(iii) Creation of educational endowments.

(iv) Attraction of many literary men, even from other countries.

(iv) Jahangir :-

Jahangir, the successor of Akbar, was himself a poet and generous patron of learning. But he was not so able a ruler as Akbar was. However, he did many

---

89. Ibid., P. 151. Also in S.M. Jaffar. Op. Cit., P. 85.
90. Ibid., P. 170.
91. Ibid., P. 152.
92. Ibid., PP. 147-152 (For detail). Also in S.M. Jaffar. Op. Cit., PP. 83-84.
93. Ibid., P. 170.

remarkable works for the progress of education. He issued an ordinance that if a wealthy man or a traveller died heirless, his property would go to the state and be utilized for the construction and repairing of schools, colleges and *khãnqãhs*.[94] He constructed several new *madrasãs* and renovated and rebuilt many old ones. In addition to all this, he :

> "repaired even those *madrasãs* that had for thirty years been the dwelling place of birds and beasts, and filled them with students and teachers."[95]

He was so fond of books that even in his journey he took books with him. Far greater than the actual price was paid to authors in order to enrich the Imperical Library and preserved the valuable books. Maktûb Khan was the librarian.

(v) Shahjahan :-

The reign of Shahjahan is widely known for its architectural developments. Several magnificent and beautiful buildings and monuments were erected. However, during his time, several *madrasãs* and mosques were also constructed. Delhi, Lahore, Sialkot,

94. Ibid., PP. 174-175. Also in S.M. Jaffar, Op. Cit., P. 93., and Krishnalal Ray Op. Cit., P. 21., Abu'Ḥasanãt Nadvi, Op. Cit., PP. 29-30., *The Encyclopaedia of Islam,* vol. V, OP. Cit., P. 1135.
95. Jãn Jahãn Khan, *Tãrikh-e Jãn-e Jahãn* , (MS). Library of the Asiatic Society of Bengal. Quoted by N.N. Law. Op. Cit., P. 175.

Ahmadabad, Jaunpur, Burhanpur, Sirhind, Thaneswar and Anbala became famous educational centres, where the students from Hirat and Badakhshan used to come and quenched their educational thirst.

He founded Imperial College[96] in the vicinity of *Jãme' Masjid* at Delhi in 1658 and for its maintenance ample endowments were granted. Two other Government schools were founded-one at Delhi and another at Agra - and for them teachers were also appointed.[97] During his reign, the former as *Madrasãh Fatḥpûrî Begum* in 1649 and the latter as *Madrasãh Akbarãbãdi Begum* in 1630 - after the name of one of the queens of Shahjahan. Proper arrangements were made for the residence of teachers and students. The shops, which were constructed around it, were used to meet the expenses of the *madrasãh.*[98]

(vi) Aurangzeb :- Aurangzeb himself was well-versed in the knowledge of Arabic, Persian ad Chughtai Turkish languages as well as several arts and sciences. He was also accomplished in *fiqh* and other Islamic sciences. Like his predecessors, he built many schools and colleges in his territory and gave pensions,

---

96. Abu'l Ḥasanãt Nadvi writes that the Imperial College was known as *Dãr ul-Baqã*. (Abu'l Ḥasanãt Nadvi. Op. Cit., P. 23). But N.N. Law and S.M. Jaffar write that Shahjahan rebuilt this *madrasãh* which was near to *Jãme 'Masjid*. (N.N. Law, Op. Cit., P. 182., and S.M. Jaffar, Op. Cit., P. 99.)
97. Krishnalal Ray. Op. Cit., P. 22.
98. Syed'Abd ul-Ḥai. Op. Cit., PP. 171-172.

allowances and land to scholars and teachers. He sent a *farmãn* (instruction) to all provincial governors that special attention should be paid for the education of every subject and stipends should be given to all meritorious students from state treasury.[99]

He took special care for the teaching of Bohra community of Gujrat and appointed capable teachers. In 1678, he sanctioned large amount for repair, and rebuilt the old *madrasãh* of Gujrat. He gave the village Sundra as *Jãgîr* to Akram ud-Dîn Khan when he requested for an endowment after the construction of a college in 1697 in Ahmadabad.[100] *Madrasãh Firangi Maḥal* at Lucknow and *Madrasãh Raḥîmîyah* at Delhi were also founded in his reign. Later, the last two named *madrasãhs* became very famous and brought about a revolution in the educational system. Mulla Niẓãm ud-Dîn Sahãlwi of Firangi Maḥal prepared a new curriculum, known as *Dars-e Niẓãmi*, which is still being taught in almost all *madrasãs*. Shãh Wali-ullãh, the son of the founder of *Madrasãh Raḥîmîyah* rendered invaluable services in the promotion and dissemination of *ḥadîth,* literature and the holy *Qur'ãn*.

After Aurangzeb, Muslim rule started declining rapidly but among his successors Bahadur Shãh (1707-12) was a patron and friend of the learned and

---

99. S.M. Jaffar, Op. Cit., P. 100.
100. N.N. Law, Op. Cit., PP. 188-189.

he encouraged education and extended financial help for its promotion such as the two colleges at Delhi. One was founded by Ghãzi ud-Dîn Khan (Prime Minister of Shah 'Âlam) near Ajmeri Gate. The college was closed in 1793 due to want of funds.[101] The other was founded by Firoz Jang. Some *madrasãs* were established outside Delhi during his reign, e.g. the *madrasãh* of Qannauj called *Fakhr ul-Marãbi.*

3. Girls' Education :-

Besiedes these, there was also some arrangement for girls' education. Some rulers and nobles established separate *madrasãs* for female education and special attention was paid to their progress. The Sultan of Hinawar, Sultan Jalãl ud-Dîn, showed his interest in this regrad. Ibn Batûta informs us that there were as many as thirteen girls schools in his capital.[102] Ghiyãth ud-Dîn Khilji (1463-1500), of Malva, was another pioneer of women's education. He founded a *madrasãh* at Sarangpur to teach arts and crafts to women.[103] Akbar established a school for girls in Fatḥpûr Sikri and made proper arrangement of education to the ladies of *haram.* Apart from *maktabs* and *madrasãs*, several ladies of the royal descent adopted teaching profession or encouraged and

101. Ibid., PP. 194-195.
102. S.M. Jaffar, Op. Cit., P. 189.
103. Krishnalal Ray, Op. Cit., P. 90.

established educational institutions. They considered it as an act of piety and divine blessings. The women in Mughal period or earlier who got fame for their literary and educational pursuits were many,[104] Razia Sultãnã, Gul Badan Begum[105] (daughter of Babar), Hamida Bãno Begum (mother of Akbar), Salmã Sultana (niece of Humayun), Nurjahan (wife of Jahãngir), Jahãn Ârã Begum[106] (eldest daughter of Shahjahan), Mumtãz Mahal (wife of Shahjahan), Zeb un-Nisa,[107] Zînat un-Nisa and Badr un-Nisa (daughters of Aurangzeb), Sati un-Nisa (tutor of Jahãn Ârã Begum), Mãham Anagã (wet-nurse of Akbar) etc.

4. High Official's Interest Towards Education:-

Apart from the Muslim rulers, governors, nobles, scholars and many rich people also took interest in

---

104. Ibid., PP. 86-91 (For detail). Also in N.N. Law, Op. Cit., PP. 200-205., and S.M. Jaffar, Op. Cit., PP. 191-192.
105. She authored ***Humãyûn Nãmah*** which was considered to be the first 'literary gem' of Mughal period. (Krishnalal Ray, Op. Cit., P. 87.)
106. She authored ***Mûnisal-Arawah***(biography of the saints of Ajmer) and ***Shahbiyah*** (life of Mulla Shãh Badakhshani, her spiritual preceptor). About her, Krishnalal writes that, "She was really one of the brightest jewels of the Mughal Royal Court". (Krishnalal Ray, Op. Cit., PP. 88-89).
107. Zeb un-Nisa, as Krishalal says, "was above all poetess and the ***Diwãn-e Makhfi*** was from her pen." She insisted on Mulla Saif ud-Din to translate Imam Razi's *tafsir* ***Tafsîr-e Kabîr*** into Persian. She also skilled in the art of calligarphy and could write elegantly *nastãliq, naskh* and *shakista.* (Krishnalal Ray, Op. Cit., P. 89).

educational activity at their own personal level. They encouraged the local people. They established schools and colleges where the children of poors and orphans received education. They made ample arrangements for stipends and freeships for the teachers and students and for *madrasãh's* maintenance. Among them, Syed Maula during the reign of Balban established a *madrasãh* at Delhi.[108] He was famous for his piousness and scholarship. Khizr Khan, Mubarak Syed 'Alã ud-Dîn of Sayyid dynasty were reputed for their endeavour in learning and their interest in the promotion of education, particularly in Badaun and Cuttair. S.M. Jaffar writes that the two cities, for a while, successfully rivalled the cities of Delhi and Firozabad in their intellectual outlook.[109] The Sayyids of Gardez Sayyid Chajju and Sayyid Ajali and the Sayyid of Bayãnah, nobles of Nauhatta and Janjãr family were famous for their interest in learning at Delhi. There were many jurists, theologians, *ṣufîs*, historians, physicians, philosophers, linguists and musicians who prospered even without the patronage of rulers and they themselves were a centre of education.[110]

Nasir uḍ-Din Qabaicha (1205-1227) ruler of Sindh, Shãh langha (1470-1503) of Multan, Shãh Beg

---

108. N.N. Law, Op. Cit., P. 37.
109. S.M. Jaffar. Op. Cit., P. 53.
110. Ibid., PP. 109-112. Also in N.N. Law, Op. Cit., PP. 37-41. (For detail).

Arghûn (1509-1522) of Multan patronised education in every possible way. They founded several schools and appointed salaried teachers.[111] In Kashmir, Sikandar Shãh (1394-1416), Zain ul-'Âbedîn (1420-70) and Ḥusain Shãh (1472-84) were very well-known rulers for their contribution in education. The founder of Ahmadabad city in Gujarat Sultan Aḥmad Shãh (1512-1580) built several schools and colleges.[112] Khwãjã Bandã Nawãz Gesu Darãz of Gulbargah was well-known *ṣufi* and accomplished in traditional and modern sciences. Prince Aḥmad Shãh Bahmani constructed a *madrasãh* to perpetuate his memory and endowed several towns and villages for its expenses.[113]

In the Bahmani Kingdom (1347-1526), Maḥmûd Gawãn, a minister of Muḥammad Shãh Bahmani-II (1463-82), was famous for his literary pursuits. ***Rauḍat ul-Inshã*** (روضۃ الانشاء) and ***Dîwãn ul-Asḥãr***(دیوان الاشعار) are the products of his pen. His patronage was not limited to the people of his Kingdom. Gifts and presents were sent by him to the scholars of Iraq and Khurasan. He built a college at Bidar after his own name as *Madrasah-e Maḥmûd Gawãn*. Mosque, library, and hostels for students and teachers were attached to it. Here both religious and rational education was imparted side by side. He

111. N.N. Law, Op. Cit., P. 105.
112. Krishnalal Ray. Op. Cit., P. 18.
113. S.M. Jaffar, Op. Cit., PP. 119-120.

appointed Shaikh Ibrãhim Multani (Saint and scholar) as the Principal of his *madrasãh.*[114]

Muḥammad Quli Quṭb Shãh, the founder of Hyderabad city, was reputed for his love of learning and his interest in dissemination of education in his Kingdom. He constructed a magnificent mosque and *Chahãr Minãr.* Along with this, he founded many *madrasãs* and seminaries and appointed there salaried teachers.[115]

It would be unjust if we overlook the contribution of Sultan Ibrahim Sharqi (1402-1440) of Jaunpur. Due to his encouragement and patronage, scholars and students flocked in Jaunpur for higher education. It has been written in ***Tadhkerat ul-Ummah*** (تذکرۃ الامّۃ) and ***Siyar ul-Mulk*** (سیر الملک), there were more than hundred *madrasãs* in Sharqi capital which were richly endowed. N.N. Law refers to lethbridge's 'Topography of Mughal Empire' and writes that,

> "During Ibrahim's reign, the court of Jaunpur far outshone that of Delhi and was the resort of all the learned men of the East."[116]

In the period of Ibrahim Sharqi, Jaunpur became a centre of education and received the honorific

---

114. Ibid., PP. 122-27. Also in N.N. Law. Op. Cit., PP. 87-89.
115. N.N. Law, Op. Cit., PP. 95-96.
116. Ibid., P. 100. Also in S.M. Jajjar. Op. Cit., PP. 62-63.

appelation of *Shirãz-e Hind.* Shahjahan used to call it "*Pûrab* (East) is our Shîraz"[117] and issued an ordinance that special care was to be taken to the *madrasãs* of Jaunpur. But in 1760/1147, Sa'ãdat Khan Nishãpuri became governor of Jaunpur who withdrew all the endowments and facilities as a result of which its educational glory gradually was dimmed day by day.

Apart form these famous schools, there were several *madrasãs* which were constructed in Lahore, Agra, Fathpur, Nirawar, Mathura, Dara Nagar, Rampur, Shahjahanpur, Bareilly, Pilibhit, Oudh, Allahabad, Farukhabad, Jaunpur, Banaras, Azamgarh, Ghazipur, Manner, Sasaram, Danapur, Patna, Bengal, Dhaka, Murshidabad, Chennai, Gulbargah, Golkundah, Bijapur, Malva, Multan, Kashmir, Gujrat etc. Abu'l Ḥasanãt Nadvi has detailed out the *madrasãs* of all these cities in his book ***Hindustãn kî Qadîm Islãmî Darsgãgheṇ*** (ہندوستان کی قدیم اسلامی درس گاہیں) and Syed 'Abd ul-Ḥai in his book ***India During Muslim Rule***.

Maxmular referring to British official documents and a missionary report concerning education exclusively in Bengal, before British occupation, says that there were then 80,000 native schools, or one school for every 400 of the population.[118] Syed Sulaiman Nadvi referring to Captain Alexendra

117. Abu'l Ḥasanãt Nadvi, Op. Cit., P. 40.
118. S.M. Jaffar, Op. Cit., P. 150.

Hamilton, a European traveller, writes that in Thatha (ٹھٹھہ) (a city of Sindh) there were 400 *madrasãs* of various arts science.[119]

5. Courses of Studies :-

If we go through the curriculum and its changes during Muslim rule in India, for better understanding, it can be divided into three stages:

(i) The first stage covers the whole Saltanat period, i.e. upto 1500. The subjects which were taught in the *madrasãs* were: *fiqh*, *uṣûl-e fiqh*, theology, *ḥadîth tafsir, taṣawwuf, naḥv, balãghat* etc. The study of *fiqh* and *uṣûl-e fiqh* were given greater importance.

ii. The second stage starts from 1500 to 1575, i.e. Sikandar Lodhi's reign to Humayun reign. In this period, the study of secular sciences such as mathematics, logic, philosophy, astronomy, medicine received more importance.

iii. From Akbar's reign marks the third stage, in which the study of other religious and rational sciences became important studies. Comparative studies of religion started and schools were open for all irrespective of caste and creed, rich and poor.

6. Why little information about education in the books of history:-

During Muslim rule in India, almost all rulers,

119. Abu'l Ḥasanãt Nadvi. Op. Cit., P.4.

courtiers, governors and nobles were themselves well educated and accomplished in prose and poetry. They were well-versed in Arabic, Persian, Turkish, Urdu and several other languages. They took active interest often in the diffusion of education. But why the books of history, which were written in those days, give very little information about their contributions in the development of education? Maulana Abu'l Ḥasanãt Nadvi tried to find the reasons behind this. He writes;[120]

i. Imparting education (*Dars wa Tadrîs*) has always been considered by Muslims as a religious act. They considered that to help students and teachers, dissemination of education, aids and endowments for this purpose, founding of *maktabs* and *madrasãs* were their religious duty and is also a source of divine blessing (*barakãh*). Thus, since it was general and routine activity in Muslim society, therefore, it did not often find special mention in the books of history except occasional mention among other things.

ii. Generally we read in the books of history, 'wells, ponds, bridges and other buildings were constructed by the Sultans or Emperors', Abu'l Ḥasanãt says that these other buildings were generally *maktabs, madrasãs,* mosques and

120. Ibid., PP. 10-12.

khãnqãhs which were used as an educational centre. It was a general practice of Sultans and Courtiers to promote education and learning as much as possible.

iii. During the early centuries of Muslim rule, there were not separate buildings for schools. Education was imparted in the mosques. Almost all the mosques were used as *madrasãs* and as academic institutions. Due to this reason big and spacious mosques were founded in every quarter of Islamic cities of India. The magnificent mosques which still exist in Delhi, Agra, Lahore, Jaunpur etc. were all used for teaching purpose. The small rooms around the courtyard of the mosques were used as residence by the students and teachers.Fatḫpuri and Akbarãbãdi mosques which were built about 1649/1060 are still used as *madrasãh* and the students still reside in their courtyard-rooms.

iv. The old *khãnqãhs* of *ṣufis* or *durveshes* were also used as *madrasãs*. *Ṣufis* and *shaikhs* along with their sufistic practices engaged themselves in dissemination of *sharî'ah* (exoteric side) and *ṭarîqat* (esoteric side) or *ẓãhir* and *bãtin* (the exterior and the interior). The state grants and private endowments to *khãnqãhs* were spent on students.

v. Rooms and cloisters, which were constructed around the tombs and graves of *sultãns* and *shaikhs*, were also used as *madrasãs*. Such as the tombs of 'Alã' ud-Dîn Khilji, Humayun and others that are still existed in Delhi, Agra, Ahmadabad, Bijapur etc. are living testimonies to this history.

Besides these schools, mosques, tombs and *khãnqãhs*, many scholars used to teach students at their homes. To some of them, they even provided free lodging and boarding. In the absence of any proper shelter, they even imparted education in open fields[121]

7. Downfall of *madrasãs* :-

After Aurangzeb, the disintegration of Muslim rule in India had rapidly started. The British took full advantage of the chaos and gradually usurped the power and administration of Mughal rulers. Due to this political change, the Muslim education was badly affected and the *madrasãs* were put to oblivion, giving way to British schools and Western education.

Under British rule, there was no definite educational policy. The education was limited to only European families. But after 1765, a decision was taken regarding the education of Indians also. For Muslims, their special attention was centred on the study of Muhammadan law, in order to facilitate the

---

121. 'Aziz Aḥmad. Op. Cit., P. 57. Also in Syed Mɛḥboob Rizvi, Op. Cit., P. 61.

smooth running of judicial administration. In 1813, rupees one lakh had been granted for the promotion and encouragement of modern education among Indians. But this was only a part of their over all policy in which missionaries played an imprtant role in the propagation of Christianity. They wanted to replace Islam and its culture with Christianity and Western culture. Governors General indirectly were providing all moral and material support to the missionaries. Their intentions became clear when in 1835 a resolution was passed that all the funds be used towards the introduction of English education alone. Behind this, their main objective was to familiarize the Indian Muslims with Christianity and thus convert them to it. Muslims who were studying Muḥammadan law to secure job in administration were deprived of their jobs when, in 1837, English language was made the language of Courts in place of Persian. During Lord Carnawalis (1786-1793) 75 per cent of Government jobs where held by Muslims but now there was no more Muslims particularly in higher ranks in Government services.[122] W.W. Hunter rightly observed regarding the Muslim plight:

> "Hundreds of ancient families were ruined, and the educational system of the Musalmans, which was almost entirely maintained by rent free grants, received

---

122. Muḥammad Ṭãhir, Op. Cit., P. 108.

> its death-blow. The scholastic classes of Muhammadans emerged from the eighteen years of harrying absolutely ruined.[123]

East India Company, on the other hand, started to destroy the centres of Indian industries for which even English men like Sir Charles Trevelyen and Montgomary Martin expressed their grief. East India Company also passed the Land Act which adversely influenced the economic condition of the Muslims. Likewise, they took over all financial sources under their control. Consequently, the revenue-collection passed from the Muslims to the English hands.[124]

Muslims' condition became still worse after the Mutiny of 1857 as the British view was that the revolt mainly was caused by the Muslims. Already, there was little consideration for Muslims to enter government jobs, but in the post-1857 period such considerations were completely withdrawn.

Apart form this, there were other reasons behind the downfall of Muslims particularly in Northern India, i.e. their racial pride. Muslims were the descendants of nobles, officers and soldiers, many of whom enjoyed privileges of large estates and pre-eminence and as such considered the British as usurpers. Another reason was religious apprehension.

---

123. W.W. Hunter. *The Indian Musalman*. Lahore, 1964, P.167.
124. M.F. Raḥman. *The Bengali Muslims and English Education (1765-1835),* Bengal Academy, Dacca, 1973. P. 17.

Due to this Muslims widely refrained from active participation in the new educational system of East India Company.

When the British became politically and economically powerful they started to interfere in the educational set-up. For example they extended all kind of support to missionaries for the propagation of Christian faith through educational institutions. They passed resolutions and favoured Western languages and learnings. They sanctioned funds to facilitate English education and modern sciences. At the same time, they confiscated or withdrew all aids, endowments and *waqf* properties of the *madãris-e islãmia* which were the source of all stipends of the teachers and the facilities of students. So with each day the number of students and teachers in the *madrasãs* began to decrease and soon led them to be the *madrasãs* closed down for ever. The scholars who used to teach at their own houses were forced to discontinue this good work as they were considered enemy of the British whose properties were often seized and they were themselves imprisioned.

CHAPTER-1

MUSLIM CONDITIONS IN INDIA DURING NINETEENTH CENTURY : WITH SPECAIL REFERENCE TO EDUCATION

1. **Background :-** Muslims used to visit India from the very beginning for trade and commerce and established their earliest colonies on the western and eastern coast-line of India. The first conquest by them was made in Sindh during the reign of Walîd bin 'Abd ul-Malik (705-715), the Umayyad Caliph, under the command of Muḥammad bin Qãsim in 711. Later, during the 11th century Maḥmûd Ghaznavi invaded India several times between 999 to 1026. But every time, he returned to his capital after fulfilling his objectives. Then came the Ghaurid whose commanders not only invaded but after conquest settled down in North Western parts of India, where they promoted education and founded *madrasãs* in their conquered areas. They were followed by the Khiljis, Lodhis, Suris and lastly the Mughals came and established their rule. Education and *'Ulamã'* were, by and large, patronized by all Muslim rulers.

The Mughals continued to rule the country until the last Mughal Emperor, Bahadur Shãh, who was deposed by the British in 1857. But after Aurangzeb, (d. 1707) the political decay of the country had clearly set in and finally ended in complete collapse under rebellions and conspiracies of high officials, governors and courtiers.

For a time, the Marãṭḥãs had become the chief political and military power in India. They unsuccessfully tried to establish their own rule in the country. In the North, the provinces of Oudh and Bengal as well as Panjab under the Khãlsã power became independent of the Mughal rulers of Delhi. The invasion of Nãdir Shãh and Aḥmad Shãh Abdãli further weakened the central rule.

Apart from this, there was a large number of small petty states scattered all over India owing allegience to some neighbouring larger states. Most of these states, whether large or small, were too weak to defend themselves against any external enemy, i.e. the British. On the other hand they often sought help from the British against their rival rulers.

2. Invasion of East India Company :-

This was the situation in which the British East India Company turned to make the most of it. The Company had come to India for trading purpose and had no desire of establishing a territorial rule. But gradually, they found that the petty Muslim states, which had sprang up as a result of Mughal weakness, were not in a position even to defend themselves. They began to realize that they could trade much more profitably and freely if they wrested the political control and established their military supremacy. With this object in mind, they had to fight first with the French who were already struggling for the same objectives in the South. In 1765, the Company also succeeded in establishing their control over Bengal province. After defeating Tipû Sultan almost all the areas of South India came under their control in 1799. Thus, from the beginning of the 19th century, the British trading company brought almost all the major parts of India under their colonial rule. Wherever the British went, they crushed and subjugated the local chiefs, disbanded their armies and took the administration of the area into their own hand or supervision.

3. Mughal Attitude Towards Christian And Education:

From the very beginning, the Mughal rulers had adopted a secular policy; welcomed the Europeans for commerce, showed liberal attitude towards Christians and permitted even to carry on missionary activities. The following lines highlight this Mughal patronage and enviable position of the Mughal nobles,

> "The extent patronage shown to the missionaries under the Emperors of the house of Babar was extra ordinary. They were the honoured guest of the

> Emperors; they enjoyed privileges which were the cause of envy to the Mughal nobility."[1]

Many Europeans had been appointed to the higher military posts in the 18th century. As 'Azîz Aḥmad observed that this showed the technical superiority of the Europeans in the manufacture and use of the more sophisticated weapons as well as in their strategy of war.[2]

The Muslim rulers from the very beginning took interest in the advancement of education. They encouraged and patronized the scholars and the people of pen. There existed many schools and *madrasãs* and ran smoothly through proper financial arrangement, i.e. endowments. But there was one demerit in the policy regarding education during Muslim rule that, to some extent, the education was limited to the children of nobles and upper classes. There was no adequate attention or provision towards the education of general masses. When the British became the political masters this situation further deteriorated as they confiscated or curtailed public trusts and endowments of *madrasãs*.

In the beginning of the 17th century, the East India

---

1. S.R. Sharma, *The Crescent in India,* Bombay, 1966, P. 731.
2. 'Azîz Aḥmad, *Islamic Modernism in India and Pakistan,* Oxford University Press, London, 1967, P.4.

Company did not take proper step for the education of the Indian people. In 1659, the Court of Directors explicitly stated that it was their earnest desire by all possible means to spread Christianity among the people of India and allowed missionaries to act boldly in this regard.[3] According to Charter Act of 1698, Chaplains were appointed in Bombay, Calcutta and Madras to look after the education of the Christian children and Anglo-Indian Children.

4. British Acts And Resolutions Regarding Education:

After 1765, when the Company became a political power in India, their educational policy got some change. Before 1765, the Company's attention was limited to the education of Europeans and Anglo-Indian subjects. But now they established some centres of higher learning for the Hindus and the Muslims also.

Warren Hastings was the first man who took a major step and founded a *madrasãh* in Calcutta in 1781. The *madrasãh* was solely meant for promoting and encouraging the study of Arabic and Persian languages. However, special care was taken to educate

---

3. W.H. Sharp, *Selection from Educational Records* , vol. 1, P.3. Quoted by Syed Ghulam Meḥiuddin, "Modern Education and the Educational Problems of the Indian Muslims",*Muslim Education Quarterly*, vol. II, No. 4, Islamic Academy Cambridge, U.K., 1985, P. 62.

the students in the Muhammadan Law. Besides the syllabi included Astronomy, Geometry, Logic, Arithmetic, Philosophy, Theology and Grammar. Syed Maḥmood had borrowed an extract from the ***"Memoir"*** of Mr. Thomas Fisher,[4] which is the most authroritative source of information available regarding the purpose;

> "The Calcutta Madrissa, or Muhammadan College, was founded at the request of several Muhammadans of distinction, in the year 1781, by the Governor General, Warren Hasting, who provided a building for it, whose cost was Rs. 57745. The Bengal Government also assigned lands of the estimated value of Rs. 29000 per annum for the support of the institution. The original intention of the Founder appears to have been to promote the study of the Arabic and Persian Languages, and of the Muhammadan Law, with a view, more especially, to the production of well qualified officers of the courts of Justice."[5]

---

4. Thomas Fisher hold the office "Searcher of the Records" at the East India Company, in London. He had written ***"Memoir"*** on Education in India, dated 7th February 1827.
5. Syed Maḥmood. *A History of English Education in India,* MA.O.College, Aligarh, 1805, P. 18

Not only did the company provide for the education of Muslims due to their intention running the judicial administration smoothly they provided for the education of Hindus also. The Resident Jonathan Duncan founded a Hindu Sanskrit College in Banaras, the sacred place of Hindus.[6] The curriculum included Hindu theology and rituals, Medicine, Mathematics, Arts, Grammar, sacred Loxicograhpy, Logic, Ethics, Philosophy etc.

In these two institutions, by going through the subjects which were taught there, it became clear that the British needed the cooperation of Hindus and Muslims in so far as the matter related to judiciary. No special care was taken to educate the people in sciences particularly Western science and English language.

However, in 1813 the Charter of the East India Company was placed before the British Parliament to make the provision of one lakh rupees for the promotion and encouragement of sciences among the inhabitants of British India.[7] In any case, it was the first ever legislative support introduced by the British for promoting modern education among Indians.

The policy of Warren Hastings on education was largely welcomed by the Hindus of Bengal as the urge to acquire the Western knowledge was strongly

6. Ibid., P. 19.
7. Ibid., P. 23.

enough among them. This is one of the reasons for which the British favoured Sanskrit over Persian and The Court of Directors wanted this amount to be spent on the promotion of Sanskrit learning alone.[8] Any way, the fact of the matter is that Muslims for a longer period of time remained inactive in accepting the Western education.

5. Secret Mission of the British and the Missionaries :-

The missionaries' main interest was to propagate Christianity. In order to promote this objective, they had established several schools. They were, however, mainly concerned with the propagation of their own religion. They tried to woo the Indians by making use of printing press and the vernacular languages. However, the educated natives opposed the steps of missionaries, as the purpose of the missionaries was neither the education of Indian natives nor the eradication of backwardness, but only the propagation of Christian ideas.

The Government took certain steps for them to desist from such activities as might lead to an escalation of agitation. But, actually, the Government's warning to the missionaries was only an outward posture. The well known paper ***Friends of India*** highlighted the conspiracies of the Government and Christian missinaries to replace Islam and its culture

8. Ibid.,. PP.23-24

with Christianity and Western Civilization. The Company Government, though interested in the translation of Christian scripture, avoided direct interference. At the same time, it allowed the missionaries to go ahead freely with their aims and objectives.[9]

6. Rãjã Rãm Mohan Roy and Modern Education:

In the Charter of 1813, rupee one lãkh per year had been sanctioned for the education among the Indian natives. In 1823, a General Committee of Public Instruction was appointed by the Government to decide whether the traditional education should be continued or it should be replaced by English education. Majority of the members of General Committee of Public Instruction were in favour of traditional education. But it was opposed particularly by the Hindus of Bengal. Rãjã Rãm Mohan Roy[10] protested against the expenditure of money on traditional education and urging that all available funds and endeavours should be devoted to the

---

9. *Friends of India*, 1838, 5th April. Quoted in Mujeeb Ashraf, *Muslim Attitudes Towards British Rule and Western Culture in India*, Idarah-e Adbiyat-e Delli, Delhi, 1982, P. 24.

10. Rãjã Rãm Mohan Roy was the founder of Brahmo Samãj and Hindu College Calcutta. He led a revolution against *Satî Praṭ ḥã*. He was expert of Persian, Arabic, Sanskrit, Latin, English and Hebrew languages. He was an enlightened and far-sighted man and a great patron of Western education.

promotion of the English language and literature and Western science, among the people of India.[11]

Rãjã Rãm Mohan Roy along with David Hare[12], Sir Edward Hyde East[13] and some of the rich Hindu natives of Calcutta formed an association for founding a seminary (*pãṭ ḥshãlã*) in which the sons of Hindus might receive education not only in Asiatic languages but also the languages and literature of England. For that purpose, a sum of rupee 113179 had been subscribed and a *vidyãlayã* had been opened in 1817.[14]

To meet the demand of local Indians and to improve their conditions, educationally and economically, the rich and educated Hindu class suggested the Government to take necessary steps. And as a result, a number of Committees of Public Instruction were appointed in Calcutta, Bombay and Madras mainly with a view to ascertain the state of education and to aid and advise the Government to take steps to mobilise people and resources for education. In Bombay in 1823, an educational society was established to do the same job. No doubt, there were differences in their view point regarding the nature of education. Some supported oriental learning

11. Syed Maḥmood, Op. Cit., P. 52.
12. David Hare was a private European Resident of Calcutta and served for the betterment of the people of the Calcutta. He was a close friend of Rãjã Rãm Mohan Roy.
13. Sir Edward Hyde East was the Chief Judge of Supreme Court, Bengal in 1816.
14. K.S. Vakil, *Education in Indian Modern Period (1540-1940)* , Kolhapur, 1940, P. 56

while others Western learning and till 1835 no decision could be taken in this regard.

7. William Bentinck's Resolution:

Lord Macaullay, legislative member of the council of Governor-General, submitted a Minute to Governor-General, Lord William Bentinck, on 2nd February 1835 in favour of English education. Lord Macaullay wished,

> "to create a class of persons who would be Indian in blood and colour, but English in taste, in opinion, in morals and in intellect."[15]

Lord William Bentinck adopted Lord Macaullay's views and on the 7th March 1835 passed a resolution, in which their special emphasis was on that all the funds be reserved for the purpose of English education alone[16]. This resolution resolved the problems of medium of instruction.

Hindus, generally, showed their inclination towards Western education and sciences. So they welcomed and appreciated the resolution passed by Lord William Bentinck[17]. The number of books sold by School-book Society[18] shows the public choice and

---

15. *The Cambridge Shorter History of India,* vol. II, ed. By H.H. Dodwell, India Edition, Cambridge University Press, 1935, P. 717.
16. Syed Maḥmood, Op. Cit., P. 51.
17. Ibid., P. 52
18. The policy of school-book society was to print only such books as were in demand, and to dispose of them only to those who pay for them.

feelings in regard to the different system of learnings. Syed Maḥmood has given the detail of books which were sold from January 1834 to December 1835.[19] They are as follow;

A.	English Books	-	31649
B.	Bengali Books	-	5754
C.	Hindi Books	-	4171
D.	Persian Books	-	1454
E.	Arabic Books	-	36
F.	Sanskrit Books	-	16 etc.

But for the Muslims, it was equally disheartening as they thought of this as an encroachment on the religious learning. In the words of H.H. Wilson.[20]

> "Upon the determination to abolish the stipends, and the proposal to appropriate all the funds to English education, there was a petition from the Muhammadans of Calcutta, signed by about 8000 people, including all the respectable Maulvis and native gentlemen of that city. After objecting to it on grounds of general principles, they said that the evident object of the Government was the conversion of the natives; that they encouraged English exclusively and discouraged Muhammadan and Hindu

19. Syed Maḥmood, Op. Cit., P.52.
20. H.H. Wilson was a famous Sanskrit scholar and a member and secretary of the Committee of Public Instruction at Calcutta.

studies, because they wanted to induce the people to become Christians."[21]

8. William Bentinck's Policy of Religious Neutrality:

William Bentinck declared the policy of religious neutrality after the petition of the Muslims of Calcutta appealing to the Government to spare the *madrasãs* and refrain from such measures as might result in the destruction of the literature and religious system of Islam.[22] Muslim *'ulamã* apprehended that the objective of the Government exclusive to the encouragement to English language and discouragement to Hindu and Muslim studies was conversion to Christianity. Their suspicion was not unfounded because the missionaries used to teach Christianity through the English education,[23] disregarding the policy of religious

21. Syed Maḥmood, Op. Cit., P. 53.
22. Ibid., P. 64.
23. Many Christian missionaries played a vital role into conversion. Such as St. Mary's Charity School at Bambay founded by Rev. Stevenson in 1717. Rev. Richar Cobbe founded a missionary school at Bombay in 1719, Chaplain Bellamy opened at Calcutta in 1719, a Female Orphan Asylum was started at Madras by Lady Campbell in 1787, Rev. Dr. Andrew Bell started a Male Asylum in 1787, Carey Missionaries in 1793, Marshman and Ward at Serampur played important role into conversion. By 1820 the Missionaries Societies were doing a lot of work in this field. The primary object of all these missionaries was not to educate the people but to preach Christianity. The missionaries realized that the spread of English language would help in the spread of Christianity in the country. Wilson College at Bombay, Christian College at Madras, St. John's College at Agra and many other missionaries colleges where the Bible classes were made compulsory.

neutrality.[24] In the words of Rev. Alexendra Duff. D.D, a missionary:

> "Our great object was to convey as largely as possible knowledge of our literature and Science to the young persons; but another and more vital object was to convey a thorough knowledge of Christianity"[25]

This isolation in the field of education, however, caused immense harm to the Muslims in competing with their Hindus compatriots. The suspicion was to remain as an obstacle in the way of Muslims and prevented them to take up the challenge of Western education. There were enough evidences which substantiated the views of Muslims. For instance, it may be seen in the willingness and the approval of the Governor of Madras, Marquis of Tweeddale, regarding the inclusion of Bible in the course of study of Government seminaries.[26] It could be noticed that high ranking official were against the local religion and were sympathetic towards missionaries.

William's Resolution of 1835 on one hand encouraged English education and on the other, it intended to stop all kinds of financial assistance to the institution of Oriental learning. This extreme measure was, however, abrogated by Lord Auckland in 1839.

---

24. Ram Gopal, *Indian Muslim,* Bombay, 1964, PP. 18-19.
25. Ibid., P. 20.
26. Syed Masroor 'Ali Akhtar Hashmi, *Muslim Response to Western Education,* New Delhi, 1989, P.6.

Lord Harding in 1844 brought a new ruling by which the students were to be given preference in services if they come from such institutions which imparted English and Western education. The Resolution of Lord Harding of 1844 is as follow:

> "In every possible case, a preference shall be given, in the selection of candidates for public employment, to those who have been educated in the institution thus established, and especially to those who have distinguished themselves therein by a more than ordinary degree of merit and attainment".[27]

This helped a great deal in creating a material preference for English education. Though the Resolution of 1844 also emphasized English as the official language in the transaction of official business. But more or less this attempt did not materialize.

9. Wood's Despatch:

Sir Charles Wood's Despatch to the Courts of Directors has been described as, 'The Magna Carta of English Education in India'. It enunciated the aim of education as the defusion of Arts, Sciences, Philosophy and the Literature of Europe. The English language was to be taught wherever there was demand for it. Both the English language and the Indian

27. Quoted by K.S. Vakil, Op. Cit., P. 101.

languages were to be given special attention and prescribed as the means for the attainment of the following objects:

1. "The constitution of separate department of the administration of education.
2. The institution of Universities at the presidency towns.
3. The establishment of institutions for training teachers for all classes of schools.
4. The maintenance of the existing Government colleges and High schools, and the increase of their number when necessary.
5. The establishment of new middle schools.
6. Increased attention to Vernacular schools, indigenous or others, for elementary education; and
7. The introduction of a system of Grants-in-Aid."[28]

The Government's commitment to higher education can be seen in that even in the event of great disturbances in North India, three Universities were established in Calcutta on 24th January 1857, in Bombay on 18th July 1857 and in Madras on 5th September 1857. It was in 1882 that an Indian Education Commission was appointed, which was headed by W.W. Hunter to enquire and to suggest

---

28. *Report of the Indian Education Commission,* 1882, PP. 22-23. Quoted by Syed Maḥmood, Op.Cit.,P.85

measures to further strengthen and widen the educational network proposed by Wood's Despatch. So, there was a sharp rise in the number of colleges and from 27 in 1857 the number rose to 72 in 1882.[29] Along with this, the Wood's Despatch also supplemented the educational institutions of private nature which were largely financed by individuals and private organisations. This policy was seen as an advantage by missionaries till 1882. But later on, due to national feeling, Private Indian enterprises came into lead. In 1901-1902, the colleges under Indian management numbered 42 as against 37 missionary colleges.[30]

10. Indian University Commission :

In 1902, Indian University Commission was appointed which was largely welcomed by the educated Indians. The recommendation of this Commission was incorporated in the Indian University Act of 1904. The act was considered a milestone in the development of higher-education. The appointment of Sadler Commission in 1917 was also a landmark as it recommended the opening up of Women's education and establishment of teaching Universities at Dacca and Calcutta. The recommendation helped in the establishment of teaching and residential Universities. From 1915 to 1920, more than half a dozen

---

29. Nurullah. S. and Naik J.P, *A Students Histroy of Education In India,* Bombay, 1956, P. 158.
30. Ibid., P. 146.

Universities came into existence. They were Mysore University in 1916, Patna University in 1917, Banaras Hindu University in 1917, Aligarh Muslim University in 1920, Dacca University in 1920 and Lucknow University in 1920.

11. Muslim's Response Towards Western Education :

Regarding the Muslim's response towards British as Mujeeb Ashraf, after evaluating, divided them into four groups,

> "One group of nobles sincerely considered friendship and alliance with the British indispensable for the continued existence of the Indian states and made it their policy to be friendly with the British... Another group was so completely impressed by the British and their culture that it sought to organise the affairs of State and the conditions of the society on British lines. A third group was loyal neither to the state nor to the British Government and followed a policy which, in its view, best suited its own personal and selfish interests. There was, finally, a fourth group which was totally opposed to British dominance and the British connexion."[31]

31. Mujeeb Ashraf, Op. Cit., P. 85.

The behaviour of the Muslims of Southern and Northern part of India differed from each other in many respects. Southern and Western sections of Muslims showed positive response towards English and Western sciences, while the Muslims of Northern India, to some extent also Hindus, refused to accept Western learnings. S. 'Abid Ḥusain discussed in detail the reasons by which the behaviours of Southern and Northern Indian Muslims differed form each other towards Western culture and sciences. The abstract of his thinking are given in the following sentence:

The Muslims of Southern and Western part of India were descendants of Arab merchants and sailors. To fulfil their material aspect, they liked peaceful society, having good relation with the Hindu rulers, ready to adjust with every new circumstance and were generally educated. While the Muslims of Northern India were descendants of nobles, officers and soldiers they were holding high posts, enjoying privileges. But after the British dominance, all the privileges were curtailed or abolished. They considered British as usurpers and openly showed their hostility due to social, cultural and political prejudice.[32]

The study of political events and their impact on Muslims are important to understand the Muslim response. The political events in the aftermath of the battle of Plassey (1757) and the battle of Buxar (1764)

32. S. 'Abid Ḥusain, *The Destiny of Indian Muslims* , Asia Publishing House, New Delhi, 1965, PP. 17-20 (For detail).

had changed the attitude of British towards Muslims. The British now onwards were highly cautious regarding Muslims. After establishing their hegemony, the British began to destroy the financial strength of the Muslims.

The commercial policy of East India Company destroyed the centers of Indian industries that even Englishmen like Sir Charles Trevelyon and Montgomary Martin felt sorry over the plight of Indian manufactures and labourers.[33] Many of the finer industrial arts of India were in the hands of skilled Muslims, were ruined. Particularly, the Muslims of Bengal were the greatest lossers.[34] In 1793, the British passed the land Act, which adversely influenced the economic condition of the Muslims. They changed the relationship with the landlords, especially in regard to the Muslims, and closed the door to their landlordism.[35]

The substitution of English language for Persian as the Court language in 1837 greatly affected the Muslim subordinate officers. Ḥafiẓ Malik rightly remarks,

"Their strategy was to oust the Muslims

33. R.C. Dutt, *The Economic History of India in the Victorian Age*, London, 1908, P.P. 99, 105, 112.
34. Ram Gopal, Op. CIt., P. 15.
35. P. Hardy, *The Muslims of British India, Cambridge,* 1972, PP. 40-50. (For detail).

> from the profession and the position of economic and administrative control."[36]

As a whole, Syed 'Amir 'Ali writes that upto this time, in 1793, high offices, fiscal as well as judicial were filled by Muslims. But now the higher executive appointments were reserved exclusively for Europeans.[37]

As a result of this biased injurious discriminating policy, the Muslims were forced to live in shabby conditions. In this circumstance, the *'ulamã* of the time such as Shãh 'Abd ul-'Azîz, Syed Isma'îl Shahîd, Muḥammad Iṣḥãq, Syed Aḥmad Barelvî, Ḥãjî Imdãd-ullãh Muhãjir Makkî, Maulana Qãsimi Nãnautavi, Sir Syed Aḥmad Khan in the Northern India and in Bengal Ḥãjî Sharî'at-ullãh, Tîtumîr, Karãmat 'Alî led the movement to teach and preach the Islamic teachings and values amongst the Muslims. They tried their level best to reform in the Muslim community.

Shãh 'Abd ul-'Azîz in the beginning of 19th century declared India as a Dãr ul-Harb in his *fatva*. He in his *fatva* said,

> "In the city (Delhi) the Imam ul-Muslemin wields no authority, while

36. Hafeez Malik, *Muslim Nationalism in India and Pakistan* , Washington D.C. 1963, P. 145.
37. Quoted by Mujeeb Ashraf, Op. Cit., P. 21.

the decrees of the Christian leaders are obeyed without fear (of the consequences). Promulgation of the commands of *kufr* means that in the matter of administration and the control of the people, in the levy of land tax, tribute, toll and customs, in the punishment of thieves and robbers, in the settlement of disputes, in the punishment of offences, the *kãfir* acts according to their discretion. There are, indeed, certain Islamic rituals, e.i. Friday and *'Id* Prayers, *ãdhãn* and cow slaughter, with which they do not interfere. But that is of no account. The basic principles of these rituals are of no value to them, for they demolish mosques without the least hesitation, and no Muslim or *dhimmî* can enter the city or its subrubs except with their permission. It is of their own good that they do not object to people going in and out, to travellers and traders visiting the city. (On the other hand), distinguished persons like Shuj'ã ul-Mulk and Wilayate Begum cannot visit the city without their permission. From here to Calcutta, the

> Christians are in complete control. There is no doubt that to the right and to the left, in principalities like Hydrabad, Rampur, Lucknow etc, they do not govern directly as a matter of policy and because the possessors of these territories have become subject to them. This is what is to be understood from the *ḥadîth*, and in accordance with the principle of following the lives and actions of the venerable companions and the great *khalîfas*."[38]

However, he was of the view that the learning of English was not against *shari'ah.* He had the view to learn English not for employment and monetary purpose. His *fatva* describes the purpose of acquiring English Knowledge:

> "Learning English for the purpose of reading, writing letters and knowing the secret meanings of words is permitted. But if any man learns English in order to unite himself with the English, he sins and transgresses the Law, as in the case of weapon. When it is made to drive

38. Shãh 'Abd ul-'Aziz, *Fatawa-e 'Azîzî*, vol. I, Maktba 'Mujtaba'-e Delhi, 1311 AH, P. 17. Quoted by M. Mujeeb, *The Indian Muslims*, London, 2nd ed., 1969, PP. 390-391.

> away thieves or to arrest them, the making of it is a pious act; but if it is made for helping or defending the thieves, then the making of it is sinful."[39]

Shãh 'Abd ul-'Azîz formed two Boards of Directors, one to look after military matters and the other to serve as a Surveillance Committee. 'Abd ul-Ḥaq Maulana Isma'îl and Syed Aḥmad Barelvî looked after military matters and Maulana Iṣḥãq and Maulana Muḥammad Yã'qûb served in surveillance committee. Syed Aḥmad Barelvî after Shãh 'Abd ul-'Azîz played a leading role in the military matters and tried to check the ill practices of the Muslim society. He fought a series of battles first against the Sikhs and then against the British rule. The movement was shaken only after the five state trials form 1864 to 1871 and saw many leaders of the movement were killed and executed.[40]

12. Mutiny of 1857 :

The hostility further got accentuated in the Resistance of 1857 and thus began a continuous struggle between the British and Muslims, in which freedom-loving Hindus also participated with

---

39. Shãh 'Abd ul-'Azîz, *Fatawã-e 'Azîzî*, Delhi, 1904, PP. 91-92. Quoted by Mujeeb Ashraf, Op. Cit., P. 122.
40. Five State trials :- First to fifth trials were held in Ambala, Patna, Maldah, Raj Mahal and Bengal consequtively.

Muslims. However, the British rulers were powerful on both the fronts, economic as well as military.

The Mutiny of 1857 had turned the Muslims as the main accused in the eyes of the British. Consequently, in the post 1857 period, Muslims were persecuted. Many were imprisioned, hanged, tortured while their properties were taken away without any consideration of his being a rebel or legal, young or old. As a result, many Muslim families perished and those who survived were not less unfortunate. Lord Canning, after the Mutiny of 1857, described the situation in the following words:

> "The discriminate hanging, not only of persons of all shades of guilt, but of those whose guilt was at the least very doubtful, and general burning and plunder of villages, whereby the innocent as well as guilty, without regard of age or sex were indiscriminately punished."[41]

From the very early time, the British regarded the Muslims as hostile but after 1857 the situation became worse. They put, right or wrong, every blame on Muslims and did not want to see them in

41. Edward Thompson, *The Other Side of the Medal* , London, 1925, P. 74. Also quoted in Syed Razi Wasti,*The Political Triangle in India (1858-1924)*, Lahore, 1976, P. 20.

administration. On the other hand, their attitude was kind towards Hindu and were even inducted in administrative services. Not only this but they now replaced Muslims by Hindus in Government services. There were some concessions for Muslims to enter in Government jobs, but after 1857 these concessions were withdrawn.

13. Muslims' Position in the Services :

Sir William Hunter in his book ***Indian Musalmans*** had given the data by which the pitiable condition of the Muslim can be understood. Hunter has shown the Muslim position in the three aristocracy department;

(A) Military Command

(B) The collection of revenue and

(C) Judicial and political employ.

Regarding the army, Hunter Says,

> "No Muhammadan gentlemen of birth can enter our regiments; and even if a place could be found for him in our military system, that place would no longer be a source of wealth."[42]

As regard to the collection of land revenue, Hunter compared the Muslim's position under Mughal and the British and quoted Mr. James O'Kinesly:

---

42. W.W. Hunter, *The Indian Musalmans*, Delhi, 1969, P. 151.

> "It (British policy) elevated the Hindu collectors, who upto that time had held but unimportant posts, to the position of landholders, gave them a proprietary right in soil, and allowed them to accumulate wealth which would have gone to the Musalmans under their own rule."[43]

Regarding the Judicial, political or civil employ, he says;

> "None of the native gentlemen who have won their way into the Covenanted Civil Services, or upto the bench of the High Court, are Musalmans."[44]

Hunter gave a detailed report that how many Englishmen, Hindus and Muslims were promoted or demoted in their posts from their grade to lower grade. He says,

> "In the highest grade in which the appointments dated from a previous generation... in April 1869 there was one Musalman to two Hindus; there is now (1871) one Musalman to three Hindus. In the second grade, there were then two

43. Ibid., P. 155.
44. Ibid., P. 157.

> Muhammadans to nine Hindus; there is now one Musalman to a total of 27 Hindus and Englishmen; there are now three Musalmans to total of 24 Hindus and Englishmen. Passing down to the lower ranks, there were in 1869 four Musalmans among a total thirty nine. Among the probationers from whom the service is recruited, there were only two Musalmans in a total of 28; there is now not a single Muhammadan in this rank."[45]

He further says,

> "In the three grades of Assistant Government Engineers, there were 14 Hindus and not one Musalman; among the apprentices there were four Hindus and two Englishmen, and not one Musalman. Among the Sub-Engineers and Supervisors of the Public Works Department, there were 24 Hindus to one Musalman; among the overseas, two Musalmans to 63 Hindus. In the Office of the Account, there were fifty five names of Hindus, and not one

45. Ibid., PP., 159-60.

Musalman, and in the Upper Subordinate Department, there were twenty two Hindus, and again not one Musalman."[46]

Hunter drew a chart of the gazetted appointments of 1871 where Englishmen, Musalmans and Hindus were having the same qualification chart is given below.

Gazetted Posts	Europeans	Hindus	Muslims	Total
Covenanted Civil Services	260	00	00	260
Judicial officers in the Non-Regulation Districts	47	00	00	47
Extra Assistant Commissioners	26	7	00	33
Deputy Magistrate and Deputy Collectors	·53	113	30	196
Income-Tax Assesors	11	43	6	60
Registration Department	33	25	2	60
Judges of Small Cause Court and Subordinate Judges	14	25	8	47
Munsifs	01	178	37	216
Police Department	106	03	00	109
Public Works Department (Engineer Establishment)	154	19	00	173
Public Works Deptt. (Subordinate Establishment)	72	125	4	201

46. Ibid., P. 60.

Gazetted Posts	Europeans	Hindus	Muslims	Total
Public Works Deptt. (Account Establishment)	22	54	00	76
Medical Department Offices attached to Medical Colleges, Jails, Charitable,Deispensaries, Sanitation and Vaccination Establishments and Medical Officers in charge of Districts etc.	89	65	04	158
Department of Public Instruction	38	14	01	53
Other Departments, such as Customs, Marine, Survey, Opium etc.	412	10	00	422
	1338	**681**	**92**	**2111**

After showing the chart Hunter says,

> "A hundred years ago, the Musalmans monopolised all the important offices of State."[47]

Further he says,

> "The proportion of Muhammadans to Hindus, as shown above, is now less than one-seventh. The proportion of Hindus to Europeans is more than one-half; the proportion of Musalmans to Europeans is less than one-forteenth.... In the less conspicuous office establishments in the Presidency Town,

47. Ibid P. 161.

> the exclusion of Musalmans is even more complete. In one extensive Department the other day, it was discovered that there was not a single employ who could read the Musalman dialect; and infact, there is now scarcely a Government office in Calcutta in which a Muhammadan can hope for any post above the rank of poster, messenger, filler of ink-pots and menders of pens."[48]

Regarding the Law Profession, Hunter says,

> "The law is even more strictly closed to the Muhammadans."[49]

And collected the statistics regarding that in 1869. According to that:

> "The Law Officers of the Crown were six in number-four Englishmen, two Hindus and no Musalman. Among the Offices of the High Court of sufficient rank to have their name published, twenty one in number, there were seven Hindu gentlemen and not one Musalman. Among the Barristers-at-Law were three Hindus and not one Musalman."[50]

48. Ibid P. 161.
49. Ibid P. 163.
50. Ibid P. 163.

Likewise, Hunter also drew up a chart of Medical Profession in 1869 which reflects the worst condition of Muslims. Such as,

> "Among the Graduates of Medicine in the Calcutta University there were four doctors; three Hindu one English man, and no Muhammadan. Among Bachelors of Medicine, ten were Hindus and one Englishmen. The hundred and four (104) Licentiates of Medicine had five Englishmen, ninety eight Hindus, and one solitary Muhammadan."[51]

The Muslim Students who had enrolled in English Colleges and Schools, as has been reported to the Education Commission of 1882, in the various provinces, shows the Muslim intention towards English. To clarify the actual condition, it is necessary to show the chart, which is as follow:

Provinces	Classes of Institution	Total Number Of Students	Musalmans	%
Madras	Colleges English	1669	30	1.7
	High Schools "	4836	117	2.4
	Middle "	18553	702	3.8
	Total	**25058**	**870**	**3.4**
Bombay	Colleges English	475	7	1.4
	High Schools "	5731	118	2.0
	Middle "	14257	781	5.4
	Total	**20463**	**906**	**4.4**

51. Ibid P. 166.

Bengal	Colleges English High Schools " Middle "	2738 43747 37959	106 3831 5032	3.8 8.7 13.2
	Total	**84444**	**8969**	**10.6**
North-Western Provinces	Colleges English High Schools " Middle "	223 } 4273	29 } 697	13.0 } 16.3
	Total	**4496**	**726**	**16.3**
Oudh	Colleges English High Schools " Middle "	126 } 1081	7 } 195	5.5 } 18.0
	Total	**1207**	**202**	**16.7**
Punjab	Colleges English High Schools " Middle "	103 453 2671	13 91 703	12.6 20.0 26.3
	Total	**3227**	**807**	**25.0**
All the above Provinces	Colleges English High Schools " Middle "	5334 } 133561	192 } 12288	3.6 } 9.2
	Total	**138895**	**12480**	**8.9**

The above table stated the percentage of Muslims, who learnt English education and showed that their number decreased as the class-wise education increased.[52] Concludingly, Hunter remarks that the statistical data of the Muslims in profession of any departement showed their negligible presence.[53]

Consequently, the Muslims of Bengal, Bihar and Orisa were relegated to a very pitiable position where they had virtually to beg from their political and beaurocratic masters. The sorrowful plight of Muslims

52. Syed Maḥmood, Op. Cit., PP. 167-168.
53. W.W. Hunter, Op. Cit., P. 164.

can be read in the following lines. The Muslims of Orissa submitted a petition to their Commissioner Mr. E.W. Malony.

> "As loyal subjects of Her Most Gracious Majesty the Queen, we have, we believe, an equal claim to all appointments in the administration of the country. Turely speaking, the Orissa Muhammadans have been levelled down and down, with no hopes of rising again. Born of noble parentage, poor by profession, and destitute of patrons, we find ourselves in the position of fish out of water."[54]

Likewise the Muslims of Delhi also addressed their sorrowful condition to the Governor-General:

> "We the Muslim inhabitants of Delhi have since sustained the extreme losses of life, property and honour. At present, we have absolutely nothing to feed our children and ourselves. There is no ceiling under which we could seek shelter against inclement weather, and no clothings to cover our bodies. Thousands of us not bearing the severities of climate perished last year and if nothing is done to protect us many more will die this season."[55]

54. Ibid., PP. 167-168.

55. Punjab. C.S. Records, Genaral Department of Proceedings of Ist January, 1859, F. No. 11-12. Quoted by Syed Razi Wasti, Op. Cit., P. 22.

The sulking mood of Muslims can also be read into the report of a Persian news paper ***Dûrbîn*** dated 14th July, 1869, which is also testimony to the agony of nightmares the Muslims had to face. The report is as follow:

> "All sorts of employment, great or small, are being gradually snatched away from the Muhammadans, and bestowed on men of other race, particularly Hindus. The Government is bound to look upon all classes of its subjects with an equal eye, yet the time has now come when it publicly singles out the Muhammadans in its Gazettes for exclusion from official posts. Recently, when several vacancies occurred in the office of the Sunderban Commissioner, that official, in advertising them in Government Gazette, stated that the appointments would be given to none but Hindus. In short, the Muhammadans have now sunk so low that even qualified for Government employ, they are studiously kept out of it by Government notifications. Nobody takes any notice of their helpless condition, and the higher authorities do not deign even to acknowledge their existence."[56]

56. W.W. Hunter, Op. Cit., P. 167.

Sir Syed Aḥmad Khan felt so distressed that on 26th May, 1875 addressing the Muslim population at Azimabad (Patna), he said,

> "Now you take a glance at the whole of India and bring before your eyes its various organisations. Look at the Government Departments! Look at the factories or Railway! Look at small shops or big trading concerns! Look at any kind of private enterprise and just find out for yourself how many of the employed are Musalmans. I dare say the proportion would not be more than one to a thousand."[57]

14. Muslim Advocacy For Modern Learning:

Muslim scholars and *'ulamã'* showed their liberal trends towards Western learnings from the last decades of 18th century. Mirza Abu Ṭãlib Landãni[58] (1752-1806), perhaps the first outspoken Indian Muslims, supported British rule and responded to the Western culture. He liked English system of education, the English legal system, the English customs and manners. He was of the view that the Muslims in India should embrace such of the Western values as were

57. Sir Syed Aḥmad Khan, *Lecturercṇ Kã Majmû'ah,* ed. By Imãm ud-Dîn, Lahore, 1900, P. 86.
58. Mirza Abu Ṭãlib Landãni was Liason Officer between Oudh Government and the British.

healthy and morally sound.[59] 'Abd ur-Raḥîm Dahrî[60] emphasized and wrote a booklet[61] on the necessity to acquire English learning by the Muslims. He, like Rãjã Rãm Mohan Roy, advocated for Western learnings and addressed a Pamphlet to Lord Hasting regarding the introduction of modern learning through the medium of English language. He was of the view that the modern knowledge cannot be disseminated through translation.[62]

Another well known scholar for his liberal and favourable attitude towards British was Lutf-ullãh (1802-1854)[63] perhaps the first Muslim who wrote an autobiography in English. He praised the technical achievements of the British and their political and military tactics. He was impressed by the civility, refinement and culture and admired their efficiency,

---

59. Mujeeb Ashraf, Op. Cit. PP. 209-210.
60. 'Abd ur-Rahîm Dahrî was an English teacher at the Fort William College and had a prolific knowledge in Arabic, Persian, Turkish, English, Latin, Pushtu etc.
61. The booklet was entitled***Arzdãsht dar Bãb-e Ḍarûrat Tarvîj-e Zabãn-e Angrezi-o 'Ulûm Firang***(An appeal for the Study and Dissemination of the English language and Western Culture.)
62. 'Abd ur-Raḥmãn Parwez Iṣlãḥi, " 'Abd ur-Rahîm Dahri ki Khud Navisht Sawãnih 'Umarî",*Jãmia*', New Delhi, April 1975, PP. 186-193. (For detail).
63. Lutf-ullãh was born at Dãrã Nagar in Malwa on 4th November 1802. He was the son of Shaikh Mıḥammad Ikrãm. He taught Persian to British Military personals, such as B. Mac. Mohan, W. J. Easturck. He also journeyed England in 1844.

their capacity for hard work, their sence of cleanliness and their punctuality and regularity.[64]

Many products of Delhi College who after completing their education advocated to acquire Western knowledge and supported British rule, such as Zaka-ullãh of Delhi (1832-1910), Maulana Muḥammad Ḥusain Âzãd (1833-1910) and Maulvi Nazîr Aḥmad (1836-1912). Maulvi Nazîr Aḥmad wrote many books, especially novels with a view to reform the Muslim society on modern lines.[65] He advocated two types of education-religious and rational sciences. British were expert in rational sciences and as a result achieved tremendous material progress. He viewed that Muslims should take up the study of the sciences but not at the cost of their religious and cultural education.[66]

15. Sir Syed's Approach Towards Western Education :

Among the Muslim reformers, Sir Syed Aḥmad Khan was one of the most towering personality in the 19th century. He launched a movement which affected every aspect of Muslim life, i.e. social, economical, political, cultural and religious. After the Mutiny of 1857, the condition of Muslim community was very

64. Mujeeb Ashraf, Op. Cit., PP. 218-225 (For detail)
65. 'Abd ul-Ḥaq, *Marhûm Delhi College* Delhi, 1945, PP. 1-2, 6-15, 61-62, 76-77, 146-149, 171-177.
66. Mujeeb Ashraf, Op. Cit., P. 231.

gloomy. He, did not know for a time inspite of all the reformist zeal and ability, as how to help and save his community from material and spiritual ruin. Finally, he reached certain conclusions and made a plan. The main objective of his plan, as Syed 'Âbid Ḥusain summed up, were as follows:

1. "To protect the Islamic religion from the onslaught of Christian missionaries, and to prove that it was the one true religion.
2. To remove the bitter enmity which had arisen between the Muslims and the British for religious and political reasons, and to establish friendly relations between them.
3. To re-enterpret the teachings of Islam and bring them in harmony with modern science and philosophy, so that educated Muslims, while holding on their religion, might see the relation and enlightened view of life and meet the demands of the new age.
4. To persuade Muslims to learn the English language and Western sciences so that they might meet Englishmen on equal terms and get a substantial share in the administration of the country.
5. To try to maintain Urdu along with English as an associate official language, and to develop it through translation and original writings so that

> it might acquire a respectable stock of modern scientific material."[67]

During the Mutiny of 1857, Sir Syed Aḥmad Khan was at Bijnor, there he saved the life of about twenty families of Europeans and Eurasians. He assured the Collector and Magistrate of Bijnor, Mr. Shakespeare by saying,

> "As long as I am alive, you have no cause to worry."[68]

With this, he earned the confidence of the British and succeeded, to some extent, in minimising their hostile attitude towards Muslims. He on one hand wrote a Pamphlet entitled ***Asbãb-e Baghãwat-e Hind*** (The causes of the Indian Mutiny) and tried to prove that the British Government itself was responsible for the Mutiny. He also refuted the British charge that Muslims were exclusively responsible for the Mutiny. On the other hand, he wanted to shut the mouth of the critics of Islaṃ through a commentary on Bible. His main purpose was to highlight as far as possible the existing correspondence between Islamic and Judo-Christian beliefs and remove the suspecions of the Christians concerning Islam.[69]

Sir Syed was of the view that the true Islamic teachings and Islamic life were in perfect harmony

---

67. S. 'Abid Ḥusain, Op. Cit., P. 231.
68. Alṭaf Ḥusain Ḥali, *Hayãt-e Jãved,* Eng. tr. K.H. Qadree and J.J. Mathew, Delhi, 1979, P. 47.
69. Ibid., PP. 75-76.

with nature and go simultaneously with the need of the age. This is clear from the fact, he asserted, that there are two types of verses in *Qur'ãn*, i.e. *moḥkamãt* and *mutashãbehãt*. According to him *moḥkamãt* verses have a clear precise meaning and *mutashãbehãt* verses have no definite meaning. But the interpretation of the *mutashãbehãt* goes with the knowledge and experience of the period. S. 'Âbid Ḥusain concludes the discussion of Sir Syed's ideas about relgious reforms as given below:

1. "In religious thought and practices, it is not enough to follow established authority. Every age requires a fresh interpretation according to the needs of the time.
2. To make Islamic teachings intelligible and acceptable to the whole of humanity, it is necessary to express them in rational terms."[70]

Sir Syed not only tried to focus on the rationalistic approach of Islamic teachings but also wanted to change the antagonistic attitude of orthodox '*ulamã*' and general masses towards the English language and Western learnings. He openly opposed those who were of the view that the door of *ijtihãd* was closed. He stressed the use of *ijtihãd* by which one would adjust with every new circumstance.

Sir Syed and his followers had to face much opposition and were even threatened but they, through

70. S. 'Abid Ḥusain, Op. Cit., P. 28.

their determination, continued to pursuade the Muslims to learn English language and advise them to adopt and respect the good things in Western culture. For this, he highlighted, time and again, the importance of Western education.

Sir Syed declared that there was no option for the subject nations but to learn the language of their rulers. He gave example of the Hindus, who were in good condition under Muslim as well as British rule by learning the language of the rulers of the day. He believed that after acquiring the Western learning, it would be possible for the Muslims to improve their social and political conditions. With this objective in mind, he formed the Scientific Society in 1862 for the translation of Western learning from English to Urdu so as it might be of help in understanding the intrinsic value of Western sciences and provide also a basis for mutual understanding and friendship between the British and the Muslims.[71] In 1866, the society started a journal, later named ***Aligarh Gazette*** which had on each page its Urdu text in one column and its English version in the other column. The main objective of ***Aligarh Gazette*** was,

> "to acquaint the British with the thoughts of the Indians and the condition of the country and to keep the Indian informed of the methods of British rule, at the

71. Alṭāf Ḥusain Ḥāli, Op. Cit., P. 85.

same time enabling them to understand and take an interest in politics."[72]

His other work was ***Khutbãt-e Ahmadiya*** (Addresses on the life of the Prophet Muḥammad) (S.A.W.), in which he refuted all the charges against the Prophet of Islam levelled by Sir William Muir.[73] Before this, he went to England and visited libraries, museums, many scholars and observed closely the Western culture and British administration. In England, he had written a small Pamphlet into English and highlighted the shortcomings and demerits of the Indian educational system.[74]

During the stay in England, he reached certain conclusions such as how to overcome the religious prejudice which had arrested the progress of his community. After returning from London, he started a journal ***Tahdhîbul-Akhlãq*** with certain objectives, which are given below:

I. "A rational approach to Islam.

II. A readjustment of Islamic traditions and customs in accordance with the changing time.

III. An active interest in the history and literature of Islam.

IV. A new approach to life, Islamic in its roots, but

---

72. Ibid., P. 91.

73. Sir William Muir Wrote *Life of Muhammad* and discredited the whole divine fabrics of Islam and presented the Prophet Muḥammad (S.A.W.) as a man of least character.

74. Alṭãf Ḥusain Ḥãli, Op. Cit., P. 123.

adjustable to modern requirements, and

V. A better understanding of the Christians and their mode of living."[75]

The sixth volume of ***Tahdhîb ul-Akhlãq*** stated the following aims of reformation of religious and cultural life of Muslims:

1. "Freedom of opinion
2. Reforms of relgious faith
3. Religious ideas and practices
4. Reserach and analysis of certain religious problems
5. Correction of certain religious matters
6. Education of the young
7. Making provision for education
8. Women's education
9. Promoting skills and the arts and crafts."[76]

No doubt, Sir Syed was much opposed by the traditional sections of the Muslims society but soon afterwards many Muslims particularly of upper classes supported him and realized the value of Western education. With their help, Sir Syed laid the foundation of Aligarh College with three major aims., i.e.

A. " to establish a college where Muslims might acquire an English education without prejudice to their religion,

---

75. Rafiq Zakaria, *Rise of Muslims in Indian Politics*,Somaiya Publications, Bombay, 1970, P. 240.
76. Qamar Hasan, *Muslim in India,* A.M.U. Aligarh, 1987, PP. 9-10.

B. to organise a boarding house to which a parent might send their children in confidence that the boy's conduct would be carefully supervised and

C. to give an education which, while developing intellect, would provide physical training, foster good manners, and improve the moral characters."[77]

Since Aligarh College was insufficient to provide the religious teachings, then Sir Syed founded 'Muḥammadan Educational Conference' in 1887 for imparting religious education. Many erudite people such as Alṭãf Ḥusain Ḥãli, Shibli No'mãni, Maulvi Nazîr Aḥmad, Nawãb Moḥsin ul-Mulk took active part.

16. Deoband Movement :

Before Sir Syed, Maulana Qãsim Nãnautavi along with his enlightened friends, after the Mutiny of 1857, decided to found a *madrasãh* at Deoband to preserve the learnings of Islam. He was of the view that the teaching of *Qur'ãn* and *ḥadîth* were necessary to the Muslims for the reconstruction of the Muslim society. The main object behind the foundation of Dãr ul-'Ulûm Deoband was the preservation and perpetuation of Islamic belief and faith, learing and culture. The Dãr ul-'Ulûm on the one hand provided

77. H.G. Rawlinson, "Sir Syed Ahmad Khan"*Islamic Culture,*vol. IV, July, 1930, P. 394.

religious education to the students so as to liberate them form polytheism, superstitions and enthused them as a community to take a leading part in the National freedom movement. Shaikḫ ul-Hind Maulana Maḥmûd ul-Ḥasan, the first student of the *madrasãh*, expressed his impression in the following words:

> "Did Maulana Nãnautavi found this *madrasãh* only for teaching and learning? It was founded in my presence. I think it was founded after the failure of the Mutiny of 1857 to teach and prepare the Muslims for making up the losses of 1857."[78]

The foundation stone of the Dãr ul-'Ulûm had been laid on 30th May, Thursday, 1866 (15 *Muḥarram* 1238). At the time of the establishment of the *madrasãh,* almost all the old *madrasãh* were either destroyed or seized or closed due to financial crisis. In this pitiable condition, Maulana Qãsim realized the gravity of situation, established the seminary of Deoband and advocated the propagation of religious instruction.

The syllabi of the Dãr ul-'Ulûm consisted of *Qur'ãn, ḥadîth, tafsîr, fiqh* and *usûl-e fiqh*. Along with these subjects grammar, Arabic and Persian literature, logic, astronomy, *kalãm,* were also included

78. Syed Maḥboob Rizvi, *Tarikh-e Deoband*, Vol. I, Idarah-e Ihtimam, Dãr ul-'Ulûm, Deoband, 1977, P. 44.

in the syllabus. The entire syllabi consisted of 106 texts and the students were classed by the text books they studied rather than the year of their study.[79]

Modern science (Physics, Chemistry, Zoology, Botany etc.) in the syllabus of the Dãr ul-'Ulûm had got no place. Maulana Qãsim Nãnautavi was of the view that, as written by 'Azîz Aḥmad, the identity and perfection of the Muslim community laid in the preservation of its traditional heritage and more so because Muslim traditional sciences (*manqûlãt*) were undergoing an unprecedented and precipitous decline.[80]

Maulana Qãsim Nãnautavi was not against the acquisition of Western language and literature. He reiterated that the *madrasãh* was not opposed the study of such education but simply wanted to avoid duplication of government efforts.[81] He was of the view that after completion of traditional Islamic learning, students might acquire modern education. His ideas for the acquisition of modern sciences were being realized and in 1903, in the meeting of *Majlis-e Shûra*, it was approved that scholarship would be given to those students who wanted to join

79. 'Aziz Aḥmad, Op. Cit., P. 105.
80. Ibid., P. 104.
81. Dãr ul-'Ulûm Deoband, Rudãd-e Salãnah, 1290 AH, Deoband, 1873, P. 16. Quoted by Barbara Daly Metcalf*Islamic Revival in British India: Deoband (1860-1900)*, Princeton University Press, New Jersy, 1982, P. 102.

government schools after completing their education from the Dãr ul-'Ulûm.[82] But unfortunately, this could not be practically introduced due to lack of fụnds.

With this view, Maulana Qãsim Nãnautavi reduced the period of courses of studies from ten years to six years.[83] He said that six years would be sufficient for the study of *Qur'ãn, ḥadîth, tafsîr, fiqh, usûl-e fiqh and farã'iḍ*. He advocated for the education of *Qur'ãn* and *hadîtḥ* rather to the study of logic and philosophy.

Dãr ul-'Ulûm was founded for the academic excellence and moral upbringing of the students. For academic excellence, the Dãr ul-'Ulûm though followed the Ḥanafi school of *fiqh* but it also accommodates the Mãliki, Shãfaî' and Hanabali schools of *fiqh*. And for moral upbringing, the *'ulamã'* of the Dãr ul-'Ulûm were being attached to one or the other *ṣufi* schools. Regarding the sufistic approach of Maulana Qãsim Nãnautavi, Maulana Qãri Muḥammad Ṭayyab said that the two orders, Chishtîya and Naqshbandiya, merged into one in the person of Ḥãjî Imdãd-ullãh Muhajir Makki anḍ through him transferred to Maulana Qãsim and Rashîd Aḥmad Gangohî.[84]

Maulana Qãsim refuted the Sir Syed's 15 guiding

82. Syed Maḥboob Rizvi, *Tarik-e Deoband*, vol. I, Op. Cit., P. 208.
83. Manãẓir Aḥsan Gilãni, *Sawãneḥ Qãsmi*, vol.II, Dãr ul-'Ulûm Deoband, 1975, P. 286.
84. Syed Maḥboob Rizvi, Op. CIt., P. 28.

principles of *tafsîr* one by one and rejected his speculative trends.[85] He was also against the political views of Sir Syed to keep separate from Indian National Congress and be loyal to the British. But at the same time, he appreciated the Sir Syed's efforts for the welfare of the Muslims. Maulana Muhammad Qãsim gave a positive response to a letter of Sir Syed, in which Sir Syed invited him for the preparation of up-to-date curriculum for the teaching of theology. Maulana Qãsim himself could not go Aligarh but he sent his son-in-law Maulana Muḥammad 'Abd-ullãh for the purpose. In 1893, Maulana Muḥammad 'Abd-ullãh joined the college as a Dean and looked after the theological education.[86]

Maulana Qãsim and Sir Syed both were advocates of remarriage of widows, women's legal right of inheritence and opposed to extravagance in ceremony, dowry, innovations (*bid'at*) and other ill-practices of the Muslim community.

Sir Syed's affection and his hight of respect to

---

85. For the fifteen guiding principles of Sir Syed see in Sir Syed, *Maktûbãt-e Sir Syed*, ed. By Shaikh Muḥammad Isma'il Pãnipati, Majlis-e Taraqqi Adab, Lahore, 1959, PP. 23-27. And for Maulana Qãsim Nãnautavi's refutation to Sir Syed's 15 guiding principles see in Muḥammad Qãsim Nãnautavi, *Tasfiyat ul- 'Aqã'id,* Dãr ul-Ashã'at Karachi, 1976.

86. Sir Syed wrote a letter to Munshi Sa'îd Aḥmad (Assistant Manager of the the College Boarding House) on 5th June, 1893 regarding the appointment of Maulana Muḥammad 'Abd-ullãh. For detail see Sir Syed, *Maktûbãt-e Sir Syed*, Op. Cit., PP. 617-622.

Maulana Qãsim Nanautavi reflects in his obituary which he wrote on the demise of Maulana Qãsim. Some lines of the obituary notice are given below:

> "People had thought that after Maulana Muḥammad Iṣḥãq (grand son of Shãh Waliullah) there would be no body who could equal him in all those qualities for which he was known, but the late Maulana Qãsim proved by his great goodness and godliness, his piety and humility, that among those who passed through the discipline of Delhi school... In this age of ours he (Maulana Qãsim) may perhaps have been a little less than Shãh 'Abd ul-'Azîz in learning but he excelled him in all other things. He was really a man of angelic qualities.... The Seminary of Deoband is a worthy memorial to his greatness. It is the duty of all of us to endeavour that the school may be placed on a stable foundation."[87]

17. Guiding Principles of Dãr ul-'Ulûm Deoband :

The Dãr ul-'Ulûm Deoband was founded in 1866 after eight years of the failure of the Mutiny of 1857. For its smooth running, Maulana Qãsim Nãnautavi made a policy of inviting public contribution because

---

87. *The Aligarh Institute Gazette*,24th April, 1880, 467. Quoted by S. 'Abid Ḥusain, Op. Cit., P. 43.

the British curtailed or even stopped the financial aids and endowments to *madrasãs* which led it closing down. In this situation Maulana Qãsim compiled the following eight fold basic principles on which the foundation of the Dãr ul-' Ulûm is based.

1. The most important thing is that the authorities of the *madrasãh* should always take utmost interest in raising more and more funds from the public. Others should also be exhorted to make efforts for constant increase in public donations. The well-wisher of the *madrasãh* should never forget this obligation of theirs.
2. Constant and serious endeavours are to be made towards a permanent and decent boarding arrangement for the students.
3. The body of the councillors (*shûra*) responsible for the management of the *madrasãh* should be devoted to its cause. Rigidity of views is undesirable. One should never try to manoeuvre in order to impose his opinions upon others. God forbid! the foundation of the *madrasãh* will be shaken if its councillors cease to be tolerant of each other's views. The *muhtamim* is bound to seek council in all advisable matters. Outsiders, also, who entertain a feeling of good-will toward the *madrasãh* and have experience and intelligence, should be given an

opportunity for constructive suggestions.

4. It is essential that the teachers of the *madrasãh* be like-minded like the worldly-minded *'ulamã'* they should not be conceited and disrespectful to others. It will be a bad day for the *madrasãh* when such a situation arises.

5. The curriculum and the method of instruction, as already proposed or afterwards agreed upon by mutal consultations, should be strictly followed; otherwise this *madrasãh* will not flourish and if does flourish it will not serve the purpose.

6. So long as the *madrasãh* does not have any regular and definite source of income, it will continue to exist-*Inshã Allãh* provided there is an honest reliance on and faith in His mercy and compassion; and when it comes to posses a definite source of income, e.g. some substantial property in the form of land or factory or a promise of permanent donation from some rich person of honest intentions, then it appears the *madrasãh* will be diverted of the feelings of fear and hope-a perennial source of submission to the will of *Allãh*-and, with this, will be deprived of the 'hidden' source of unfailing assistance; and its workers will start quarrelling amongst themselves. Therefore, in matters of income and constructions, there should always

remain a lack of certainty of means.

7. The participation of government and rich person is also harmful.
8. The donations of persons who want to remain unknown, I believe, is a source of *barakah* (blessing). Their sincerity seems a more permanent means of income.[88]

Maulana Qãsim Nãnautavi from the very first day was against the government's interference in the Dãr ul-'Ulûm's affairs. In his eight guiding principles, two principles are related to the prohibition of acceptance of government grant and the denial of permanent income form any organisation or individual. According the guide-lines of Maulana Qãsim, the *Majlis-e Shûra* of the Dãr ul-'Ulûm created a network of donors who formed a base not only for financial support but also for the preaching of their teaching. As Barbara Daly Metcalf writes about their sources of income:

> "Most of their income was derived from popular contributions pledged by their many supporters.... Deoband also solicited single gifts in both cash and kind. Especially in the early days of school people donated books, food for the students, and household items to

88. Z.H. Faruqi, *The Deoband School and the Demand for Pakistan* Asia Publishing House, New Delhi, 1963, PP. 25-26. Also in Maulana Muḥammad Tayyab, *Azãdi-e Hindustan Kã Khamosh Rahnuman*, Dãr ul-'Ulûm Deoband, 1957, PP. 9-11. And Maḥboob Rizvi, Op. Cit., PP. 116-117.

furnish the school. Group of people organised collections of hides of animals left from the *'Id* Sacrifice (*'Id ul-Aḍḥa*), selling them and sending the proceeds to the school. People were encouraged to designate their contributions as *zakãt.*"[89]

18. Aims and Objectives of the Dãr ul-'Ulûm :

The aims and Objectives of Dãr ul-'Ulûm are as under :

1. To teach the Holy *Qur'ãn*, the Quranic exegesis, the *ḥadîth*, the Islamic beliefs and their traditionally accepted interpretation and all the necessary and useful allied subjects; to provide complete Islamic information to the Muslims; and to render service to Islam through spiritual instruction, guidance and preaching.
2. To give training in Islamic actions and morals and to infuse the Islamic spirit in the lives of the students.
3. To preach and disseminate Islam and to preserve and defend the religion; to propagate Islam through writing and speech; and to cultivate in the Muslims through education and preaching the morals, actions and sentiments as those of "the best of decades" and the pious ancestors.
4. To keep off and avoid the influences of the government and to maintain the freedom of thought and knowledge.
5. To establish Arabic schools at different places

89. Barbara Daly Metcalf, Op. Cit., P. 97.

for the dissemination of the religious sciences and to affiliate them to Dãr ul-'Ulûm.[90]

The ideal of Dãr ul-'Ulum consists in the revival and renewal of the above said objectives. Regarding the aims of Dãr ul-'Ulum and the regrettable condition of the Muslims of that time Maulana Yã'qûb Nãnautavi[91] said in the function of prize distribution in 1883/1301 that Dãr ul-'Ulum was founded for the teaching and preaching of Islamic learnings and its values. Due to the British policy almost all the *madrasãs* were closed. In such a state Mualana Qãsim established it and tried to revive the Islamic traditional learnings.[92] Maulana Qãri Muḥammad Ṭayyab said about the simplicity and conduct of the students of Dãr ul-'Ulum that not only their high morality and selflessness but all the characteristics of Dãr ul-'Ulum could be seen in their practical life.[93]

Maulana Qãsim Nãnautavi was the man who played a key role in the establishment of their educational movement. He has rendered glorious and

---

90. Syed Mɛḥboob Rizvi, Op. Cit., P. 108.
91. Maulana Yã'qub Nãnautavi was one of the founder member of Dãr ul-'Ulum Deoband. He was the first man who was appointed as the Principal of Dãr ul-'Ulum in 1866. He was born in Nãnauta on 13th *Ṣafar* 1249/2nd July 1883, and learnt from his father Maulana Mamlûk Ali and *Ḥaḍrat* Shãh 'Abd ul-Ghani *Mujaddidi.* He took *ba'it* at the hand of Ḥãji Imdãd-ullãh Muhãjir Makkî. He performed *ḥajj* twice in 1860 and 1877. He was also a good poet. His poetical compositions in Persian and Urdu have been recorded in ***Bayãz-e Yã'qûbi*** He died of cholara on 3rd Rabi ul-Awwal 1302/31 December, 1894.
92. Syed Mɛḥboob Rizvi, Op. CIt., P. 109.
93. Ibid., P. 110.

invaluable services to the Muslims in the academic, educational, political and social fields. Due to his efforts, Dãr ul-'Ulum has attracted the students not only from every corner of the country but also from the foreign countries. It is the credit of Dãr ul-'Ulum that to render selfless service for the cause of Islam, to refute the unbelievers' attacks, to give legal verdicts on the emerging questions and problems and weeding out of innovations in religion and maintaining the fervour of faith among the Muslims masses.

19. Shibli No'mãni Towards Modern Education:

Apart from the untiring efforts of Sir Syed and Maulana Qãsim Nãnautavi, another personality who devoted his whole life for the reconstruction of Muslim society was Maulana Shibli No'mãni. He completed his education on traditional pattern and worked as a professor in M.A.O. College, Aligarh. Therefore, he got the opportunity to study Western Science and literature very closely. He came to the conclusion that for Muslims it was equally necessary to acquire knowledge in both institutions traditional *madrasãs* and modern schools. He desired such educatinal institutions where there ought to be a combination of traditional and modern education. He wished to produce such '*ulamã*' who could add western researches to Islamic learnings and could explain Islamic faith and beliefs through the medium of English language.[94]

Shibli was highly influenced by the ideas of Sir

94. Shibli No'mãni, *Maqãlãt-e Shibli*, vol.III, ed. by Syed Sulaiman Nadvi, Dãr ul-Mụsannefin, Azamgarh, 1938, P. 163.

Syed. But after a few years, differences developed between Sir Syed and Shibli No'mãni. The former was deeply influenced by the Western view, while the latter stressed the primacy of Islamic *sharî'ah*. Shibli often advocated to Sir Syed for the inclusion of Islamic sciences and literature in the syllabi. One such letter, he wrote to Sir Syed in which he tried to make him realize that no real success is possible without the acquisition of knowledge in both institutions.[95] On the other hand, he lectured among the '*ulamã*' that they need not worry about modern education for it is not against Islam, nor it poses any obstacle to Islamic faith.[96]

20. Efforts of other Muslim Scholars to Modern Education :

The efforts for the promotion of modern education were not confined to Northern India only. There were several other lesser lights who worked for the propagation of education among Muslims in Southern and Eastern part of India. Such as Badr ud-Dîn Ṭayyab in Bombay, Syed Amir 'Ali, and Nawãb 'Abd ul-Laṭîf in Calcutta who made good efforts to persuade the Muslims to realize the importance of Western education and be able to share in Government sevices. Nawãb 'Abd ul-Laṭîf opened 'Muḥammadan Literary Society' in Calcutta in 1863. Syed Amir 'Ali founded 'Central National Muḥammadan Association' in 1877 for the protection of the future of Muslim Community.

---

95. Shibli No'mãni, *Makãtib Shibli*, vol. I, ed. by Syed Sulaiman Nadvi, Dãr ul-Muṣannefin, Azamgarh, 1971, P. 4.
96. Shibli No'mãni, Khutbãt-e Shibli, ed. by Syed Sulaiman Nadvi, Dãr ul-Muṣannefin, Azamgarh, 1965, P. 10.

In Bombay, *Anjuman-e Islãm* was established in 1876, in which Badr ud-Dîn Ṭayyab served and tried to awaken the sleeping minds.

The main purpose of all these organisations was to impart English language and Western sciences to improve their material well-being, i.e. politically, economically and educationally.

Consequently, it can be said that Muslim masses had been persuaded for education from three angles. One was pro-British, who advocated the Western learning and modern sciences. The second group showed resentment against the British and they criticized Western customs and manners and championed the cause of traditional learnings. The third group adopted the middle way. They gave preference to Islamic learnings on the one hand and accepted the Western knowledge on the other. They approached Western values from the point of view of Islam. They were of the view that without having knowledge of both of the fields, the Muslims stand no chance of real progress.

After 1857 the social, political, economical and educational position of the Indian Muslims was so bad that their existence in Government services was almost nil. They were ignorant, lost their social dignity and political existence. In this period of gloom and misery, quite a few social reformers and educationists appeared in the Muslim society and rendered untiring services for the upliftment of Muslim Community through the establishment of institutions, schools, colleges, *madrasãs* and organisations and through their valuable speeches.

CHAPTER-II

ESTABLISHMENT OF DÃR UL-'ULÛM NADVAT UL-'ULAMÃ

1. Background :

With the decline of Mughal Empire, the Europeans gradually came to power. Their state policy by and large aimed at crushing and demoralizing the Muslim Community in every walk of life - social, economical, political, educational as well as religious. They even blocked the financial resources of Arabic *madrasãs* such as trusts (*auqãf*) and at the same time provided full support to the missionaries. The resolution of William Bentinck, Governor General, dated 7th March 1835, clearly shows their outwardly support to English language and Western education. According to the resolution,

> "The great object of the Birtish Government ought to be the promotion of European Literature and science amongst the natives of India, and that all the funds appropriated for the purposes of education would be best employed on English alone."[1]

---

1. Syed Maḥmood, *A History of English Education in India (1781-1893)*, M.A.O. College, Aligarh. 1895, P. 51.

Apart from this resolution, many British officials openly aligned themselves with proselytising activities of the missionaries and some of them even were so out-spoken as to declare that it was duty of every Christian to assist the mission.[2] By the resolution and the support of government authorities, the missionaries played a vital role in every corner of the country. As Hunter says, there were about 30,000 scholars in the missionary schools.[3]

So to reverse the effect of the British policies towards the Indian Muslim society particularly in the field of education and culture, Maulana Muḥammad Qãsim Nãnautavi with other '*ulamã*' of the time established a *madrasãh* at Deoband and started what came to be known as Deoband Movement in 1866. Its curriculum was purely based on Islamic traditional learnings-*Qur'ãn, ḥadîth, tafsîr, fiqh, uṣûl-e fiqh*, Arabic-Persian grammar, logic, *kalãm*. *Qur'ãn, ḥadîth, tafsîr* and *fiqh* covered the major part of the curriculum. However, Dãr ul-'Ulûm Deoband combined *kalãm* and philosophy of Khyrabad school, *fiqh* specialization of Firangi Maḥal, Lucknow, with specialization of *ḥadîth* and *tafsîr* of the Waliullahi school of Delhi.[4]

---

2. Syed Ghulam Mohiuddin, "Modern Education and the Educational Problems of the Indian Muslims", *Muslim Education Quarterly*, vol. II, No. 4, Islamic Academy, Combridge, U.K. 1985, P. 64.
3. W.W. Hunter, *Report of the Indian Education Commission*, Calcutta, 1982, PP. 10-11.
4. K.A. Nizami, "Deoband", *The Encyclopaedia of Islam*, (new edition), vol. II, Leiden, 1960, P. 205.

Dãr ul-'Ulûm, though follows, the Ḥanafi school of *fiqh* but it also accomodates the Mãliki, Shãfaî' and Hanabali schools of *fiqh* for the academic excellences, For the sake of ethical and spiritual training, the *'ulamã'* of Dãr ul-'Ulûm were gradually attached to one or the other mystical (sufistic) order, i.e. Chishtî, Naqshbandî orders. These orders apparently differed with each other in their methodology but their main aim and ideal was one and the same, i.e. sincere devotion to *sunnah*, love of Allãh and ethical excellence. Maulana Qãsim Nãnautavi was not against the acquisition of English education. In fact, he did not want any interference of the Government in the affairs of the *madrasãs*.[5]

The credit goes to Deoband that it distinguished itself in serving selflessly for the cause of Islam, defending the Islamic faith against Christian missionaries, weeding out the innovations in faith and producing pious and illustrious *'ulamã'*.

Sir Syed Aḥmad Khan, on the other hand, devoted his whole life for the upliftment of the Muslim Community. He journeyed many places in India as well as England for the cause of his community and tried to awaken the Muslims. After the failure of the rebellion of 1857, Sir Syed wrote a book entitled ***Asbãb-e Baghãwat-e Hind*** (The causes of the Indian

---

5. He advocated that first the students completed their study in Islamic *madrasãs* and then they might take admission in modern schools.

Mutiny) in which he criticized British policies and tried to prove that the British Government itself was responsible for the Mutiny. Besides he also refuted the British that Muslims were not exclusively responsible for the Mutiny of 1857. Further he stressed that a section of Muslim remaind loyal to the British Government and gave a long list of such loyal Muslims.[6] At the time of the Mutiny, Sir Syed was at Bijnor, there he saved the lives of about 20 families of Europeans. With this, he eraned the sympathy of the British and succeeded to some extent in lessening the hostile attitude towards Muslims.

Sir Syed and Maulana Qãsim Nãnautavi both tried to revive the Muslim Community through education. Their aim was one, upliftment of Muslims, but their approaches were different. The former was loyal to the British and advocated for the acquisition of English language and Western education and advised to adopt and respect the good things of the West. The latter stressed religious education rather than Western learning in the wake of political domination and missionary onslaught of the Christian West.

In these circumstances, a group of '*ulamã*' realized that the modern education and traditional education had to be studied side by side. Among them Maulana Muḥammad 'Ali Mongeri, Maulana Shibli No'mãni, Ḥabîb ur-Raḥmãn Khan Sherwãni, Maulana Maḥmûd

---

6. Sir Syed Aḥmad Khan. *Asbãb-e Baghãwat-e Hind* , Karachi, 1957, PP. 110-113.

ul-Ḥasan, Maulana Ashraf 'Ali Thãnwi, Maulana Lutf-ullãh of Aligarh, Mualana Shãh Sulaimãn Pḥulwãrwi were in agreement that the curriculum of the *madrasãs* needed reform and effort should be made to evolve an up-to-date curriculum.

2. Realisation for the need of Nadvat ul-'Ulamã'

In this social and political atmosphere, the *'ulamã'* of the day realized the need of forming an organisation where an update curriculum and the elimination of sectarian misunderstandings should receive greater emphasis. So on the occasion of Annual Convocation (*dastãrbandi*) of *Madrasãh-e Faiḍ-e Âm*, Kanpur in 1892/1310, a decision was taken by the *'ulamã'* [7] to form an organisation (*anjuman*) for two main purposes:

7. The *'ulamã'* who were present in the ceremony of *dastãrbandi of Madrasãh-e Fai ḍ-e Âm* are as follow-Shaikh ul-Hind Maulana Ma ḥmûd ul-Ḥasan (*Mudarris* Ist, Dãr ul-'Ulûm, Deoband), Maulana Ashraf Ali Ṭ ḥ ãnvi (Teacher in *Madrasãh Jãmi'ah Dãr ul-'Ulûm*, Kanpur,) Maulana Khalîl Aḥmad Sahãranpuri (*Mudarris* 2nd, Dãr ul-'Ulûm, Deoband), Maulana Shãh Mu ḥammad Ḥusain Allahabadi. Maulana Syed Mu ḥammad 'Ali Mongeri, Maulana Lutf-ullãh Aligarhi, Maulana Thanã-ullãh Amritsari, Maulana Noor Mu ḥammad Panjabi (Head Master of *Madrasãh-e Islãmiyah* Fat ḥpur), Maulana A ḥmad Hasan Knapuri, Maulana Shãh Sulaiman Phulwarwi, Maulana Syed Ẓahur ul-Islam Fat ḥpuri, Maulana 'Abd ul-Ghani Khan Murshidabadi, Maulana Fakhr ul- Ḥ asan Gangohi, Maulana Shãh Tajamm ul-Ḥusain Dasnui, Maulana Mushtaq 'Ali (Teacher in Faizabad) etc. See in Seyd Mu ḥammad al-Ḥasani, *Sirat Mualana Mu ḥammad 'Ali Mongeri,* Shahi Press, Lucknow, 1964, P. 116., and M ḥammad Iṣ ḥãq Jalis Nadvi, *Tarikh-e Nadvat ul-'Ulamã'* , Vol. I, Lucknow, 1983, P. 96.

I. to reform in the prevalent educational system as the time required,

II. and to eliminate the differences among Muslim groups on different religious issues.

The organisation was named Nadvat ul-'Ulamã' (the religious scholars' forum). It was founded by a gruop of scholars and its first *nãẓim* was Maulana Syed Muḥammad 'Ali Mongeri.[8] Here a question arose as who first of all inspired the idea of Nadvat ul-'Ulamã'. Regarding this, Maulana Ḥabîb ur-Raḥmãn Khan Sherwãni, in a letter, wrote to Maulana Lutf-ullãh, son of Maulana Mongeri, that Mongeri, was the man who had given the idea for the formation of Nadvat ul-'Ulamã.'[9] But Shaikh Muḥammad Ikrãm in his book ***Mauj-e Kauthar*** writes that 'Abd ul-Ghafûr[10] was the prime mover while Maulana Mongeri gave it its final shape.[11]

Maulana Mongeri did his best to achieve the said objectives of Nadvah. He wrote letters and essays in the newspapers regarding the necessity of Nadvah and highlighted its objectives.[12] To acquaint the people

8. He was the desciple of Maulana Lutf-ullãh and made the *bai'ah* at the hand of Faḍl ur-Rahmãn Ganj Muradabadi. See in Syed Sulaiman Nadvi, *Ḥayat-e Shibli*, Dãr ul-Muṣannefin, Azamgarh, 3rd ed., 1970. P. 305.

9. Syed Muḥammad al-Ḥasani, Op. Cit., P. 117.

10. 'Abd ul-Ghafur was Deputy Collector in British Government Services.

11. S.M. Ikram. *Mauj-e Kauthar,* Matia Mahal, Delhi, 1998, P. 187. Also in 'Aziz Aḥmad, *An Intellectual History of Islam in India*, Edinburg University Press, 1969, PP. 58-59.

12. Syed Muḥammad al-Ḥasani, Op. Cit., P. 118.

with its aims and objectives, a delegation was sent, headed by Maulana Mushtãq 'Ali[13], to different parts of India with a letter[14] of Maulana Mongeri. He journeyed Deoband, Rampur, Patna, Nagina, Najibabad, Etawah, Aligarh[15], Jhansi, Bhopal, Bombay. From there he went to Jeddah (Makkah and Madinah) through Karman.

3. Objectives of Nadvat ul-'Ulamã' :

The basic objectives by which Nadvah had started its journey are as Abu'l Ḥasan 'Ali Nadvi wrote

i. "To unite Muslim Community;

ii. to reform educational systme for Islamic renaissance;

iii. to produce men of high character and integrity;

iv. to abolish unIslamic practices;

v. to form a common platform (*Ahl-e Sunnat wa'l Jamã't*) for solving the emerging problems;

vi. to chart out such syllabi, in the light of Islamic principles, and *sharî'ah*, as could fulfil the need of the day;

---

13. Maulana Mushtaq 'Ali Naginavi was a teacher in *Madrasah-e Islamiyah*, Faizabad. He studied *ḥadîth* from Maulana Muḥammad Y'aqûb Nãnautavi, Maulana Syed Aḥmad (*Mudarris* 2nd, Deoband) and Maulana Aḥmad 'Ali *Muḥaddith* Saharanpuri. He also participated in the ceremony of annual convocation in *Madrasãh-e Faiḍ-e Âm* in 1892.

14. Maulana Mongeri had written a letter on behalf of the members of Nadvat ul-'Ulamã' who were present at the ceremony of *dastãrbandi* in 1892 of *Madrasãh-e Faid-e Âm.*

15. The delegation, led by Mushtãq 'Ali reached Aligarh. Here they met Shibli and explained their purpose. Shibli at that time was a teacher in M.A.O. College, Aligarh.

vii. to upgrade the intellectual standard of *'ulamã'*; and

viii. to produce such *'ulamã'* who enjoy the trust and confidence of the people so that they may guide and advise them in relgious as well as educational field."[16]

But in the letter of Mushtaq 'Ali, mainly two objectives had been emphasized:

i. "The students who completed their education from Arabic *madrasãs* are, on the one hand, not aware of the ways of the world. So they often are dependent on others. On the other hand, they do not have such religious knowledge as the time requires. This organisation, therefore, wants to reform the courses of studies in such a manner that it may fulfil the need of the time.

ii. The organisation should try to lessen the differences among the *'ulamã'* of different sects and try to unite them. Due to their confrontations, the Islamic teachings and values along with them are humbled down in the eyes of the opponents."[17]

These two objectives further widened its scope and were discussed on five points :

i. Development of education;

---

16. Muḥammad Iṣḥãq Jalis Nadvi, Op. Cit., P. 11.

17. *Report of Nadvat ul-'Ulamã' 1894,* Kanpur, n.d. PP. 23-24, Also qouted in Muḥammad Iṣḥãq Jalis Nadvi, Op. Cit., PP. 101-102., and Syed Muḥammad al-Ḥasani, Op. Cit., P. 119.

ii. Necessity to reform educational system;
iii. Ethical development;
iv. Minimization of mutual disagreements;
v. Necessity of the welfare of the Muslims.

These points were further explained by the Managing Committee of Nadvat ul-'Ulamã', which are as follows:

i. "There are many *'ulamã'* in India but there is total absence of any system by which they may came close and know each other. The efforts and activities of each other are not known by the *'ulamã'* of different areas. Due to this gap, *'ulamã'* are not in a position to check the deterioration of religious and moral life. So the main efforts of Nadvat ul-'Ulamã' should be to cordinate in estbalishing the missing relationship among *'ulamã'*.

ii. "The second objective of Nadvat ul-'Ulamã' is the elimination of differences among the different Muslim sects (it does not mean that these Muslim sects will become one.) But the main aim behind this effort is to unite them on one platform and react collectively against the Europe's invasion and domination.

iii. "The third objective is to reform and modify in the syllabi of Arabic *madrasãs* according to the need of the day. There had been many changes in the curriculim and the prevalent courses of studies were prepared by Mulla Niẓãm ud-Dîn.[18] Now the time has changed and it requires some addition and deletion in the curriculum. For instance, to refute the attacks of contemporary atheistic ideas a new *'ilm-e Kalãm* is needed. Greater emphasis should be laid on Arabic Literature and Qur'ãnic studies.

iv. "To establish a *madrasãh* of high standard where the education will be provided upto higher levels, so that the students may become expert in their respective fields of education, is the fourth objective of Nadvat ul-'Ulamã'. There would be separate teachers of separate fields of education. There should be a big library. It requires a huge amount of money and selfless devotion. It is not the work of one or two *'ulamã'*. So Nadvah, where hundreds of *'ulamã'* will work together, has taken the responsibility to establish such *madrasãh*.

18. Mulla Niẓãm ud-Dîn (d. 1784) was the son of famous scholar Mulla Quṭb ud-Dîn (d.1691). He belonged to the village of Sihali, 32 miles away from Lucknow. After completing his education, he settled at Firangi Ma ḥal and began his career as a teacher. He became famous by his mathod of teaching and students were attracted from different areas and Firangi Ma ḥal soon became the centre of Islamic learning. Many *'ulamã'* of repute, e.g., Mulla Baḥr ul-'Ulûm (d. 1819), Maulana 'Abd ulḤai (d.1923) and Maulana 'Abd ul-Bari (d. 1960) were the products of Firangi Maḥal. It has been known for its specialisation in *fiqh* and *uṣul-e fiqh*. Due to the fame of Mulla Niẓam ud-Din the course taught here came to be known as *Dars-e Niẓãmi*.

v. "The fifth objective is the propagation of Islam in India as well as in foreign countries. Nadvah will manage the expenses and other requirements for those preachers who will journey for the cause of Islam.

vi. "The sixth objective is related to the department of *fatva* (legal verdict). Nadvah wants to establish a *Dar ul-Iftã'* for the convenience of the people.[19]

4. First Meeting of Nadvat ul-'Ulamã' :

After wide publicity of Nadvat ul-'Ulamã' in India as well as in foreign countries its first meeting was held on 22, 23, 24 April 1894 in *Madrasãh-e Faiḍ-e Âm,* Kanpur. Having kept their differences aside the Muslims of almost all the sects and groups participated in the meeting. Maulana Ḥabîb ur-Raḥmãn Khan Sherwãni writes,

> "Many certified '*ulamã*' of different Muslim sects were present in the meeting. Along with the scholars of Ḥanafi school, Maulana Ibrãhim Ârwi[20], Maulana Muḥammad Ḥusain Baṭãlawi of *Ahl-e Ḥadîth* and among Shi'ah *mujtahids* Maulvi Ghulãm ul-Ḥasnain Kantûri participated in the meeting."[21]

---

19. *Maqãsid Nadvat ul-'Ulamã'* , Kanpur, n.d., PP. 2-7
20. Maulana Muhammad Ibrãhim Ârwi was the manager of *Madrasãh-e Ahmadîya*, Âra.
21. Habîb ur-Rahmãn Khan Sherwãni, *Ustãz ul-'Ulamã',* Aligarh, 1937, P. 42.

Maulana Shãh Muḥammad Ḥusain Âzãd Allahãbadi[22] gave an argumentative lecture on the aims and objectives of Nadvat ul-'Ulamã' and counted the shortcomings of the prevalent system of education. Next day, Maulana 'Abd ul-Ḥaq Ḥaqqãni[23] gave a provocative speech on the necessity of Nadvat ul-'Ulamã'. On 24th April 1894, after *Maghrib salãt, Dastûr ul-'Âmãl* (Plan of action) of Nadvat ul-'Ulamã' had been presented in the general body meeting.[24] Along with this, four resolutions were approved, Which are as follows:

1. "The present system of educations is out-dated and reformable, so efforts should be made in this regard.
2. "The *madrasãh* authorities will be persuaded that either the *muhtamim* (Principal) or other representatives of *madãris-e islãmiyah* (Islamic Seminaries) should participate in the annual meetings of Nadvat ul-'Ulamã'.

---

22. Shãh Muḥammad Ḥusain Âzad Allãhabadi was very renowned scholar of his time. After completing his education, he went for *ḥajj* and studied *ḥadith* from Shaikh Aḥmad Bin Zain wa Hallãn as-Shafa'i al-Mãliki. He was very simple and pious.
23. Abd ul-Ḥaq Ḥaqqãni was from Anbala in Punjab. He studied from Maulana Lutf-ullah Aligarhi in Kanpur. He learnt *ḥádîth* from Maulana Nazir Ḥusain Muḥaddith. After completing his studies he started his career as a teacher in *Madrasãh-e Fatḥpuri*. He authored a book on *tafsir* known as ***Tafsir-e Ḥaqqãni***.
24. Muḥammad Işḥãq Jalis Nadvi, Op. CIt., P. 105. Also in Syed Muḥammad al-Ḥasani, Op. Cit., P. 129.

3. "For proper coordination among *madâris-e islãmiyah* two or three *madrasãs*[25] would serve as a Dãr ul-'Ulûm and all other *madrasãs* be affiliated to them.

4. "Fourth resolution appeals for the donation to *Madrasã-e Faiḍ-e Âm,* especially for hostels."[26]

First resolution was proposed by Muḥammad Ḥusain Allahãbãdi and 'Allãmah Shibli seconded it. Then Ḥabîb ur-Raḥmãn Khan gave an argumentative lecture and a committee of twelve members[27] was formed so that they may advise regarding the present curriculum and system of education. After the approval of third resolution, according to the article No. II of Nadvat ul-'Ulamã', sixteen members for Managing Committee were appointed and four scholars[28] were nominated as honorary members.

---

25. Three big *madrasahs* to which the status of Dãr ul-'Ulûm had been given were Deoband, *Fai-e Âm* and *Ahmadiyah Madrasah* of Âra.
26. Syed Sulaiman Nadvi, Op. Cit., PP. 307-309.
27. Twelve members of the Committee are as :- 1. Maulana Lutf-ullah Aligarhi, 2. Maulana 'Abd ul-Ḥaq Ḥaqqãni, 3. Maulana Aḥmad Raḍã Khan Barelvi, 4. Maulana Ghulam Ḥasan Kanturi, 5. Maulana Muḥammad Ibrahim Ârwi, 6. Maulana Ṣhãh Muḥammad Ḥusain Allahãbãdi, 7. Maulana Shãh Muḥammad Sulaiman Phulwãrwi, 8. Maulana Shibli No'mãni, 10. Maulana 'Abd ul-Ghani, 11. Maulana Muḥammad Ḥusain Baṭãlwi, 12. Maulana 'Abd-ullãh Ansãri.
28. Four honorary members were Maulana Lutf-ullah Aligarhi, Maulana Muḥammad Shãh Muḥaddith Rampuri, Maulana Muḥammad 'Âdil and Maulana Muḥammad Wahid Kanpuri.

After the first meeting of Nadvat ul-'Ulamã' many renowned scholars[29] took active part in the propagation of aims and objectvies of Nadvah in India and abroad. The steps of Nadvat ul-'Ulamã' were welcomed and appreciated by the modern intellectuals in Muḥammadan Educational Conference in 1894 in Aligarh[30], in 1895 in Shahjahanpur[31] and in 1906 in Dhaka.[32] Sir Syed also favoured the establishment of Nadvah and distributed the resolutions passed by the Conference in the form of thousands of copies among

---

29. Shãh Muḥammad Sulaiman Phulwãrwi, 'Abd ulḤaq Ḥaqqãni, Ḥabîb ur-Raḥman Khan Sherwani, 'Abd ul-Ḥai, Ḥakim Syed Ẓahûr ul-Islãm, Fatḥ Muḥammad Tã'ib Lucknowi, Shibli No'mãni, Lutf-ullãh Aligarhi, Mıḥammad 'Âdil, 'Abd ul-Wahid, Muḥammad Shãh Muḥaddith etc. Muḥammad Iṣḥãq Jalis Nadvi,Op. Cit., P. 107.
30. *Pachãs Sãlah Tãrikh; All India Muslim Educational Conference* , Nizami Press, Badaun, 1937, Resolution No. 2, P. 55. (Nawab Moḥsin ul-Mulk proposed the resolution in favour of Nadvah and appealed to the Muslims to support it by money and by pen. Justice Syed Maḥmood seconded it.)
31. Ibid., Resolution No. 5, P. 59. (Editor of Najm ul-Akhbãr, Etawah, Maulvi Bashir ud-Ɖîn proposed a resolution that the idea of Arabic Dãr ul-Ulûm of Nadvat ul-'Ulamã' was very useful and this conference realised its necessity and supported it. The resolution was seconded by Munshi 'Abd ul-Razzaq Kanpuri.)
32. Ibid., Resolution No. 17, P. 117. ("This conference considers Nadvat ul-'Ulamã' a very important *anjuman* and its objectives are very useful in the improvement of education and religion of the Muslims. So it is the duty of every Muslim to support it". Nawab Mohsin ul-Mulk was the proposer and Nawab Viqãr ul-Mulk was the seconder of this resolution.)

Muslims.[33] In one letter to Syed Muḥammad 'Ali Mongeri, on 6th April, 1894, Sir Syed appreciated and prayed for the good result of Nadvat ul-'Ulamã',[34] *Anjuman-e Himãyat-e Islãm*, Lahore also approved a resolution in its support.[35] Not only in India, resolutions in support of Nadvat ul-'Ulamã' were also passed in Syria and Egypt[36]. As Syed Muḥammad al-Ḥasani writes that reforms in syllabus and inclusion of modern sciences into courses of studies were the two main things in which the scholars of the Arab world showed their interest.[37]

On 12, 13, 14 April (1895 16, 17, 18 *Shawwãl* 311), in the second annual meeting of Nadvat ul-'Ulamã', according to the Resolution No.2, passed on 24 April 1894, twenty one representatives of different *madãris-e islãmiyah* took part.[38] *Dastûr ul-'Âmãl* of Nadvat ul-'Ulamã' was read by Maulana Shãh Muḥammad Sulaiman Phulwãrwi and it was approved on 14 April 1895. In the same meeting, a

---

33. Syed Muḥammad al-Ḥasani, Op. Cit., P. 142. Also in Mıḥammad Işḥãq Jalis Nadvi, Op. Cit., P. 113.
34. *Aligarh Institute Gezette*, 6th April, 1894, P.358.
35. Syed Muḥammad al-Ḥasani, Op. Cit., P. 142.
36. Ibid., P. 142.
37. Ibid., P. 143. Also in Mıḥammad Işḥãq Jalis Nadvi, Op. Cit., P. 135.
38. Muḥammad Iqbal Ansari, "Nadvat ul-'Ulamã' : Eik Dînî wa T'ãlîmî Taḥrîk", *Islãm Aur 'Aṣr-e jadid,* Jamia Millia Islamia, New Delhi, April, 1975, P. 37.

new Managing Committee consisted of 34 members was formed.[39]

From the very first day of the establishment of Nadvah, the necessity of *Dãr ul-Iftã'* (Judgement on religous questions) was being felt for the solution of emerging worldly and relgious issues. Maulana Mongeri reiterated that now Nadvat ul-'Ulamã' became widely known in India as well as in foreign countries, therefore for the convenience of the people it was necessary to establish a *Dãr ul-Iftã'*.[40] He, later, presented an outline of this plan which consisted of eleven articles. Munshi Aṭhar 'Ali lectured in its favour.[41] The then Managing Committee approved the resolution of *Dãr ul-Iftã'*.

5. Outline of Dãr ul-'Ulûm *(Musavvidãh-e Dãr ul-Ulûm)*

Reform in syllabi of *madãris-e islãmiyah* is one of the main objectives of Nadvat ul-'Ulamã'. In, almost every meeting, every lecture and very pamphlet of Nadvah, the emphasis had been laid on the upto-date

---

39. Muḥammad Iṣḥãq Jalis Nadvi, Op. Cit., P. 132. (For the names of 34 members, see PP. 132-133.)
40. On 13th April, 1895, Maulana Mongeri put the resolution for the establishment of *Dãr ul-Iftã'*. 'Abd ul-Ḥaq Ḥaqqãni and Shãh Sulaiman Phulwarwi were in the favour but it was not approved by Managing Committee. Muḥammad Iqbal Ansari, Op. Cit., P. 40.
41. Syed Muḥammad al-Ḥasani, Op. Cit., P. 146. Also in Mıḥammad Iṣḥãq Jalis Nadvi, Op. Cit., P. 138. (Munshi Aṭhar 'Ali said, "Earliar I was against but the argumentative lecture of Maulana Mongeri changed my ideas.")

curriculum. But they (members of Nadvah) realised and experienced that without establishment of new Dãr ul-'Ulûm, it was impossible to introduce the reformed curriculum. In the first meeting of Nadvat ul-'Ulamã' on 24 April 1894, the Resolution No.1, regarding the reforming of the curriculum, committee of twelve members was formed. In this, 'Allãmah Shibli was one of the members, who instead of preparing the curriculum came out with an outline for a Dãr ul-'Ulûm.[42]

Here lies a controversy who had chalked out the plan of Dãr ul-'Ulûm called *Musavvidãh-e Dãr ul-'Ulûm*? According to Maulana Abu'l Kalãm Âzãd Shibli prepared *Musavvidãh-e Dãr ul-'Ulûm* and gave it to Maulana Mongeri that he should publish it on his behalf.[43] But on the other hand, Syed Muḥammad al-Ḥasani writes in his book ***Sîrat Maulana Muḥammad 'Ali Mongeri*** that the *musavvidãh* was prepared by the Maulana (Mongeri) himself.[44]

---

42. Syed Sulaiman Nadvi, Op. Cit., P. 310.
43. *Al-Hilãl,* 11the March, 1914, Calcutta P. 177.
44. Syed Muḥammad al-Ḥasani, Op. Cit., P. 146. (People were informed about the *Musavvidãh-e Dãr ul-'Ulûm* through letters and newspapers to propagate their intentions. In response 80 people sent their views. 69 of them expressed their appreciation and supported whole heartedly. Muḥammad Iṣḥãq Jalis Nadvi, Op. Cit., P. 152.) The proposal of *Musavvidãh-e Dãr ul-'Ulûm* had been read in the meeting of Managing Committee on 12th *Muḥarram* 1313/6th July, 1895 which was organised in banglow of Ḥãji Muḥammad Kifãyat-ullãh (business man of sticks). After discussion, it was approved. *Annual Report of Nadvat ul-'Ulamã' - 1926*, Lucknow, n.d., P. 44.

In this *musavvidãh,* major emphasis was put on two objectives;

(i) Production of such *'ulamã'* who would be expert in religious sciences, especially in *'ilm-e kalãm* and *'ilm-e fiqh,* by which they might be able to defend Islam and issue *fatvãs* (legal verdicts)

(ii) Acquaintance with world affairs among the *'ulamã'* so that they may help the people.[45]

Along with this, the *musavvidãh* discussed, in detail, about classes, system of education, arragement of subjects, hostel's life, dinning hall etc. Regarding the hostle's life as written in the *musavvidãh*;

> "separate room for every student... and instructions for them to keep their rooms clean and to carry the activities, e.g. *salãt*, reading, exercise-all should be in time."[46]

Exercise and recreation would be a part of education. Extra-curricular activities like riding, rowing and shooting or whatever they can freely take part in.[47] For debate, seminar and symposium, according to the *musavvidãh*, a separate hall would be there and it would be necessary for every student to take part twice or thrice in a month. In addition to this, it is also mentioned that there would be no distinction between

45. Ibid., P. 147.
46. Ibid., P. 149.
47. Ibid., P. 150.

rich and poor students in the standard of living, dress and food. Rich students would bear their expenses and for poor students the *madrasãh* would arrange.

6. Selection of the place for Dãr ul-'Ulûm :-

In the third annual meeting[48] of Nadvat ul-'Ulamã' after the forceful speech of Shibli No'mãni establishing the necessity of a Dãr ul-'Ulûm, the *Musavvidãh-e Dar ul-'ulûm* was approved [49] and it was decided to form a Managing Committee for the same.[50] On 21 March, 1897, 'Abd ul-Ḥaq Ḥaqqãni proposed and Syed Muḥammad Shãh Rampuri seconded that Delhi would be the most suitable place for Dãr ul-'Ulûm. Shah Sulaiman Phulwãrwi opposed it [51] but after discussion Delhi was selected.[52] But when they found themselves unable to give it the final shape in Delhi, then Ḥabîb ur-Raḥmãn Khan Sherwãni advocated that Lucknow

---

48. The 3rd annual meeting of Nadvat ul-'Ulamã' was held in Bareilly on 11-13 April, 1896.
49. On 12th April, 1896 'Abd ulḤaq Ḥaqqani read out the proposal of Dãr ul-'Ulûm and Shibli seconded it.
50. *Annual Report of Nadvat ul-'Ulamã'- 1896,* Kanpur, n.d., P. 48.
51. Shãh Sulaiman Phulwãrwi was in favour of Lucknow. He said Lucknow would be better than Delhi, because of its open and favourable atmosphere. In his reply 'Abd ul- Ḥaq Ḥaqqãni quoted the Government's report that Delhi was more hygenic, less populated area and the death rate was also comperatively less here than other regions of the country. Moreover, he said, the building of the *Madrasãh-e Ghãzi ud-Dîn Ḥaider* and its property could be acquaired with a little effort. Muḥammad Iṣḥãq Jalis Nadvi, Op. Cit., PP. 192-196 (For detail).
52. *Annual Report of Nadvat ul 'Ulamã'-1897,* Kanpur, n.d., P. 89.

would be a more appropriate place. Later, the decision in favour of Lucknow was finalised[53] and a delegation was sent to Lucknow for the selection of suitable land for Dãr ul-'Ulûm.

The delegation[54] reached Lucknow on 10th March, 1898 from Kanpur for the selection of a piece of land for Dãr ul-'Ulûm. Soon afterwards Munshi Iḥtishãm 'Ali Kãkorwi[55] agreed to give his land of *Ḥasan Bãṛî,* West of Lucknow city, for Dãr ul-'Ulûm.[56] But it is not known why this offer could not be utilized. As Masroor Hashmi Writes.

---

53. Maulana Ghulãm Muḥammad Fâḍil Hoshiyãrpuri opposed it but the majority favoured the selection of Lucknow. Mushir ul-Ḥaq (Honorary Secretary, Edinbara Islamic Society) wrote that Lucknow was selected in place of Delhi for Dãr ul-'Ulûm for two reseans,

    1. "Since last two hundred years Firangi Mahal of Lucknow was playing a leading role among the *madãris-e islãmiyah.*

    2. Many prosperous *nawãbs, zamindãrs* and business men lived in and around Lucknow."

    See in *Al-Nadvah*, vol. V, No. 7. August, 1908, P.1.

54. In the delegation Ḥabib ul-Raḥmãn, Ẓahûr ul-Islãm Fatḥpuri, Khalil ur-Raḥmãn Saharanpuri, Masiḥ uz-Zamãn Khan Shãhjahanpuri, Muḥammad Yûnus Datãlvi, Ḥafiẓ-ullãh, Ghulãm Muḥammad Hoshiyãrpuri under the leadership of Muḥammad 'Ali Mongeri, had gone to Lucknow.

55. Munshi Iḥtishãm 'Ali Kãkorwi was the son of Munshi Imtiãz 'Ali, who was minister in the State of Bhopal. Iḥtishãm 'Ali served Nadvat ul-'Ulamã' as a treasurar.

56. Iḥtishãm 'Ali showed his two lands : one was in *Ḥasan Bãṛi* and other was in *Âfãq Bãgh*. The delegation had chosen the land of *Ḥasan Baṛi.*

"One of the reason for none utilization of the offer might be paucity of funds."[57]

7. Opening of Primary Classes of Dãr ul-'Ulûm

In the annual meeting of 1898, Ḥabîb ur-Raḥmãn Khan Sherwãni said that it was very difficult to start all the classes at the same time. So in the first place, primary level classes should be started at the earliest. This proposal was approved. Maulana Mongeri appealed for the donation for primary classes for one year. In addition to this, Shibli said that *'ulamã's* were blamed that they themselves did not give any donations. Therefore, the expenses of the primary classes were to be borne by *'ulamã'*. At that time, only thirteen members[58] were present and the sum of their donations was more than a thousand rupees.[59]

The proposal of primary classes of Dãr ul-'Ulûm was approved that it would be started in a rented

---

57. Syed Masroor 'Ali Akhtar Hashmi, *Muslim Responses to Western* Education, New Delhi, 1989, P. 127.
58. 1. Maulvi Masîḥ uz-Zamãn Khan = 200/-, 2. Maulvi Mıḥammad Yûnus Khan Datãlvi = 200/- 3. Maulvi Ḥabib ur-Raḥmãn Khan Sherwãni=125/-, 4. Maulvi Shibli No'mani=100/-, 5. Maulvi Syed Muḥammad 'Ali (*nãẓim*)=50/-, 6. Maulvi Khalil ur-Rḥman Saharanpuri=50/- 7. Maulvi Shãh Abu'l Khair Ghazipuri=50/- 8.Maulvi Mushtaq 'Ali (Teacher in Faizabad)=25/- 9. Maulvi Ḥakim Ronaq 'Ali Rudaulvi=25/- 10. Mualvi Mḥammad Dã'ud (Advocate Mirzapur) =25/- 11. Maulavi Mufti Raḥim Bakhsh (Teacher in Almora)-25/- 12. Khan Bahadur Munshi Aṭhar 'Ali=150/-, 13. Maulvi Syed Ashraf 'Ali =125/-
59. Syed Sulaiman Nadvi, Op. Cit., P. 317.

building till the construction of Dãr ul-'Ulûm's own building. Munshi Ihtisham 'Ali purchased a big house, known as *Khãtoon Manzil*, in Golaganj, Lucknow in rupee 9000/- and gave it to Nadvat ul-'ulamã.[60] The head office of Nadvah was shifted to Lucknow from Kanpur[61] and primary classes started functioning. The inaugural ceremony of the *madrasãh* took place on October 4, 1898 in *Khãtoon Manzil.* Many people of the pen, businessmen, advocates, land lords along with Deputy Commissioner Mr. Giri and Commissioner Mr. P. Hardy were present in the ceremony.[62]

In the ceremony, Munshi Aṭhar 'Ali (advocate and honorary Magistrate of Lucknow) read the prepared report of Maulana Mongeri, the *nãẓim* of Nadvat ul-'Ulamã'.[63] The report elaborated four objectives as the moving force behind the establishment of Dãr ul-'Ulûm;

60. It was written in the *Annual Report of Nadvat ul-'Ulamã'-1910,* that by the generosity of Munshi A ṭhar 'Ali and Munshi Iḥtisham 'Ali Kakorwi a building called, *Khãtoon Manzil* , costing repees 9200/- in Golaganj had been handed over to Nadvah, for primary classes, which started functioning from 6th September 1898/9th *Jumadi ul-Awwal* 1316. See in *Annual Report of Nadvat ul-'Ulamã' 1910* , Lucknow, n.d., P. 86.
61. The head office of Nadvah was in Kanpur since 1897/1315 and on 2nd September 1898 it was shifted to Lucknow.
62. Maulana 'Abd ul-Bãri Firangi Maḥali, Maulana 'Ain ul-Quḍḍãt, Maulana Na'im Firangi Maḥali, Maulana Fatḥ Muḥammad Ta'ib Lucknowi, Ḥakîm 'Abd ul-'Aziz, Hakim 'Abd ul-Wali, Mḥammad Nasim (Advocate High Court), Dr. 'Abd ur-Raḥim, Shaikh Aṣghar 'Ali Lucknowi (Business men of fragrance) etc. particpated actively in the inaugural ceremony of the Dãr ul-'Ulûm.
63. Muḥammad 'Ali Mongeri (*nãẓim*) and Maulana Syed 'Abd ul- Ḥai (assistant *nãẓim*), were not present in the inaugural ceremony.

(i) "Completion of arts and sciences.

(ii) "To produce the '*ulamã*' of *fiqh* and '*ilm-e kalãm*, so that they may defend Islam from foreign attacks and solve the emerging problems through *fatvãs*.

(iii) "To promote a moral sense and patience among Muslims.

(v) "To create broadmindedness and bravery among students."[64]

Maulana Ḥafîẓ-ullãh had been appointed as a Principal of the *madrasãh* but due to his long absence from *madrasãh* without information Maulana 'Abd ul-Fãrûq Chiryãkotî, mentor of Shibli, took the charge of Principalship. Along with him Maulana 'Abd us-Shakoor Kãkorwi, Maulana 'Abd ul-Laṭîf Sambhali and Maulana Syed 'Abd ul-Ḥai served as teachers.

To achieve the aims of Dãr ul-'Ulûm, the courses were mainly divided into three stages;

(i) Primary classes (*Darjãh-e Ibtidã'i*). The duration of the courses was three years.

(ii) Secondary level (*Darjãh-e Faḍîlat*)- The curriculum consisted of five years of study.

(iii) Higher classes (*Darjãh-e 'Âlã*) - It was equivalent to M.A. and duration of the courses was two years.

After completing *Darjãh-e Faḍîlat* students are

64. Muḥammad Işḥãq Jalîs Nadvi, Op. Cit. P. 218. Also in Syed Muḥammad al-Ḥasani, Op. Cit., P. 201.

awarded the Degree of 'Âlim.[65] *Darjãh-e 'Âlã* is the stage of specialization, e.g; *ḥadîth, tafsîr, fiqh*, literature (*adab*). So according to the nature of their specialization, the Degree of *Muḥaddith, Mufassir, Faqîh, Adîb* is awarded.[66] The classes of *Darjãh-e Faḍîlat* and *Darjãh-e 'Âlã* were started from 1902 and 1909 respectively.

In 1903, plague broke out in Lucknow and students of Dãr ul-'Ulûm started fleeing home. To check the loss of education, it was decided to shift Dãr ul-'Ulûm in the house of Shaikh Mushîr Ḥusain.[67] Dãr ul-'Ulûm remained there for two and half months.[68] Due to hot season and shortage of hostel facility students were facing many problems. So most of the members of Managing Committee wanted to transfer it to Shahjahanpur. But later the advice of Munshi Aṭhar 'Ali, Munshi Iḥtisham 'Ali, Ḥakîm 'Abd ul-'Azîz, Shaikh Qãdir Bakhsh Faiḍãbadi was accepted and the Managing Committee entrusted the responsibility of its management to Munshi Iḥtishãm 'Ali for one year.[69]

---

65. *Annual Report of Nadvat ul-'Ulamã' -1910,* Lucknow, n.d., P. 87.
66. Muḥammad Iqbal Ansari, Op. Cit., P. 49.
67. Shaikh Mushir Ḥusain was *T'aluqadãr*. His house was on the road adjacent to the station of Badshahnagar.
68. Syed Muḥammad al-Ḥasani, Op. Cit., PP. 264-265.
69. Shamsh Tabrez Khan. *Tarikh-e Nadvat ul-'Ulamã',* Vol. II, Daftar Niẓãmat, Nadvat ul-'Ulamã', Lucknow, 1983, P. 38.

8. Relation between Government and Nadvah:

Earlier the relation between Government and Nadvat ul-'Ulamã' was not good. The Lieutenant Governor of United Provinces Lord Mac. Donnel considered himself as the lord of Muslims' destiny. Any move or the voice of the '*ulamã*' was considered as anti-British Government. On the other hand, some Muslims,[70] for their personal cause and benefit, informed exaggeratedly about the activities of Nadvah.[71] But later on, the Government's attitude became relatively liberal. On 13th March, 1902 Vaqãr ul-Mulk met Lieutenant Governor of United Provinces of Agra and Oudh in Aligarh and told the real condition and minimised the suspicion of the government and helped in preparing a smooth ground for Nadvah. The governor responded positively saying that there was no more suspicions about Nadvah as he had been already informed about the good intentions by the Government Officials who were present in the annual meeting of Nadvat ul-'Ulamã' in Calcutta.[72] Nadvat ul-'Ulamã' also took care to publicize through pamphlets and statements that it was only an academic institution and had nothing to do with politics.[73]

---

70. Chaudhary Nuṣrat 'Ali, rival of Munshi Aṭhar 'Ali, supported to Antony Mac. Donnel. Due to this Munshi Aṭhar 'Ali left Lucknow and went to Madinah through Hyderabad, where he died. Shibli also left for Hyderabad.
71. Syed Sulaiman Nadvi, Op. Cit., P. 352
72. Syed Abu'l Ḥasan 'Ali Nadvi, *Ḥayat-e 'Abd ul-Ḥai*, Nadvat ul-Muṣannefin, Delhi, 1970, P. 150.
73. Syed Muḥammad al-Ḥasani, Op. Cit., P. 266.

9. Decentralisaton of Power :

After the resignation of Maulana Mongeri, Maulana Masîḥ uz-Zamãn Khan became *nãẓîm.*[74] But after two years, he resigned on 21 April, 1905. Hence forth, Nadvah came to be administered under three heads;[75] e.g.,

(i) Registrar Office (*Daftar Murãsalãt*)
(ii) Finance Office (*Daftar Mãl*)
(iii) Dean Office (*Daftar T'ãlîm*)

Maulana Shibli took the charge of Deanship (incharge of academic activities) in April, 1905. Due to his hard work and efforts, students started taking interest in reading and writing. Shams Tabrez Khan writes,

> "He gave a new impetus to the students."[76]

During his Deanship, some such resolutions[77] were passed which created the impression that Nadvat

---

74. Maulana Masîḥ uz-Zaman Khan took the charge of *niẓãmat* on 17th *Shabãn* 1321/28th November, 1903. *Annual Report of Nadvat ul-'Ulamã'*- 1904, Madras, n.d., PP. 31-32.

75. Syed Abu'l Ḥasan 'Ali Nadvi writes that there was no such person in Nadvah who dealt, at a time, religious as well as worldly mattars and stayed permanent in Nadvah. So Nadvah's work had been divided into three departments. Munshi Iḥtisham 'Ali Kakorwi became Finance Officer, Shibli took the charge of Deanship and Syed 'Abd ul-Ḥai became Registrar. Syed Abu'l Ḥasan 'Ali Nadvi, Op. Cit., P. 150 (For detatil).

76. Shams Tabrez Khan, Op. Cit., P. 52.

77. 1. Formation of Law of heriditry endowments and effort to its approval. 2. A reformatic and intellectual view on the translation of *Qur'ãn*. 3. A completion of an authentic Eng. tr. of *Qur'ãn*. 4. The arrangement of the teaching of theology in the Government schools under the supervision of Nadvat ul-'Ulamã'.

ul-'Ulamã' was not only a Dãr ul-'Ulûm but it practically toucned every aspect of Muslim life.

10. Appeal for Donations :

However, still there was no regular source of income of Nadvat ul-'Ulamã'. The financial requirements were fulfilled by the donations collected in the annual meetings and journeys for this purpose. The States of Bahawalpur and Hyderabad had extended some financial aid. Through the efforts of Shibli, the State of Bhopal provided a fixed sum of fifty rupee per month. Although the Government was ready to extend a grant of five hundred rupee per month, but it did not materialise because of a resolution which laid down that no external agency should be allowed to intervene in the activities of Dãr ul-'Ulûm.[78]

As the time passed, Nadvah felt the need of a big building. Shibli came out with a well-thought out idea

---

78. Office of Nadvat ul-'Ulamã' under its regular contact with the Government. A letter releated to Nadvah's donation was published in the ***Indian Telegraph*** of Lucknow by Shaikh Mushir Ḥusain (Barristar and T'aluqadãr.) With reference to this letter, the Director of Public Instruction of United Provinces on January 21, 1909, concerning grant to the Nadvat ul-'Ulamã'. Regarding this, many letters were written and published from both sides. According to the letter of June 21, 1909, "Government will not intervene in any matter of *madrasãh*". Later in Novermber, 1909, a resolution was published that the Lieutenant Governor of United Provinces was ready to grant an aid of 500 hundred per month. For detail see in *Annual Report of Nadvat ul-'Ulamã'*-1910, n.d. Lucknow, PP. 49, 50, 92.

regarding the situation of Dãr ul-'Ulûm.

According to him,

(i) "Nadvah requires at least 30-40 *bighã* land in such a place where there is a possibility of further expansion.

(ii) "Area of land should be free of pollution.

(iii) "Neither it should be far from the city nor too near.

(iv) "It should be donated."[79]

For this, an appeal for the donation of rupee 50,000 had been sent to Bahãwalpur State through Maulvi Ghulãm Muḥammad[80] (advocate of Nadvat ul-'Ulamã'). Maulana Shibli on the other hand tried to get a piece of land for Dãr ul-'Ulûm from the Government.[81] When the grand mother of the Nawab of the State of Bahãwalpur came to know of the appeal, she decided to donate the whole amount (50,000 rupee) out of her own purse.[82]

---

79. Shibli No'mãni, *Maqãlãt-e Shibli* Vol. VIII, ed. by Syed Sulaiman Nadvi, Dãr ul-Muṣannefin, Azamgarh. 1983. P. 78. Also in *al-Nadvah*, vol. V, No.7, August, 1908, PP.1-2.

80. Maulvi Ghulãm Muḥammad Shimlavi, an advocate, was very active supporter of Nadvat ul-'Ulamã'. By his effort, the grandmother of the *nawab* of Bahãwalpur State donated rupee 50,000/-. For his selfless service for Nadvah, Munshi Iḥtisham 'Ali, Finance Officer of Nadvah, awarded him a silver medal.

81. *Al-Nadvah,* vol. V, No. 7, August, 1908, P. 2.

82. Ḥãji Raḥîm Bakhsh (C.I.E. Bahawalpur State), an admirer of Nadvah, after becoming President of the Council of Bahawalpur State invited to the members of Nadvah. On his invitation Maulvi Ghulam Muḥammad Shimlavi went there. He very soon with the help of Dr. Muḥammad Dîn (Medical Officer and advisor to treasurar of Bahawalpur State) put the proposal of Dãr ul-'Ulûm Nadvat ul-'Ulamã' to the grandmother of the *Nawab* Ḥaji Ṣadiq Muḥammad Khan (5th descendant of Bahawalpur State). She agreed to donate the entire sum of money from her own treasury. For detail see *Annual Report of Nadvat ul-'Ulamã'-1910,* Lucknow, n.d., PP. 48, 56, 107.

This unexpected assurance led them to search a suitable piece of land for Dãr ul-'Ulûm. In this regard, they selected a piece of thirty *bighã* land across the river Gomti.[83] The rent of said land amounted rupee 1920/-annualy (as per by-laws of Municipality rupee 60 per *bigha*). But by the effort of Colonel 'Abd ul-Majîd Khan (Foreign Minster of the state of Patiala) and the intervention of Japling (the Deputy Commissioner), the Lieutenant Governor (United Provinces of Agra and Oudh) Hawett granted the land on a nominal charge of rupee two hundred annually.[84]

Due to the non-availability of land and building Shibli mentions that we were not in a position to start new classes. Not only this but we were unable even to provide a chair in the library to our guests. In such situation of dire need, the Government provided us with a piece of land on nominal rent. Shibli appealed, therefore, to the Managing Committee of Nadvat ul-'Ulamã' in particular and the Muslim Community in general to pay the vote of thanks[85] to the government.

11. Ceremony of Foundation Stone :

The ceremony of laying the foundation stone of

83. The land is situated adjacent to the Âhni Bridge. On one side, there is Gomti river and on the other side the hostel of Canning College.
84. *Al-Nadvah,* vol. V, No. 11, Lucknow, December 1908, PP. 2-3. Also in *Annual Report of Nadvat ul-'Ulamã'- 1910* , Lucknow, n.d., P. 107. (Masroor Hashmi wrote that Government granted the land on nominal rent of rupees 60/- per year). For detail See Syed Masroor Akhtar Hashmi, Op. Cit., 128.
85. Shibli No'mãni,*Maqãlãt-e Shibli* , vol. VIII, Op. Cit., PP. 78-79.

Dãr ul-'Ulûm was held on November 28, 1908 by Sir John Perscot Hawett, the Lieutenant Governor of United Provinces, between 4 to 5 in the evening.[86] The address of welcome (*sipãsnãmah*) had been read out to the honorable guest into urdu (the original text of the *sipãsnãmah* was in Arabic.)[87] Maulvi Shams Tabṛez Khan writes in the footnotes of his book ***Tãrîkh-e Nadvat ul-'Ulamã'***, vol-II, that in the book ***Yãd-e Ayyãm*** (the Memoirs) of Maulvi Ḍia ul-Ḥasan Alvi Nadvi, it is written that the real foundation of Dãr ul-'Ulûm was laid by Maulana Najm ud-Dîn Fatḥpuri Naqshbandi (successor of 'Abd us-Salãm Hinsawi).[88]

However, a section of the *'ulamã'* and some others of the same view strongly criticized that how pertinent it was that a Christian laid the foundation of a *madrasãh*. In order to tone down their resentment Shibli referred to the Pulpit of *Masjid-e Nabvi* which was constructed by a Christian.[89]

---

86. Ibid., PP. 89-90. Also in Syed Sulaiman Nadvi, Op. Cit. P. 483. and *al-Nadvah*, vol. V, No. 11, Lucknow, December, 1908 PP. 3-4. (Maulvi Shãh Abu'l Khair, Colonel 'Abd ul-Majid Khan, Honourable Raja of Muradabad, Nawab Viqãr ul-Mulk, Ḥafîz 'Abd ur-Raḥîm (*Rais* Kanpur), Nawab 'Ali Ḥasan Khan (*Rais* Bhopal), Munshi Iḥtisham 'Ali Kãkorwi, Munshi Aṭhar 'Ali, Kãkorwi (Advocate Lucknow), Ḥakîm 'Abd ul-'Azîz, Ḥakîm 'Abd ul-Wali, Ḥabib ur-Raḥmãn Khan Sherwãni, Maulvi Muḥammad Nasim (Advocate), and the *Qãḍi* (*Qãḍi's* name is not known) of Nadvat ul-'Ulamã' were the members who accompanied the Lieutenant Governor at the foundation site.
87. *Annual Report of Nadvat ul-'Ulamã'-1910,* Lucknow, n.d., PP. 109-125 (For detail about the *Sipãsnãmah's* Arabic Text, its Urdu tr. and the Urdu tr. of the speech of Lieutenant Governor.)
88. Shams Tabrez Khan, Op. Cit., P. 81.
89. *Al-Nạdvah* vol. V. No. 11, Lucknow, 1908. PP.1-2.

At the ceremony, *'ulamã'*, *nawãbs*, businessmen, scholars of Aligarh[90], and the members of Muḥ ammadan Educational Conference were present. Maualna Shibli expressed his feelings in the following words:

> "This was the first time when the people of Turkish cap and the people of turbans stood shoulder to shoulder. This was the first time when the *'ulamã'* respected and sat together with the Christian Soverign. This was the first time when Shiã and Sunni both participated in the celebration of a religious institution. This was the first time when the foundation stone of a religious institution was laid by a non-Muslim. In short, this was the first time when Christians, Muslims-Shiã, Sunni-Hanafi, Wahhabi, *ṣufi, zãhid* all came together under one roof." [91]

In the annual meeting of Nadvat ul-'Ulamã', which was to take place the next day, 29 November 1908, a proposal for the construction of, at least, one room by

---

90. Viqar ul-Mulk, Ḥãji Musa Khan, Aftab Ahmad Khan, Dr. Ḍiã ud-Dîn etc. for the first time attanded the ceremony of Nadvat ul-'Ulamã'. See Sulaiman Nadvi, Op. Cit., P. 486.

91. *Al-Nadvah,* vol. V No. 11, Lucknow, December, 1908, PP. 1-2. Also in Shibli No'mãni, *Maqãlãt-e Shibli,* vol. VIII, Op. Cit., PP. 88-89.

the people of each city was put forth by Shibli No'mãni and was seconded by Ḥabîb ur-Raḥmãn Khan Sherwãni and Ghulãm Muḥammad Shimlavi.[92] 'Allãmah Shibli required some more money especially for religious studies. For this, he wrote a letter to Munshi Muḥammad Amîn of Bhopal on February 7, 1909,

> "Still the regular income of Nadvah is only two hundred rupee for religious studies whereas an aid of five hundred rupee comes from the Government for modern studies. State of Hyderabad promised to pay rupee five hundred but presently the State itself is in debt."[93]

The Sultan Jahãn Begum of Bhopal increased the donation from fifty rupees to two hundred fifty rupees per month.[94] From 1910, Nawãb Ḥamid 'Ali Khan of Rampur State agreed to grant five hundred rupees annually.[95]

After the foundation ceremony, the architectural plan of Dãr ul-'Ulûm was prepared by Khan Bahãdur

---

92. Syed Sulaiman Nadvi, Op. Cit., P. 487.
93. Shibli No'mãni, *Makatib Shibli*, vol. I, Comp. by. Syed Sulaiman Nadvi, Dãr ul-Mıṣannefin, Azamgarh ed. 2nd, 1928, P. 234. (Letter No. 3)
94. Syed Sulaiman Nadvi, Op. Cit., P. 489.
95. Ibid., P. 490. Also in*Annual Report fo Nadvat ul-'Ulamã'-1910*, Op. Cit., P. 34.

Mîr J'ãfar Ḥusain of Jhansi, which consisted of thirty rooms along with a big central hall. This was approved by Managing Committee on 2 May, 1909.[96] To lookafter the construction work, a sub-committee was formed. It was headed by Munshi Iḥtisham 'Ali Kakorwi. The construction work was started under the supervision of Syed Hãdi Lucknowi, the overseer, and it was continued upto 1913.[97] When the construction work was going on, Shibli along with the students and other teachers of Dãr ul-'Ulûm went to the site in February, 1910 and said,

> "The formal foundation of Dãr ul-'Ulûm had been laid by the ruler of the time, now we will lay the real foundation"[98]

Then he laid the foundation of *Dãr ut-Tafsîr*. Shibli No'mani himself wrote regarding the event that the day was Ist *Muḥarram*. 1328, Friday, when all the students of Dãr ul-'Ulûm came together to the site and helped labourers.[99]

On the invitation of 'Allamah Shibli, Sir Agha

---

96. Khan Bahãdur Mir Jãfar Ḥusain along with the architecture of Dãr ul-'Ulûm gave a detailed report (spread upon 50 Pages) regarding expenses. The architectural plan of*Dãr ul-Iqãmah* (hostels) also made by him. See*Al-Nadvah*, vol. VI, No. 3, April, 1909, P.1. Also in *Al-Nadvah*, Vol. VI, No.5, June, 1909, PP. 1-2.
97. Syed Sulaiman Nadvi, Op. Cit., P. 490.
98. Ibid., P. 491.
99. Ibid., P. 491-492. Also in*Al-Nadvah*, Vol. VII, No. 2, February, 1910, PP. 2-3.

Khan attended the meeting of Nadvat ul-'Ulamã', which was held in the incomplete central hall of Dãr ul-'Ulûm on February 3, 1910.[100] He granted rupee five hundred per year to Nadvah. The editor of ***al-Manãr*** 'Allãmah Rashîd Raḍã was also received on April 6, 1912 in the same hall. In 1914 Dãr ul-'Ulûm was shifted in this incomplete building from *Khãtoon Manzil.*

100. *Al-Nadvah,* vol. VII, No. 3, March, 1910, PP. 1-2. Also in Shibli No'mani, *Maqãlãt-e Shibli,* vol. VIII, Op. Cit., P. 96.

CHAPTER-III

COURSES OF STUDIES

Reformation in the courses of studies and system of education was one of the main factors behind the formation of Nadvat ul-'Ulamã', because with the advent of British in India Western influence in the field of culture and civilization, arts and sciences started playing a leading role in the society. Particularly for Muslims, it was the period of confusion and conflict that how they would be able to preserve Islamic civilization and to adopt Western education at the same time.

In these circumstances, Muslims in general were divided into two groups. One opposed the acquisition of modern education and advocated for the restoration and preservation of Islamic learnings. They were of the view that turning to Western education meant renouncing Islam itself in favour of Christianity and gradually it would weaken their faith and belief. The other group advocated for the acquisition of modern education to meet the needs of the day. They considered it was the only means of enlightenment and modernisation for the Muslim Community. In the following years, the gap between these two conflicting groups further widened and blocked their way of progress.

This situation led to the emergence of a third group which was convinced of the necessity of adopting the middle way and of trying to reconcile between Islamic values and modernistic views. They advocated for the acquisition of such modern education which was not against the Islamic teachings. The man who played, in this, a key role was Maulana Shibli No'mãni. He observed minutely the ideological compulsions of the *'ulamã'* and concluded that the out-dated courses of studies were the main reason of the rejection of modern knowledge.

In this context, their ideas and views took a practical shape in the annual convocation programme of *Madrasãh-e Faiḍ-e Âm*[1] in Kanpur with the approval of four resolutions[2] regarding the reformation in the curriculum and organisation of Islamic institutions. Along with this, a committee of twelve members[3] was formed to advise on necessary modifications in the curriculum after examining the prevalent courses of studies and system of education. They were also suggested to take help from Maulana Rashîd Aḥmad Gangohî.[4]

---

1. *Madrasah-e Faiḍ-e Âm* was founded by *Mufi* 'Inayat Ahmad Kakorwi, desciple of Maulana Buzurg 'Ali, at Kanpur in 1271/1854.
2. Supra., PP.98,99.
3. Supra.,P.99 (Foot Note)
4. Syed Muḥammad al-Ḥasani. *Sirat Maulana Muḥammad 'Ali Mongeri*, Shahi Press, Lucknovv/1964, P. 130.

In the same convocation programme, Maulana Shah Muḥammad Husain of Allahabad focussed on the aims and objectives of Nadvat ul-'Ulamã' and pointed out comprehensively to the demerits of the out-dated syllabi of Islamic institutions. He also emphasized that the system of education needed urgent reformation. His ideas and views were greatly supported by Shibli No'mani.

In his speech, Shibli replied argumentatively to the following questions:

> "What was the system of education in Islam? Why changes took place in the courses from time to time? How and why *mã'qulãt* became a part of curriculum? what were the reasons behind the popularity of *Dars-e Niẓãmi* and demerits of the *madrasas'* curriculum."[5]

> Maulana Alṭãf Ḥusain Ḥãli also sent an article on the 'necessity of curriculum reform', in which he laid more emphasis on the teaching of History, Geography and Arabic language and Literature.[6]

1. Views of Shibli No'mani Regarding Syllabi :-

Maulana Shibli realized that the acquisition of English language and Western sciences were necessary

5. Muḥammad Iṣḥaq Jalis Nadvi, *Tarikh-e-Nadvat ul-'Ulama*, vol. I, Lucknow, 1983, P. 105'
6. Ibid., P 106.

for the cause of Islam. He highlighted the Western spirit in English interpretation of Islamic faith and ethics. So it was the prime duty of the *'ulamã'* that they:

1. Rectify the wrong interpretation of the Qur'ãnic injunctions by orientalists.
2. Acquire the science of Western sciences and literature to refute the Westerners' attack.
3. Check the unbridled interpretation of Islam by Westernised Muslim scholars.
4. Prepare an up-to-date syllabi for *madaris-e islãmiya.*[7]

Moreover, in the support of the above point Shibli gave an example that as in the 'Abbãsid Kingdom, Greek Philosophy was being taught for the defence of Islam and it was considered as a religious act, in the same way it was time to study Modern Philosophy and understand its theories for refuting their attacks.[8] In the words of Shibli No'mãni,

> "These Greek sciences were neither our theological sciences nor an understanding of our religion is dependent upon their knowledge. Imam Ghazãli had included them

---

7. Shibli No'mani *Maqal'at-e-Shibli,* vol. III, ed. by Syed Sulaiman Nadvi, Delhi, 1923, P. 142.
8. Syed Sulaiman Nadvi, *Hayat-e-Shibli,* Dar ul-Muṣannefin, Azamgarh, 3rd ed., 1917, P. 22. (Pereface). Also see Shibli No'mani, *Khutbãt-e-Shibli,* Dar ul-Muṣannafin, Azamgarh, 1941, PP. 89-92. (for detail).

in the syllabus of our theological schools so that our *'ulamã'* would not remain ignorant of the Greek sources of the Philosophical concepts propagated largely by the followers of the Batini Sect and could provide be fitting answer to the agnosticism of their time. But now these agnostics have disappeared and so have the Greek sciences. The Rationalists have lost faith in the soundness of the issues raised by them. Their influence has waned in the course of time and they have ceased to be a threat to Islam. In their place, there are new sciences, new problems and new discoveries and what the *'ulamã'* of today need is to master them in order to remove the current difficulties of Islam and to dispel the doubts and misconception of modern age in a scientific manner."[9]

'Allãmah Shibli never hesitated to borrow any thing from Western arts and sciences if they were beneficial and advantageous for the regeneration of Islam.[10] He in his educational planning combined the modern subjects and religious sciences. At one time-he opined that the spread of modern education amongst the Muslims was largely dependent upon the support

---

9. Syed Sulaiman Nadvi, *Hayat-e-Shibli,* Op. Cit., P. 20 (Preface)
10 Rafiq Zakariya, *Rise of Muslims in Indian Politics,* Bombay, 1970, P. 251.

of *'ulamã'* and, at the same time the religious movement needed the support of English educated Muslims for its success.[11]

2. Shibli's Appreciation to Hindu Response to Modern Education :-

'Allãmah Shibli examined that modern education was introduced in the Hindu *pãṭḥ shãlãs* and *vidyãlays* as an instrument for the preservation of their cultural identity.[12] Through these *pãṭḥ shãlãs,* they were being trained to undergo many hardships of deprivations, the cause of Hindu solidarity and advancement. The Hindu preachers at the same time were well-versed with their religious values as well as modern philosophies. Shibli highlighted that this modern education and knowledge did not create any hindrance in their development. The Hindus who knew English preached their religion in a better way. The acquisition of modern education was not an impediment in their revivalism.[13]

3. Characteristics of *Dars-e Nizãmi* :

'Ulamã' and scholars of the time realized that the prevalent syllabi, popularly known as *Dars-e Niẓãmi,* failed to fulfil the need of the day. Many out-dated

---

11. Neyaz Aḫmad 'Azmi, "Shibli on Muslim Education and Politics", *Islam and the Modern Age,* vol. 25, No. 3, August 1994, New Delhi, P. 195.
12. Shibli No'mãni,*Maqalat-e-Shibli,* vol. III, Op. Cit., P. 145.
13. Ibid., P. 147.

books were included in the *dars*. More emphasis was put on the study of *mã'qulãt* rather than on the study of *Qur'ãn, ḥadîth, tafsîr, fiqh*. Consequently, the products of the *madrasas* were not having proficiency in arts and intellectual skills. Shibli highlighted the demerits of the syllabi of *madãris-e islãmiyah;*

i. "Few books are on these subjects and disciplines which are necessary to study and more emphasis is given to those aspects whose acquisition is not needed. Such as knowledge of *ṣarf* and *na ḥv* is required to only such extent as may enable the students to acquire proficiency in Arabic language and literature. But much more time is given to the study of *ṣarf* and *na ḥv* whereas literautre as such is neglected.

ii. "Books on philosophy and logic covered major parts of the curriculum and the books on *tafsîr, ḥadîth, fiqh* and *uṣûl-e fiqh* are in much smaller number.

iii. "Many books are confusing and full of ambiguous interpretations as regard to its subject-matter. Such as ***Ḥamd-ullãh*** (حمداللہ), ***Mir Zãhid*** (میرزاہد), ***Mullã Ḥasan*** (ملاحسن), ***Qãḍî Mubãrak*** (قاضی مبارک) etc. are books on logic but in them philosophical problems have been dealt at length which hinders proficiency in the art of logic.

iv. "Only two books on *tafsir*-***Jalãlain*** and ***Baiḍãwi*** are included in the syllabi. ***Jalãlain*** is so short that its words are equal in number to the words of *Qur'ãn*.

v. *"Ilm ul-'Aqã'id* is very important subject but only ***Sharḥ 'Aqãi'd-e Nasafi*** (شرحِ عقائدِ نسفی) is prescribed. It is a book meant for primary level only. Although another book ***Sharḥ Mawãfiq*** (شرحِ مواقف) is also included but the portion of ***Umûr-e Ammah*** which has no concern with *kalãm*, is taught,

vi. "Not a single book is included on modern subjects in the curriculum.

vii. "There is no place for English in the syllabi."[14]

Maulana Syed 'Abd ul-Ḥai also discusses in detail regarding the courses of studies of Indian *madrasas*. He writes,

"The following books on logic had been included in the syllabus without any consideration, e.g. ***Ghulãm Yaḥyã*** (غلام یحیٰ), ***Mullã Ḥasan*** (ملاحسن), ***Ḥamd-ullãh*** (حمد اللہ), ***Qãḍî Mubãrak*** (قاضی مبارک), ***Sharḥ Sullam***

14. *Annual Report of Nadvat ul-'Ulamã'-1910,* Lucknow n.d. PP. 87-88. Also in Syed Sulaiman Nadvi, Op. Cit., PP. 413-414.

Abd ul-'Ali Bahr ul-'Ulûm (شرح سلم عبدالعلی بحرالعلوم), ***Hãshiyah-e Mîr Zãhid*** (حاشیۂ میرزاہد), ***Sharḥ Sullam Mullã Mobîn*** (شرحِ سلم ملامبین) etc."[15]

He further writes that two books on *tafsir*,[16] fifteen books on logic,[17] two books on *balãgha*[18] (rhetoric) had been included in the courses of studies. Geography, history and *'Ilm-e 'Aijãz ul-Qur'ãn* have got no place in the syllabus. Most of the books lack in clarity and lucidity in the treatment and subject matter they deal with.[19]

After taking into consideration the courses of studies of *madãris-e islãmiyah,* it becomes clear that students gave major part of their student's life in the

---

15. Syed 'Abd ul-Ḥai, *Islãmi 'Ulûm-O funûn Hindustãn Mei ṇ,* Dãr ul-Muṣannefîn, Azamgarh, 1970, P. 19.
16. ***Jalãliam*** (جلالین) and ***Baiḍãwi*** (بیضاوی). Two and half chapters of ***Baiḍãwi*** were includded in the course.
17. 15 books on logic are as : 1. ***Ṣughrã*** (صغریٰ), 2. ***Kubrã*** (کبریٰ), 3. ***Îsã Ghauji*** (ایساغوجی), 4. ***Qãla Aqûl*** (قال اقول), 5. ***Mizãn-e Manṭiq*** (میزانِ منطق), 6. ***Tahdhîb Shaḥ Tahdhîb*** (تہذیب شرح تہذیب), 7. ***Quṭbi*** (قطبی), 8. ***Mîr Quṭbi*** (میرقطبی), 9. ***Mullã Ḥasan*** (ملاحسن), 10. ***Ḥamd-ullah*** (حمداللہ), 11. ***Mîr Zãhid Risalah*** (میرزاہد رسالہ), 12. ***Ghulãm Yaḥyã*** (غلام یحییٰ), 13. ***Mîr Zãhid*** (میرزاہد), 14. ***Mullã Jalãl*** (ملاجلال), 15. ***Qãḍî Mubãrak*** (قاضی مبارک).
18. **Mukhtaṣar** (مختصر) and **Muṭawwal** (مطوّل). One forth of Muṭawwal was included in the syllabus.
19. Syed 'Abd ul-Ḥai, Op. Cit. PP. 20-21. Also in Mıḥammad Iṣḥãq Jalîs Nadvi, Op. Cit., PP. 66-67.

acquisition of *mã'qulãt*, which is of no use, and very little attention is being paid to religious studies. For exapmle ***Sharḥ Mullã Jãmî*** (شرح ملا جامی) comprised 400 pages took eight months, ***Mukhtaṣar ul-Ma'ãni*** (مختصر المعانی) comprised 340 pages and took seven months but the time alotted to ***Ṣaḥîḥ Bukhãri*** (صحیح بخاری) is 6¾ months only while it comprises 1128 pages.[20]

Gradually, the courses of studies of *madãris-e islãmiyah* were moving on the path of deterioration. The books, which were being included, year after year, were almost all ***Shurûḥ*** (شروح) and ***Ḥawãshi*** (حواشی). Scholars devoted most of their time in writing down ***Shuraḥ*** and ***Ḥawãshi***. Syed 'Abd ul-Ḥai wrote that there were 117 books on ***Sharḥ*** and ***Ḥawãshi*** on logic. Thirty seven ***Shurûḥ*** had been written only on ***Sullam*** (سلم) of Muḥib-ullãh Bihãri.[21] Moreover, Maulvi Muḥammad Fãrûq Chiryãkotî narrated from his mentor Mufti Muḥammad Yûsuf, as referred by Syed 'Abd ul-Ḥai in ***al-Nadvah***, that in his childhood ***Sharḥ Sullam*** was not included in the courses of every madrasãh. But the desciples of Qãḍî Mubãrak used to teach ***Sullam*** and ***Sharḥ Sullam Qãḍî***

20. Syed Muḥammad al- Ḥasani, Op. Cit., P. 71.
21. Muḥammad Iṣḥãq Jalis Nadvi, Op. Cit., P. 72. Also in Syed Muḥammad al- Ḥasani, Op. Cit., P. 81.

Mubãrak and ***Sharḥ Sullam Mullã Ḥasan*** was being taught by the desciples of Mullã Ḥasan. In the circle of Baḥr ul-'Ulûm ***Sharḥ Sullam Baḥr ul-'Ulûm*** had been taught and Ḥamd-ullãh's desciples used to teach ***Sharḥ Sullam Ḥamd-ullãh***. For polemical discussions, they often used to consult each other's ***Sharḥs***. Consequently, in the later years, all the ***Shurûḥ*** became a part of the curriculum.[22]

4. Shãh Wali-ullãh's Contribution to Education :

It was Shãh Wali-ullãh who realized this deplorable state and especially the total neglect of *ḥadîth*. On his return from *ḥajj*, he devoted his life to the teaching of *ḥadîth*. Upto now, there were only two books, i.e. ***Mashãriq ul-Anwãr*** (مشارق الانوار) and ***Mishkãt Maṣãbih*** (مشکوٰۃ مصابیح) which had been included in the syllabus of *madãris-e islãmiyah* in the field of *ḥadîth*. Shãh Wali-ullãh introduced *ḥadîth* in a big way and thus the teaching of ***Ṣiḥãḥ Sitta*** (صحاح ستہ) (Six authentic books of *ḥadîth*) was started in the *madrasãh*.

Moreover, he also prepared a syllabi, in which he on one hand, included *ḥadîth, tafsîr, taṣawwuf* and *fiqh* in the religious sciences and on the other he

---

22. *Al-Nadvah,* vol. VI, No. 1, February, 1901, P. 14. Also in Syed 'Abd ul-Ḥai, Op. Cit., PP. 19, 20 and 33.

chose grammar, logic, philosophy, astronomy and mathematics for rational science. But due to political disturbances in Delhi, he could not give it a practical shape.[23] The centre of state patronage of intelectual and educational accomplishments had shifted now from Delhi to Lucknow-where logic and philosphy had already attained position of importance.

5. Emergence of Progressive *'Ulamã'* :

Dars-e Niẓãmiyah hindered the way of progress of Muslim education and failed to keep pace with the changing modern world. The Muslim in general suffered from an inferiority complex and felt themselves helpless against the aggressive Western thought. But, later, in the last decades of the 19th century, a group of *'ulamã'* emerged, who were convinced that Islam was superior and our deterioration was due to the out-dated syallbus of *madãris-e islãmiyah.*

In 1894, in the convocation function of *Madrasãh-e Faiḍ-e Âm* in Kanpur Nadvat ul-'Ulamã' was formed and it was decided to review and reform the whole syllabus. After a year in 1895, in the meeting of Nadvat ul-'Ulamã' Shibli No'mãni read its annual report that the syllabus, which was being taught

23. S.M. Wazeh Rashid al-Nadvi, "Traditional Muslim Education in India: Origin, Curriculur, Revisions and the Present day Condition", *Muslim Education Quarterly* , vol. II, No. 4, Islamic Academy, Cambridge, U.K., 1985, p. 45.

in *madãris-e islãmiyah* for the last two hundred years, could not be changed within a year. However, it was our good fortune that most of the *'ulamã'* realized the need of reform in the curriculum.[24] In addition to this, he stated that only two suggestions had been sent regarding the reformation of courses of studies. One was from Maulana Shãh Muḥammad Ḥusain of Allahabad who compiled a treatise of 175 pages entitled ***Tanẓîm e-Nizãm-e T'allum wa'l T'ãlîm*** (تنظیم تعلیم والتعلیم) (Systematization of study and teaching). The other one was of Maulvi 'Abd ul-'Ali Ãsi of Madras.

In his treatise, Maulana Muḥammad Ḥusain wrote that Islamic institutions confined themselves only to *mã'qulãt* (rational sciences meaning here : logic, old philosophy, *kalãm* etc.) studies. There attention towards religious studies was negligible. There was not agreement regarding the changes of curriculum. History, Geography, Socio-economic subjects failed to secure only place in the syllabus.[25] Finally, all accepted that the course of *madrasãs*, in comparison to modern sciences, were stagnant and rigid. Shibli in his speech supported to the views of Muḥammad Ḥusain and that Arabic language and literature should be given greater importance in the light of *Qur'ãn* and its science having the key place in the syllabi. In addition to this,

24. *Annual Report of Nadvat ul-'Ulamã'-1895,* Kanpur, n.d., PP. 36-37.
25. Muḥammad Ḥusain, *Tanzim-e Nizam-e T'allum wa'l T'alim*, Matba'Anwar Aḥmad, Allahabad, 1895,PP. 20-25 (For detail).

Shibli also emphasized to improve the system of education and its method.

The majority of the '*ulamã*' were in favour of the inclusion of modern subjects[26] in the curriculum of *madãris-e islãmiya,* though some of them opposed the resolution when it was being approved. Besides, it was also decided that the period of education would be ten years and medium of teaching should be Arabic.[27]

6. Categorisation of the Students :

As per the need, choice and ability of the students the Executive Council of Nadvat ul-'Ulamã' on 6th July, 1895/13th *Muḥarram,* 1313 had categorised the students into three groups:

(i) "Those who wanted to complete all the prescribed syllabi of (ten years) *'Ulûm-e 'Arabiyah.*

(ii) "Those who wanted to study any particular discipline.

(iii) "Those who wanted to acquire some basic and necessary knowledge to achieve their aim."[28]

The outline and the main features of the new syllabi approved for the students of each group were as follows:

---

26. *Tafsir,* economics, history, *rijal, usul-e rijal,* Arabic language and literature, *'ilm-e kalãm* etc. see in *Annual Report of Nadvat ul-'Ulamã'-1895,* Kanpur, n.d. PP. 36-37.
27. *Annual Report of Nadvat ul-'Ulamã'-1895,* Op. Cit., PP. 118-119. Also in Syed Sulaiman Nadvi, Op. Cit., PP. 309-311.
28. Muḥammad Iṣḥãq Jalis Nadvi, Op. Cit., P. 146.

(i) In the higher category, there should be three types of books for every discipline:

A. Books related to intellectual understanding and general awareness.

B. Books related to philosophical problems and their clarification.

C. Books related to difficult and ambiguous passages so that the students may improve their understanding level.

(ii) Apart from works on *tafsir,* some other books related to *'Ulûm-e Qur'ãn* should be prescribed in the syllabus, e.g. ***'Aijãz ul-Qur'ãn*** (اعجاز القرآن)of Baqillani.

(iii) For primary classes, greater emphasis must be laid on ths study of theology and literature.

(iv) The *dîwãn* (compositions) of *Jãhili* poets and *Jãhili* literature should be made a part of the syllabus as it would enhance the understanding of Qur'ãnic styles.

(v) Study of those parts of Islamic history which focus on the moral excellences, sacrifices of Muḥammad (S.A.W.), brotherhood of *ṣaḥãbah*, *'ulamã'* and the common Muslims.

(vi) Study of Geography of Islamic states.

(vii) Books related to literature and theology should be prescribed in place of the outdated philosophy and logic.

(viii) More attention should be paid towards *'ilm-e kalãm* with books like ***Taḥãfat ul-falãsafah*** (تحافتہ الفلاسفہ) ***Sharḥ Maqãṣid*** (شرحِ مقاصد) ***Sharḥ Mawãqif*** (شرحِ مواقف), ***Sharḥ Tajrîd*** (شرحِ تجرید) which should be included in the course.

(ix) To purify the inner self (heart and soul) ethics and *taṣawwuf* should be studied. For this, some parts of ***'Awãrif ul-Ma'ãrif*** (عوارف المعارف) and ***Iḥyã' 'Ulûm ud-Dîn*** (احیاءعلوم الدین) should be prescribed.

(x) Unavailable books on any particular subjects would be compiled.

(xi) For an up-to-date curriculum, revision of the courses should be undertaken from time to time.[29]

And along with all these, there should be a regular arrangement of debates and symposia in Urdu as well as in Arabic. All types of Arabic newspapers should be available in the reading room to keep the students aware of the current situations of the world and also of the latest idioms and phrases of Arabic language.[30]

7. Mongeri's *Musavvidãh-e Niṣãb-e'Arabi* :

Maulana Muḥammad 'Ali Moṇgeri, the first *nãẓim* of Nadvat ul-'Ulamâ', also delivered a lecture on the need of change and reform in the prevalent syllabi. He says,

29. Ibid., PP. 147-148.
30. Ibid., PP. 146-149. (For detail).

> "The conditions have changed in the modern times. The objections and questions raised in the classical philosophy have lost their relevance and it has become quite unnecessary to study them or their possible answers. We live in different world. The critics of Islam have invented new arguments against it based on modern philosophy. It is not possible to refute them effectively on the strength of knowledge of ancient philosophy. The reason is that a satisfactory reply to a critic can be given only when his motives are clearly understood, and the grounds on which he has built up his case are properly appreciated."[31]

Maulana Mongeri, on 14th *Jum'adi Awwal*, 1313/25th July, 1895 produced a draft of the curriculum entitled, *Musavvidãh-e Niṣãb-e 'Arabi* for *madãris-e islãmiyah* in the meeting of Executive Council of Nadvat ul-'Ulamã'. In this, after analysing critically the development of the syllabi of Indian *madrasãs*, proposed twenty desciplines and also

31. Abu'l Ḥasan 'Ali Nadvi, *Western Civilization-Islam and Muslims,* Eng. tr. Muḥammad Asif Kidwai, Academy of Islamic Research and publications, Lucknow, 1969, P. 64.

prescribed the relevant books for each descipline. He also discussed the reasons behind the selection of each descipline. Among them, fourteen desciplines were being taught already in *madrasãs*. The rest six new desciplines were: *tãrikh* (History), *uṣûl-e lughãt* (grammar), *tajvîd* (phonetics), *'arûḍ* (Prosody), *sulûk wa tahdhîb-e nafs, taṣawwuf* and *asrãr-e aḥkãm* (ethics).[32] Syed Muḥammad al-Ḥasani writes that this was the first manifesto of Nadvat ul-'Ulamã' by which its aims and objectives were brought to light.[33]

Muḥammad 'Ali Mongeri in his *musavvidãh* emphasized that unnecessary portion of philosophy and logic should be excluded from the curriculum so that *Qur'ãn*, *tafsîr*, *ḥadîth*, *fiqh* may find greater part in the syllabi. The study of *ḥadîth*, *tafsîr*, and *fiqh* was made compulsory with every descipline so that the students may have regular touch with these subjects.[34]

After examining the *Musavvidãh-e Niṣãb-e 'Arabi* it became clear that Maulana Mongeri realized the need of modern philosophy, modern history, modern astronomy, geography, mathematics, political-

---

32. Muḥammad al- Ḥasani, Op. Cit., P. 153.
33. Ibid., P. 153. (He made many deletions and additions in his *musavvidãh,* particularly in phylosophy, logic and astronomy. For the study of history, he prescribed ***Tarikh ul-Khulafa*** and ***Muqaddimah ibn Khaldun***(مقدمہ ابن خلدون). He added modern philosophy, modern astronomy and modern history in the syllabi.)
34. Ibid., P. 159.

economy (*mã'shiyãt*) and *uṣûl-e saltanat* (Principles of Governance).[35]

8. Systematic Arrangement of the Curriculum :

The proposed curriculum of Maulana Mongeri along with the other twenty more copies (submitted by '*ulamã*') had been discussed in the meeting of Executive Council on 9th Rajab, 1313/26th December, 1895. After a long discussion, many deletions were made but unfortunately it could not be finalised. Notwithstanding some similarity, all the drafts were widely different from each other. This variety of syllabi led the members of Nadvah to frame some guiding principles for a final selection of subjects and books. These guiding principles had been laid down in the meeting of Nadvah at Amritsar in October 1902. [36]

---

35. Ibid., PP. 155-158. For detail.

Muḥammad al-Ḥasani counted the following reasons which made Maulana Mongeri unable in the prescription of books on the subjects:

1. The books of political-economy had not been yet compiled in a systematic way.
2. Books and matarials were not available in Urdu .
3. European compiled the books on these desciplines according to their patterns of thought. So the desciplines were not free from Western spirit and outlook. In such circumstances it was not possible and beneficial to adopt them as they were.
4. Their (Europeans) literary standard was very high in comparison to the students of *Madãris-e 'Arabiyah,* particularly because the students were unfamiliar with even the alphabets of the modern subjects.

36. Syed Sulaiman Nadvi, Op. Cit., P. 392. (One such principle was that all those books which dealt with an admixture of subject should be deleted from the curriculum.)

But due to some reasons the new curriculim could not be finalised and introduced. Shibli showed his unhappiness in a letter to Maulana Ḥabîb ur-Raḥmãm Khan Sherwãni on 22nd June, 1903.

> "You are syllabi-incharge but, even then, it has not been introduced till now which is rather very sad."[37]

At Madras in January 1904, (*Shawwãl* 1321) in the meeting of Nadvat ul-'Ulamã' Shibli talked rather decisively with Maulana Mongeri and Maulana Masîḥ uz-Zamãn Khan (*nãẓim*),

> "If you want at all to run Nadvah, then you administer it on the right line. Otherwise I would have no touch with it."[38]

At that time, a separate committee of three members was formed in order to give the final shape to the courses of studies. It was directed to them that it should be finalized on the approved guiding principles. Mullã 'Abd ul-Qayyûm of Hyderabad, Maulvi Syed 'Abd ul-Ḥai and Shibli No'mãni were the three members of the committee.[39] Syed Sulaiman Nadvi wrote that the major part of the curriculum had been prepared by Shibli.[40]

37. Shibli No'mãni, *Makatib Shibli* , vol. I, ed, by Syed Sulaiman Nadvi, Matba' Ma'arif, Azamgarh, 1928, P. 149.
38. Ibid., P. 154. Also in Syed Sulaiman Nadvi, Op. Cit., P. 398.
39. *Annual Report of Nadvat ul-'Ulamã'-1910,* Op. Cit., P. 88. Also in Syed Sulaiman Nadvi, Op. Cit., P. 414.
40. Syed Sulaiman Nadvi, Op. Cit., P. 414

The new curriculum had been approved in 1904 but its teaching was not started practically in the Dãr ul-'Ulûm because people were still not ready to accept any change in the old syllabi. Teachers used to teach the old books. The implementation of the new curriculum practically took place in 1905 after the arrival of Shibli No'mãni in Dãr ul-'Ulûm Nadvat ul-Ulamã' as the Dean.[41]

9. Guiding Principles for the Preparation of New Curriculum:

The guiding principles which had been laid down in 1902 at Amritsar broadly covered in the curriculum the following areas and fields by the three committee members, viz Maulana 'Abd ul-Qayyûm, Maulana 'Abd ul-Ḥai and 'Allamah Shibli.

(i) More emphasis had been placed on rhetoric (*fann-e balãghat*) and literature (*adab*). Along with ***Mukhtaṣar ul-Ma'ãnî*** (مختصرالمعانی), ***Dalã'il ul-'Aijãz*** (دلائل العجاز), ***'Aijãz ul-Qur'ãn*** (عجازالقران) of Baqillani and ***Naqd us-Shi'r*** (نقدالشعر) were also included.

(ii) 15 Paragraphs of ***Tafsir-e Baidawi*** (تفسیربیضاوی) and other book entitled ***Ṣirãt ul-Mustaqim*** (صراط المستقیم)[42] were included.

---

41. *Annual Report of Nadvat ul-'Ulamã'-1910*, Op. Cit., P.90. Also in Syed Sulaiman Nadvi, Op. Cit., P.415.

42. ***Ṣirãt ul-Mustaqim*** (صراط المستقیم) was authored by Shaikh Aḥmad Zamani and published from Egypt. It deals with those *ayahs* of the holy *Qur'ãn* which were related to *fiqh, kalãm, akhlãq*.

(iii) For the teaching of *'aqaid,* the book ***Ma'ãlim fi uṣûl ul-Dîn*** (معالم فی اصول الدین) of Imãm Rãzi was introduced in place of Ibn Rushd's ***Kashf ud-Daulah*** (کشف الدولہ) and Imam Ghazali's ***Al-Iqtiṣãd*** (الاقتصاد).

(iv) The book ***Hadiyah Sa'îdiyah*** (ہدیہ سعیدیہ) ***Sharḥ Ḥikmat ul-'Ain*** (شرح حکمت العین) and ***Sharḥ Ḥikmat ul-Ishrãq*** (شرح حکمۃ الاشراق) were prescribed for philosophical teaching. The philosophy of ***Ishrãq*** was not being taught in the old curriculum.

(v) For the teaching of *asrãr-e sharî'ah* the book ***Ḥujjat-ullãh ul-Bãlighah*** (حجت اللہ البالغہ) was prescribed.

(vi) ***Durûs ul-Awliyah***[43] (دروس الاولیۃ) was prescribed for the teaching of *falsafãh-e Jadîdah.*

(vii) Teaching of English language was made compulsory.[44]

10. Inclusion of English Language in the Curriculum :

The main objective of Nadvat ul-'Ulamã' was the production of such *'ulamã'* who were trained to keep alive their dignity, preach Islam in India as well as in foreign countries, refute the infidel's attack on Islam

---

43. It was published in Bairut and dealt such modern problems which are related to science.

44. *Annual Report of Nadvat ul-'Ulamã'-1910,* Op. Cit., P. 89. Also in Syed Sulaiman Nadvi, Op. Cit., PP. 414-415.

and stand side by side to modern intellectuals, Shibli reiterated that it was imposible to achieve these objectives without the knowledge of English. He advocated for the inclusion of English in the curriculum of Dãr ul-'Ulûm Nadvat ul-'Ulamã. In 1899, Shibli expressed the desire to Ḥabib ur-Raḥmãn Khan Sherwãni that 'inclusion of English in the course' should be an item of discussion in the meeting of Executive Council of Nadvat ul-'Ulamã'. But Maulana Sherwãni did not take it seriously and ignored it.[45]

It was again proposed in the meeting of Executive Council of Nadvat ul-'Ulamã' in February, 1900/*Shawwã!*, 1317 and it was approved, with some opposition, by the majority votes. Maulana Mongeri was also in favour of English teaching for the better prospects of *'ulamã'*.[46] But practically English was not included in the course. Then Shibli showed his unhappiness and wrote a letter to Maulana Sherwãni on 25th May, 1901 that after facing a lot of difficulties and obstacles we succeeded to win the vote of people and you, I do not know why, did not implement it in Dãr ul-'Ulûm.[47] However, in the midst of this rift in June, 1901/*Rabi ul-Awwal* 1319 the teaching of English language was started in the primary classes, and a teacher was appointed on a salary of 15 rupee

45. It is clear from the letter of Shibli to Maulana Ḥabîb ur-Raḥman Khan Sherwãni on 10th December, 1899 from Aligarh. For detail see letters No. 21 & 22. Shibli No'mãni*makãtib Shibli,* vol. 1, Op. Cit., PP. 122-123.

46. Muḥammad al-Ḥasani, Op. Cit., P. 194.

47. Shibli No'mani*makatib Shibli*vo. I, Op. Cit., P. 126. (Letter No. 26).

and 4 to 5 students started to learn alphabets of English.[48]

But before the settlement of Shibli in Nadvah as a Dean in 1905, April, the teaching of English was only nominal. He paid his attention towards its development and a resolution was approved by the Executive Council that English language would be compulsory subject for every student. Maulvi Syed Ẓahûr Aḥmad[49] was appointed as a member of the Executive Council to look after the teaching of English language. At that time, it was difficult even to appoint a teacher for English due to want of money. But when the Government approved to grant rupee 500/- per month in 1908 for the education of modern subjects, four English teachers were appointed[50] and the Nadvah started to impart English education upto the matriculation standard[51].

The students who completed their studies were appreciated in the circle of intellectuals. In the annual

---

48. *Annual Report of Nadva -ul-'Ulamã'-1910,* Op. Cit., P.90.
49. Maulvi Ẓahûr Aḥmad belonged to Allahabad. He was a social worker, later he became secretary of Muslim league. But by profession he was an advocate and practised in Lucknow. He was very simple and pious man. He died in 1942. See in *Annual Report of Nadvat-ul-'Ulamã' 1910,* Op. Cit., P. 91. Also in Syed Suliaman Nadvi, Op. Cit., P. 418.
50. Qãḍi Talmîz Ḥusain, who did M.A. and was the member of Royal Asiatic Society London, Syed Bãqar Ḥusain, B.A., were appointed for higher classes. The other two teachers had been appointed for lower classes. See in *Annual Report of Nadvat ul-'Ulamã' 1910,* Op. Cit., P. 91. and *Al-Nadvah,* vol. VI, No. 3, April, 1909, P.2.
51. For detail see *Al-Nadvah,* vol. V. No.8, September, 1908, PP. 1-2.

meeting of Nadvat ul-'Ulamã' in 1910, in Delhi, two students namely Syed Muḥammad and 'Abd ul-Majîd delivered speeches on religion in English. Maulvi Ḍiya ul-Ḥasan Alvi who after completing his study from Nadvah did Post Graduation from Aligarh and later in 1916 he was appointed as Inspector of Arabic *madrasãs*. He took many steps for *madrasãh* development. Maulana 'Abd ul-Bãri due to English education along with other contribution translated the books on Modern Philosophy of Barklay and Hume into Arabic and also wrote an English treatise on miracles. Maulvi Zain ul-'Âbedin and Maulvi Aḥmad-ullãh Journeyed to America and London respectively and served there for the cause of Islam. As a matter of fact, Shibli wanted to give a significant place to English language in the curriculum so as to produce trained theologians acquainted with modern intellectual trends through English education.

Moreover, Shibli's thirst for the education of English in Islamic institutions did not come to an end. He had an idea that the education of English should be upto the level of *Darjãh-e Takmîl* (Post-graduate studies). So he, in the annual meeting of Nadvat ul-'Ulamã' in 1907, 1908, 1909 expressed his desire that after completion of eight years of Arabic courses students must study English for two years[52] so that they became well-versed also in English.

52. Ibid., P. 2. (Maulvi Mcḥi ud-Dîn, honorary Director of The Department of Education, prepared and outline of the curriculum for English teaching. It was approved unanimously in the meeting of Executive Council of Nadvat ul-'Ulamã'.)

He said,

> "After studying exclusively English language for two years our students would be able to stand side by side with the English school graduates"[53]

But unfortunately, the objective of Shibli was not fulfilled as yet.[54]

11. Education of Hindi, Sanskrit and Modern Arabic :

(i) Hindi and Sanskrit : It was the efforts of Shibli that the teaching of Hindi and Sanskrit should also start in the Dãr ul-'Ulûm. The reason behind this was mainly the desire to defend Islam because at that time Aryans were openly attacking on Islam and were always ready to criticize it as and when they got opportunity to defame Islam. In this situation, 'Allãmah Shibli advocated for the teaching of Hindi and Sanskrit in Dãr ul-'Ulûm in order to enable the Muslim '*ulamã*' to understand the nature of Âryan's attack on Islam and counter-pose the ideological weakness of Hinduism and also preaching Islam among Hindu Communities.[55]

As a result, in 1908, a class of Hindi and Sanskrit education was opened. For creating interest among the

---

53. Quoted in Syed Sulaiman Nadvi, Op. Cit., P. 420.
54. For English Education see, *Annual Report of Nadvat ul-'Ulamã' 1910,* Op. Cit., PP. 90-94. Also in Syed Sulaiman Nadvi, Op. Cit., PP. 415-421.
55. *Al-Nadvah,* vol, V No. 6, July, 1908, P.4.

students, Shibli wrote letters to his friends by way of collecting some funds for scholarship to the students of Hindi and Sanskrit. He also appointed a *Panḍit* for the teaching of Hindi and Sanskrit.[56]

Muḥammad Sãkin of Azamgarh and Syed Imdãd Ḥusain of Hoshiyãrpur were the two students who at first opted for this subject and also acquired expertise. But unfortunately, its teaching could not be continued after the resignation of Shibli from Deanship of Dãr ul-'Ulûm. However, after some years, Hindi was again introduced in the curriculum. It is still being taught in the last three classes of primary stage and in class first of the secondary stage.

(ii) Modern Arabic : Arabic is the day-to-day speaking language of almost all the Islamic countries. As the time passes away many new words and terminologies, idioms and phrases are being added to the language. Without the knowledge of these new words and terminologies, it is very difficult to understand today's Arabic newspapers, magazines, journals and books. In this way, the new Arabic language is much different from the classical Arabic.

Shibli No'mãni after his return from Egypt and Syria compiled a glossary of these new words which

56. 'Allama Shibli himself and Maulvi Nawãb 'Ali (Professor Baroda College) and Maulvi Manẓar, (Advocate High Court, Calcutta) were ready to pay Rs. 5/- per month for Sanskrit teacher. See in *Al-Nadvah,* vol, V, No. 8, September, 1908, P. 2. And in *Al-Nadvah,* vol. V, No. 9, October, 1908. P.1.

he added at the end of his book ***Safar Nãmah Rome wa Miṣr wa Shãm***[57] (سفرنامہ روم ومصروشام). Shibli had a wide collection of books and magazines which he, during his Deanship of Dãr ul-'Ulûm, used to distribute among the students and directed them to translate and review them. Along with this, a topic was also given for discussion, speech or writing for which he also provided correction and guidance. He had established a big library with many sections of special study.

Syed Sulaiman Nadvi was among those who got the full opportunity to benefit from Shibli's books and guidance. He had been taking interest in the study of literature from the very early age. He was regular reader of the newspapers and magazines of Egypt and Syria which were being brought by Shibli. Therefore in 1908 Syed Sulaiman Nadvi himself wrote that this was the first chair of its kind in the *madaris-e islãmiyah.*[58] Shibli wanted to send him Egypt for compiling new words and terminologies. But due to the political disturbances in Egypt he could not go there. It was the result of Shibli's advice and guidance that two treatises into Arabic on new words and terminologies entitled ***Durûs ul-Adab*** (دروس الادب) were compiled by Syed Sulaiman Nadvi. These treatises were taught and still are being taught in many Arabic *madrasãs*. In 1910, in the meeting of Nadvat ul-'Ulamã', it was decided to compile a dictionary of

57. For detail see Shibli No'mãni,*Safar Namah Rome wa Mi ṣr wa Shãm,* Matba Ma'arif, Azamgarh, 1940, PP. 232-242.
58. Syed Sulaiman Nadvi, Op. Cit., P. 423.

new words and Syed Sulaiman Nadvi was assigned this task. He compiled it under the tittle of ***Lughãt-e Jadîdah*** (لغاتِ جدیدہ) and presented it in the annual meeting of Nadvat ul-'Ulamã' in 1912. Later it was published.[59]

One of the objectives of Nadvah was to equip the *'ulamã'* to meet the challenges of the contemporary world. Shibli desired English, Hindi and Sanskrit ought to be studied to provide an effective answer to the critics of Islam in India and abroad. The advocacy of Shibli for the inclusion of English, Hindi and Sanskrit in the curriculum amply shows his farsightedness and practical wisdom.

12. Opening of *Darjãh-e Takmîl* : It was discussed and decided at the very beginning in the second annual meeting of Nadvat ul-'Ulamã' in 1895 that the total duration of studies would be ten years and the last two years should be dvoted to the study of especialised course. A continuous effort in this direction finally showed result and in 1909, it was decided by the Executive Council of Nadvat ul-'Ulamã' to open *Darjãh-e Takmîl* in *'ilm-e kalãm* and *'ilm-e adab*.[60] Later in 1912 a decision was also endorsed in the meeting of Executive Council for starting *Darjãh-e Takmîl* in *tafsîr* followed by *fiqh* and *uṣûl-e fiqh*. In the preparation of curriculum of *Darjãh-e Takmîl*, Shibli's role was remarkable. The books which were

59. Ibid., PP. 418-437. (For detail).

60. *Al-Nadvah,* vol., VI, No. 3, April, 1909, P. 2. Also in *Annual Report of Nadvat-ul-'Ulamã' 1910,* Op. Cit., P. 95.

prescribed for the different *Darjãh-e Takmîl* were as under:

1. ***'Ilm-e Kalãm :- Sharḥ Maqãṣid*** (شرح مقاصد) of 'Allãmah Taftãzãni, ***Kitãb us-Ṣifãt*** (کتاب الصفات) of Imam Baihaqi, ***Taḥãfah*** (تحافتہ) of Imam Ghazali and Ibn Rushd, ***Rasãil Araba'*** (رسائل اربعہ) of Imam Ghazali, ***Baḥath 'Iṣmat-e Ambiya*** (بحثِ عصمتِ انبیاء) of Allãmah ibn Hazm, ***Talkhîṣ ul-Maqãl wa Kashaf ul-Adillah*** (تلخیص المقال وکشف الادلتہ) of Ibn Rushd, ***Hadiqah-e Fikrîyyah*** (حدیقۂ فکریہ), ***Kutub-e Âriyah*** (کتب آریہ) ***Iẓhãr ul-Ḥaq*** (اظہار الحق) ***Kitãb ur-Rûḥ*** (کتاب الروح) of Ibn ul-Qayyim.

2. ***'Ilm-e Adab :- Diwãn Imra ul-Qais wa Nãbighah Dhubyãnî Wa 'Alqamah al-Fahl Wa 'Urwah bin Wurd wa Farazdaq*** (دیوان امرالقعیس و نابغہ ذبیانی وعلقمۃ وعروۃ بن وردوفرزدق) ***Kitãb us-Ṣanã'teiṇ*** (کتاب الصناعتیں) of Abu Hilal 'Askari', ***Asrãr ul-Balãghah*** (اسرار البلاغہ) *of 'Abd ul-Qahir Jurjani,* ***Mawazanah Abi Tammam wa Buḥtiri*** (موازنۃ ابی تمام وبحتیری) ***'Iqd ul-Farîd*** (عِقد الفرید) ***Mashq Naẓm wa Nathar*** (مشق نظم ونثر).[61]

3. ***'Ilm-e Tafsîr :- Tafsîr Ibn Kathîr*** (تفسیر ابن کثیر), ***Baiḍãwi*** (بیضاوی), ***Kashshãf*** (کشاف), ***Kitãb un-Nãsikh wa'l-Mansûkh*** (کتاب الناسخ والمنسوخ), ***Al-Itqãn fi 'Ulûm ul-Qur'ãn*** (الاتقان فی علوم القران), ***'Aijãz ul-Qur'ãn*** (اعجاز

61. *Annual Report of Nadvat ul-'Ulamã' 1910,* Op. Cit., P. 95. Also in Syed Sulaiman Nadvi, *Ḥayãt-e Shibli,* Op. Cit., P. 429.

القران) of Baqillani, ***Tafsîrat-e Aḥmadiyah*** (تفسیراتِ احمدیہ) of Mulla jîwan.[62]

4. ***Fiqh and Usûl-e Fiqh :- Taḥrîr Ibn Humãm*** (تحریرابنِ ہمام), ***Musallam us-Thabût*** (مسلم الثبوت) of Mullã Muḥib-ullãh, ***Ma'ãni ul-Âthãr*** (معانی الآثار) of Tahãwi, ***Bidayat ul-Mujtahid*** (بدایۃ المجتہد) of Qãḍi ibn Rushd.[63]

13. Revision of Curriculum :

The revision of courses of studies had been made in 1923 and 1931 during the *niẓãmat* of Maulvi Syed 'Ali Ḥasan Khan and Dr. Syed 'Abd ul-'Ali respectively.[64] The latter improved the standard of instruction in English and introduced few more branches of modern sciences. He persuaded Dr. Zakir Ḥusain (at that time Vice-Chancellor of Jamia Millia Islamia) to prepare new course of study in Politics, Economics and English.[65] His desire was to introduce a new curriculum which could impart education up to the graduation standard of the modern universities along with the teaching of relgious desciplines.[66]

14. Division of Courses of Studies :

The ten years of courses of studies had been divided into three stages; primary stage, secondary stage and higher stage (*Darjãh-e Takmîl*). Primary

62. Syed Sulaiman Nadvi, *Ḥayãt-e Shibli* , Op. Cit., P. 430.
63. Ibid., P. 430.
64. 'Abd us-Salãm Kidwãi, *85 years of Nadvat ul-'Ulamã',* Daftar-e Ijlãs, Nadvat ul-'Ulamã', Lucknow, 1975, PP. 8-9.0.
65. Ibid., P.9.
66. Ibid., P. 9.

stage covered a period of three years whereas the secondary stage covered five years. The last two years were meant for higher stage. The student who completed secondary stage were awarded the degree of *Fãḍil.* At the completion of higher stage, the degree of post-graduation under the title of *Mufassir, Muḥaddith*, *Faqîh* and *Adîb* as per their course, was awarded.

But now-a-days, Dãr ul-'Ulûm Nadvat ul-'Ulamã' provides education from primary level to University level covering a period of sixteen years. The new division is as under:

1. **Primary stage :** It covers a period of six years including one year for pre-primary classes. In these classes Urdu, Hindi, English, Arithmatic, Geography and General Science of elementary level are taught.[67]

---

67. The following subjects are being taught at the pre-primary and primary stages:

Pre-Primary stage : - The elementary books on Theology, Urdu, Arithmatic are included along with physical training.

Primary stage : - Ist year : Theology: *Qur'ãn* (recitation); Islamic Creed, Urdu (reading and writing), Arithmatic, Physical training.

2nd year : Theology : *Qur'ãn* (recitation), Islamic Creed, Urdu (reading and writing). Arithmatic, Physical training and Gardening.

3rd year : Theology : *Qur'ãn* (recitation), Islamic faith and practice, Urdu (reading and writing), Hindi (elementary) Arithmatic, General Knowledge (Civics), Gardening and Physical training.

4th year : Theology : *Qur'ãn* (recitation), Islamic faith and practice, Urdu (reading and writing), Hindi (reading & writing) Arithmatic, General Knowledge (Civics), Gardening and Physical training.

5th year : Theology : *Qur'ãn* (recitation), Islamic faith and practice, Urdu (reading and writing), Hindi (reading & writing), English (elementary) Arithmatic, General Knowledge (social sciences).

2. **Secondary stage :-** This is a three years course. Along with English, Urdu, Arabic, Hindi, Persian this stage imparts Arabic Grammar, Literature and composition.[68]

3. **Higher Secondary Stage :-** It is of two years and provides instruction in Arabic, Persian and English besides relgious sciences and Islamic history.[69]

4. **Graduation Stage ('*Âlimîyat*):-** This is a four years course. It imparts instruction in *tafsîr, ḥadîth, fiqh* along with Arabic literature and other branches of Islamic learning. Higher efficiency in Arabic literature and the knowledge of English

---

68. The following subjects are devided in three years : Ist year : Theology : *Qur'ãn* (recitation & memorisation); Islamic faith and practice, Urdu (reading and writing), Hindi (reading & writing), English (reading & writing), Mathematics. General Knowledge (geography/history), Arabic (elementary).2
2nd year : Theology : *Qur'ãn* (recitation & memorisation), Islamic faith and practice, Urdu (reading and writing), Arabi (reading & writing & Grammar) English (reading & writing), Mathematics. General Knowledge (geography/history), Science.
3rd year : Theology : *Qur'ãn* (recitation & memorisation), Islamic faith and practice, Urdu (reading and writing), Arabi (reading & writing & Grammar) Persian (reading & writing), English (reading & writing) Mathematics. General Knowledge (geography/history), General Science.

69. Subjects which are studied at higher secondary stage are as under :-
Ist year : Arabic (reading & writing and grammar), Arabic literature, English (reading & writing), General Science, Religious Sciences (*Sirah and fiqh*).
2nd year : Arabic literature, Arabic (composition & grammar) English (reading & writing), General Science, Religious Sciences (*ḥadîth and fiqh*), Islamic History.

equivalent to the matriculation class are the special features of this stage.[70]

5. **Post-Graduation Stage (*Faḍîlat*) :-** This is a two years course, imparts instruction in theology and Arabic literature, of which one subject has to be offered by the students for intensive study. The students have also to submit a thesis in the subject of their choice.[71]

6. **Doctorate stage (*Takmîl*) :-** Facilities are also provided for undertaking research, known as *Takmîl*, in the subject taught at Post-Graduate

---

70. The division of four years are as follows: Ist year: Religious Sciences (*tafsîr*, *ḥadîth,* and principles of *ḥadith* criticism, *fiqh*) Arabic litrature, Arabic composition and grammar, English literature, Civics (general science and geography).
2nd year : Religious Sciences (*tafsîr*, *ḥadith,* and principles of *ḥadîth* criticism, *fiqh*) Arabic litrature, History of Arabic literature, English (literature, grammar, composition), Logic, Islamic History and Islamic culture.
3rd year : Religious Sciences (*tafsîr*, *ḥadîth,* and its principles), Arabic (*litrature* and *balãghat*), English (literature, grammar, composition), Islamic History, Social Sciences (Philosophy, economy).
4th year : Religious Sciences (*tafsîr*, *ḥadith, (intensive study), fiqh* and its principles), Arabic (litrature, history and criticism), English (literature & composition), History of Islamic Thought.

71. The division of two years are as follows : A: Theology : Ist year: Religious Sciences (*tafsîr*, *ḥadîth,*-one to be offered as the main subjects). Arabic literature, Islamic *Shari'ah* and its wisdom.
2nd year : Religious Sciences (*tafsîr*. *ḥadîth,*-one to be offered as the main subjects), Comparative Religion, Arabic literature, B: Arabic Literature : Ist year : Arabic Prose (classical and modern), Arabic Poetry (classical and modern), History of Arabic literature, Grammar (*naḥv*, Rhetorics). 2nd year : Arabic Prose (classical and modern), Arabic Poetry (classical and modern), History of Arabic literature, Criticism (rhetorics).

level. The duration of the research being normally two years, it is conducted under the guidance of competent teachers.

7. **Special Courses :-** Apart from these courses, the Dãr ul-'Ulûm made an arrangement of special courses which are as under:

   (i) *Ḥuffãẓ* have been appointed to impart instruction to such students as want to memorise the Holy *Qur'ãn* along with Urdu, Arabic and *fiqh* of primary level. It covers a period of four years.[72]

   (ii) (a) Provision for five year condensed course in Arabic and Theology for those students who have studied upto graduation in Government colleges or have at least passed the intermediate exam with first or good second division. After completion of the course, they become entitled to the degree of *'Âlim*.

---

72. Four years of *ḥifẓ* course have been divided into following ways:
Ist year : Memorisation of the Holy *Qur'ãn* (first seven *parahs*), Recitation (*qir'ãt*), Urdu (reading & writing).
2nd year : Memorisation of the Holy *Qur'ãn* (next ten *parahs*), Recitation (*qir'ãt*), Urdu (reading & writing).
3rd year : Memorisation of the Holy *Qur'ãn* (*parahs 18th to 30th*), Recitation (*qir'ãt*), and *Tajwid,* Urdu (reading & writing), *Fiqh* (preliminary).
4th year : Revision of Memorisation, Urdu and Mathematics, Arabic (language and grammar), *Fiqh* (preliminary).

(b) A special condensed course has also been started for those students whose mother-tongue is English and know neither Arabic nor Urdu.

(iii) A Department of Islamic Thought and Comparative Religion is being started from those who want to preach Islam.

(iv) An institute of teachers training has also been established to meet the requirements of institutions imparting education in religious sciences within the country. Because Nadvah realised, without it the Arabic *madrasãs* and other Islamic institutions cannot be saved from stagnation and decay.

Apart from these Dãr ul-'Ulûm Nadvat ul-'Ulamã' also runs a few Academies and Institutions of study and research, Which are as follow:

(A) Academy of Islamic Research and publications (*Majlis-e Taḥqiqãt wa Nashriyat-e Islãm*) :

Propagation of Islam in modern context, the primary object of Nadvat ul-'Ulamã', led it to establish this Academy in May 1957. It is basically an institution of study and research and publication. It works mainly for the cause of Islamic faith and propagates Islamic belief and ideology among Muslims and also introduces the basics of Islam to the non-Muslim seekers of truth.

The Academy published its books in Arabic, Urdu, English as well as in Hindi. Mostly, the English and Hindi books are the translation of Arabic or Urdu books. Its main purpose is to highlight the fundamental teachings of Islam, social customs and manners, and social evils of today's modern society. Any one can be the member of this Academy and it accepts donations and grants from individuals, institutions and libraries.

(B) Academy for Research of Islamic Law (*Majlis-e Taḥqiqãt-e Shari'ah*) :

It was established mainly to meet the demanding needs for a reoriented interpretation and education of *fiqhî* injunctions in the content of the fast-moving society under the supervision of Maulana Abu'l Ḥasan 'Ali Nadvi.

(C) Publishing House *(Maktabãh-e Dãr ul-'Ulûm)* :

It publishes text books as well as other books prepared under the auspices of various departments of the institution. The Nadvah has its own Printing press with facilities for Arabic printing. The press was started in 1957. It provides training to interested students in the composing-work of Arabic matter.

After analysing the syllabi and Academies of Dãr ul-'Ulûm Nadvat ul-'Ulamã', it can be said that the dreams of the founders of Nadvat ul-'Ulamã' have largely come true. The syllabi of this historical institution have helped the Islamic learning to recover from gradual decay and to redeem the Muslim Community from the growing menace of irreligiousness, scepticism and even apostasy. It has provided true guidance at the right time and contributed tremendously in preserving the integrity and character of the Muslim Community and the true picture of Islamic faith and practice.

CHAPTER-IV - A

FOUNDERS-MEMBERS OF NADVAT UL-'ULAMÃ

1. Maulana Syed Muḥammad 'Ali Mongeri (1846-1927) :

Syed Muḥammad 'Ali Mongeri, first *nãẓim*(Rector) of Nadvat ul-'Ulamã', who refuted Christian and Qadyãni attacks very strongly, was born on 28th July, 1846/3rd *Sh'ãbãn* 1262 in Kanpur. His ancestral chain goes back to Shaikh 'Abd ul-Qãdir Jilãni.[1] His forefathers lived in Bukhara who later migrated to Multan and afterwards to Muzaffar Nagar. Gradually, the families multiplied and settled in several cities of Uttar Pradesh and Bihar.

Life : He became an orphan when he was two years old. He was looked after by his grand father Syed Shãh

1. His geneological table is as follow : Syed Muḥammad 'Ali bin Syed 'Abd ul-'Ali bin Syed Ghauth 'Ali bin Syed Rãḥat 'Ali bin Syed Aman 'Ali bin Shãh Noor Muḥammad bin Shãh Muḥammad 'Umar bin Shãh 'Ashiq Muḥammad bin Muḥammad Shãh bin Bandagi Shãh Aṭiq-ullãh bin Shãh Qutb ul-Dîn Abu Bakr Charmposh bin Shãh Baha ul-Ḥaq Ḥabib-ullãh Multani bin Syed Ḥasan bin Syed Yûsuf bin Syed Jamãl ul-Ḥaq bin Syed Ibrahim bin Syed Rãji Ḥamid bin Syed Musa Aḥmad Shibli bin Syed 'Ali bin Syed Muḥammad bin Syed Ḥasan bin Syed Abu Sãleh bin Syed 'Abd ur-Razzãq bin Ḥaḍrat Shaikh Muḥi ud-Dîn 'Abd ul-Qãdir Jilãni.

Ghauth 'Ali. He started learning Holy *Qur'ãn* by his uncle Syed Ẓahûr 'Ali, and Maulana Syed 'Abd ul-Wahid Belgrãmi taught him some basic books of Persian. In 1861/1277, he was admitted to *Madrasãh-e Faiḍ-e Âm*, Kanpur. Where he learnt ***'Ilm us-Ṣeghah*** (علم الصیغہ) by Mufti 'Anãyat Aḥmad. Maulana Syed Ḥusain Shãh taught him ***Kãfiyah***(کافیہ) ***Sharḥ Miṣbãḥ*** (شرح مصباح), ***Sharḥ Mullã Jãmî*** (شرح ملا جامی) and ***Manṭiq*** (منطق). He studied ***M'ãqûl*** (معقول) and ***Ṣiḥãḥ Sitta*** (صحاح ستہ) by Maulana lutf-ullah Aligarhi and ***Mu'aṭṭa Imãm Mãlik*** (موطاء امام مالک), ***Mu'aṭṭa Imãm Muḥammad*** (موطاء امام محمد), and ***Ṣiḥãḥ Sitta*** by Muḥaddith Aḥmad 'Ali Sahãranpûri. After completing his education, he started teaching in the mosque of Dulãri in Kanpur. Later, he joined *Madrasãh-e Faiḍ-e Âm* but due to his illness his teaching was discontinued.

Refutation of Christian Attacks :- Maulana Mongeri realized the danger of Christian missionaries and in order to check their advance started a paper viz, ***Manshûr Muḥammadî*** (منشور محمدی) in 1880/1298. At the same time, he opened orphanages so as to rescue the orphans and poors from Christian influence. He wrote several books and treatises in its refutation such as ***Mirã't ul-Yaqîn*** (مراۃ الیقین) ***Âin-e Islãm***[2] (آئین اسلام),

2. In 1879/1297 he wrote it in the reply of ***Niyãz Nãma*** (نیاز نامہ) of Munshi Safdar 'Ali, a saint.

Tarãnã'-e Ḥijãzi[3] (ترانۂ حجازی), ***Dafa' ul-Talbiset***[4] (دفع التلبیات), ***Sãṭe'ul-Burhãn*** (ساطع البرهان) and ***Burhãn-e Qãṭi'*** (برهان قاطع). But his most famous book in this regard was ***Paighãm-e Muḥammadi*** (پیغامِ محمدی).

Maulana Mongeri and Nadvat ul-'Ulamã' :

It was Maulana Syed Muḥammad 'Ali Mongeri who first gave the idea of the formation of Nadvat ul-'Ulamã'. In 1892, in the annual convocation of *Madrasãh-e Faiḍ-e Âm*, Kanpur, where several '*ulamã*' and scholars were present, a decision was taken regarding the formation of Nadvat ul-'Ulamã'. He was appointed as its first *nãẓim*. He was one of the members who were appointed in the meeting of Nadvat ul-'Ulamã' to prepare an up to date curriculum for *madãris-e islãmiyah*. He made several journeys to different areas for the propagation of the aims and objectives of Nadvat ul-'Ulamã', such as to Kanpur, Fathpur, Hinswa, Rai Bareilly, Delhi, Ghazipur, Patna, Madras etc.

In 1897, due to his old age and weakness, he had resigned from the *niẓãmat*, which was not accepted by the Managing Committee of Nadvat ul-'Ulamã'. Instead, for his help an assistant *nãẓim* (Maulana Syed 'Abd ul-Ḥai) was appointed. Later in July 1903,

3. In this he answered the questions raised in ***Naghmah-e Ṭunbûri*** (نغمۂ تنبوری).
4. In 1884/1302, in the refutation of ***Tã'liqat*** (تعلیقات) of Imam ud-Din.

he again put his resignation which was accepted in the annual function of Nadvat ul-'Ulamã' at Madras in June 1904. Even after that he had regular contact with it and worked for it. Before the function of Nadvat ul-'Ulamã' at Madras, he went there and introduced the people with Nadvah's objectives. He admitted his son Maulana Noor-ullãh and Maulana Minnat-ullãh Raḥmãni in Dãr ul-'Ulûm Nadvat ul-'Ulamã' for their education.

Refutation of Qadyãni Activities :

He boldly checked the increasing Qadyãni influence particularly in Monger and Bhagalpur. He not only delivered lectures against it but also wrote more than hundred books and treatises for the refutation of Qadyãni thoughts.[5] In these books, as Maulana Mongeri considered, *Jihãd* was the best way to check the Qadyãni's advancement. Through his writings, he awakened the Muslims to realize its danger. He wrote voluminous books viz ***Faiṣala'-e Âsmãni*** (فیصلۂ آسمانی) (3-volumes) and ***Shahãdat-e Âsmãni*** (2-volumes) (شہادت آسمانی) in refutation of Qadyãni sect. Other works such as ***Chashma'-e Hedãyat*** [6] (چشمۂ ہدایت), ***Challenge***

5. Muḥammad al-Ḥasani writes that only 40 books had been published after his name.
6. At the end of the treatise ***Chashma-e Hidayat*** (چشمۂ ہدایت) an appeal was made that there was reward of ten thousand to those who would reply to the questions raised in it.

Muḥammadiya[7] (چیلنج محمدیہ), ***Mi'yãr-e Ṣadãqat*** (معیارِ صداقت) ***Mi'yãr-e Masiḥ*** (معیارِ مسیح), ***Ḥaqîqat ul-Masîḥ*** (حقیقت المسیح), ***Tanzîḥ-e Rabbãni*** (تنزیح ربّانی), ***Âinã-e Kamãlãt-e Mirza*** (آئینۂ کمالاتِ مرزا), ***Nãma'-e Ḥaqqãni*** (نامۂ حقّانی), ***Mirzãi Nubûwwat ka Khãtimah***[8] (مرزائی نبوت کا خاتمہ) were very famous. Some of these treatises were so famous that they were translated into English, Gujrati, Bengali ect.

The impact of the writings of the Maulana in the refutation of Qadyãni was not limited to Monger and Bhagalpur only but the Muslims of Panjab, Bengal, Madras, Bombay, Gujrat, Hyderabad, Dhaka, Katak, Nuakhali etc. had also realized the danger of Qadyani-claims.

Maulana Mongeri and Sufism:- From the very beginning, he was quite inclined towards sufism. He was much influenced by Shaikh Karãmat 'Ali, a *ṣufi* of Qãdiriyya order, and learnt sufistic teachings from him. After his death, Maulana Mongeri met Maulana Faḍl ur-Raḥmãn Ganj Muradabadi and made *bai'ah* to him and became his *Khalîfa* (spiritual successor). Regarding Maulana Faḍl-ur Raḥman's disciples, Shãh Tajammul Ḥusain writes in his book ***Kamãlãt-e Raḥmãni*** (کمالاتِ رحمانی) that they estimated about four lakhs. Maulana Mongeri wrote a book on sufism viz.

---

7. ***Challange Muḥammadiya*** was published in Arabic, persian as well as in Urdu in 1919.
8. It was published from New Delhi in 1914.

Irshãd-e Raḥmãni (ارشادِ رحمانی) which dealt with the *sulûk*, *ãdãb* and *tarîqat* and mainly consisted of *malfuzãt* and *irshãdãt* of Mualana Faḍl ur-Raḥman Ganj Murãdabãdi.

Death :- During his life time, he performed *ḥajj* twice 1900/1318 and 1908/ 1326. He took his last breath on 13th September, 1927, at 2 o' Clock.

In this way, we can say after analysing his contribution particularly his refutation of Christian missionaries and Qadyãnis, his efforts for Nadvat ul-'Ulamã' and also in the field of *taṣawwuf* that he alone accomplished such remarkable works as even an academy could hardly achieve.

2. 'Allamah Shibli No'mãni (1857-1914) :

"One of the most striking personalities of this age......a versatile genius and had a remarkable career,"[9] having profound knowledge in Arabic, eloquent speaker and powerful writer 'Allamah Shibli No'mãni was born in a prosperous family at Bindaul in the district of Azamgarh in May 1857. His father Shaikh Ḥabîb-ullãh was a lawyer, landlord and indigo merchant. His forefathers were *Rãjpût*.[10] The quality of *Rãjpût* was very much evident in his life style, i.e.

9. Ram Babu Saxena, A History of Urdu Literature, Allahabad, 1928, P. 287.

10. His ancestral chain is as follows:Shibli No'mãni bin Shaikh Ḥabib-ullãh bin Munshi Shaikh Ḥasan 'Ali bin Shaikh 'Ibãd-ullãh bin Shaikh Karim ud-Dîn bin Shaikh Mıḥammad Radã bin Shaikh Muḥammad Fakhr-e Jahãn bin Shaikh Amãn-ullãh bin Shaikh Muḥammad Isma'il bin Shaikh Meḥdi Chaudhary bin Shaikh Lãl Muḥammad bin Shaikh Aḥmad Chaudhary bin Shaikh Sohrab bin Shahbaz bin Sirãj ud-Din (Shiv Raj Singh).

sharpness of wit, intense self-respect and idealistic ambition.

He received education on traditional pattern. He learnt Islamic science from Maulana Fãrûq Chiryãkoti and *Muḥaddith* Ahmad 'Ali Sahãranpûri. He was also taught by Faḍl ul-Ḥasan Sahãranpûri and Irshãd Ḥusain Rãmpuri.

He was very much influenced by Sir Syed Aḥmad Khan and his liberalism and Dr. Thomas Arnold, Professor of Philosophy, at Aligarh where he had reached in 1882 and joined as lecturer of Persian and Arabic in M.A.O. College. He served there for 16 years. He had, during the last few years of his stay at Aligarh, some differences with Sir Syed, regarding the place of traditional education in the curriculum. Then he diverted his attention towards Nadvat ul-'Ulamã' which was the meeting point of Deoband movement and Aligarh movement.

In 1892, he went Turkey and form there he visited Egypt, Syria and Rome and minutely observed the political, educational and economical conditions of the Muslims. After Sir Syed's death, he left Aligarh and in 1901, he worked as secretary in the Department of Arts and letters under the *niẓãm* of Hyderabad. In 1903, when *Anjuman-e Taraqqi Urdu* was founded, he became its first secretary.

'Allâmah Shibli, being a student of traditional learnings and professor of M.A.O. College, came to conclusion that for Muslim, it was equally necessary to learn in *madrâsas* as well as in modern schools. He attached himself with Nadvat ul-'Ulamã' whole heartedly. He did remarkable reforms in the courses of studies and prepared an outline of Dãr ul-'Ulûm Nadvat ul-'Ulamã'. In 1905. he became Dean of Nadvat ul-'Ulamã' and gave a new impetus to the students. By his effort, Nadvah was distinguished not only as an educational institution but it practically touched every walk of life. He introduced English, Hindi, Sanskrit in the curriculum and appointed able teachers for them.

After the death of his younger brother Muḩammad Işḩaq in 1914, he came Azamgarh and stayed there till his death. Shibli had also aspired to *Dãr ul Muşanne -fin* (Academy of writer). But he did not live long so his desciple Seyd Sulaiman Nadvi founded it and fulfilled the dreams of his mentor.

He died on 18 November 1914 and was buried in the campus of *Dãr ul-Muşannefin.*

Works :- He wrote several books, treatises and articles in various fields. Among his contemporaries, he was an outstanding and versatile scholar. For a cursory view, his writings may be divided here according to their subjects.

1. Biographies :- ***Sîrat un-Nabî*** (2 volumes) (سیرت النبی), ***Al-Fãrûq*** (الفاروق), ***Al-Mãmûn*** (المامون), ***Sîrat un-No'mãn*** (سیرت النعمان), ***Al-Ghazãli*** (الغزالی), ***Sawãneḩ Maulana Rum*** (سوانح مولانا روم).

2. Literature :- ***She'r ul-'Ajam*** (5 volumes) (شعرالعجم) and ***Mawãzana-e Anîs-o Dabîr*** (موازنۂ انیس ودبیر).

3. Philosophy :- ***'Ilm ul-Kalãm*** (علم الکلام) and ***Al-Kalãm*** (الکلام).

4. Travelogue = (*Safarnãmah*) **:-** ***Safarnãmah-e Rum wa Miṣr wa Shãm*** (سفرنامہ روم ومصروشام).

5. Letters and articles :- ***Makãtîb-e Shibli*** (مکاتیب شبلی) (2-volumes), ***Maqãlãt-e Shibli*** (9-volumes) (مقالاتِ شبلی).

6. History of Islamic culture :- ***Intikhab-e Tãrikh-e Tamaddun-e Islãm*** (انتخابِ تاریخِ تمدن اسلام).

7. Poetry :- ***Dîwãn-e Shibli*** (دیوانِ شبلی), ***Bu-e Gul*** (بوئے گل), and ***Dastãn-e Gul*** (داستانِ گل).

3. Maulana Syed 'Abd ul-Ḥai Ḥasani (1869-1923)

He was born on 22nd December 1869/18th *Ramaḍãn* 1286 in Rai Bareilly. His father was Maulvi Ḥakim Syed Fakhr ud-Dîn Khayãli.[11] He received his education in Rai Bareilly, Hinsuwa, Allahabad, Bhopal and Lucknow. His teachers were Maulana Muḥammad Ḥusain Allahabadi,[12] Maulvi Amir 'Ali, Maulvi Fath Muḥammad Tãib, Maulana Muḥammad Na'îm Firangi Maḥali, Maulana Syed Aḥmad Dehlawi, Muḥaddith Ḥusain bin Moḥsin al-Yamani, Ḥakim 'Abd ul-'Ali

---

11. He was himself a poet, thinker, writer and a Persian scholar. Among his books ***Mehr-e Jahãntãb*** (مہرِ جہاں تاب) (3-volumes) in Persian was very important. It was an encyclopeadia of history of religion.
12. *Khalifah* of Ḥãji Imdãd-ullãh Muhãjir Makki.

and Ḥakîm 'Abd ul-'Azîz. He visited many important academic centres and attended the lectures of several known scholars.[13] He made his *bai'ah* (spiritual pledge before a *Shaikh*) at the hand of Faḍl ul-Raḥmãn Ganj Murãdabadi and Ḥãjî Imdãd-ullãh Muhãjir Makkî.

He attached himself with Nadvat ul-'Ulamã' from the very beginnign and journeyed several places for the cause of Nadvah. Due to his devotion, he was appointed as assistant *nãẓim* on 25 December 1895. On 13 April 1915, he was unanimously appointed as *nãẓim* of Nadvat ul-'Ulamã' and served till his least breath. During his *niẓãmat,* many resolutions were passed such as alumni would be members of the managing committee of Nadvat ul-'Ulamã', increament in the salary of the teachers, erection of mosque and that no government's grant would be taken etc.

The country had to face many problems and hardships due to the first world war and *Khilãfat* Movement. On the one hand, economic condition of the country was in very bad shape so it had become very diffifult to arrange annual meeting of Nadvat ul-'Ulamã' which looked into and solved its financial

---

13. He visited Delhi, Panipat, Sirhind, Anbala, Deoband, Saharanpur, Gangoh, Nagina and attended the lectures of Maulana Dhulfiqar 'Ali Deobandi (father of Shiakh ul-Hind Maulana Maḥmûd ul-Ḥasan), Rashid Aḥmad Gangohi, Syed Aḥmad Amrohi, 'Abd ul-'Ali, Qãri 'Abd ur-Raḥeem Panipati etc. (In these visits, he used to write daily events which were published in ***al-Ma'arif***(January, 1939-June 1939) under titled ***Armaghãn-e Aḥbãb*** (ارمغانِ احباب). Later, it was published in a book-form under the title***Dehli aur Uske Aṭrãf*** (دہلی اوراس کے اطراف).

problems and urged people to help. On the other hand, due to *Khilãfat* Movement student's mind diverted towards politics from education. In this uncontrollable condition, he took steps with patience and prepared ground for Nadvah to run smoothly.

Works :- *Gul-e R'ãnã* (گلِ رعنا), ***Yãd-e Ayyãm*** (یادِ ایّام) (History of Gujrat), ***Nuzhat ul-Khwãṭir*** (8-volumes) (نزہۃ الخواطر), ***Ma'ãrif ul-'Awãrif*** (معارف العوارف) ***Jannat ul-Mashriq*** (جنۃ المشرق), ***As-Thaqãfat ul-Islãmiya fi'l -Hind*** (الثقافت الاسلامیہ فی الہند) ***Al-Hind fi 'Ahde ul-Islãmi*** (الہندفی عہدالاسلامی).

He died on 2nd February, 1913/15th *Jamãdi us-Thãni* 1341 and was buried at Bareilly. He had two sons Dr. Syed 'Abd ul-'Ali and Syed Abu'l Ḥasan 'Ali Nadvi ('Ali Miyãṇ) and two daughters.

4. Maulana Ḥabîb ur-Raḥman Khan Sherwãni

He was born on 5th January 1867/28th *Sh'ãbãn* 1283 at Bekhampur in Aligarh. His father was Muḥammad Taqui who was very generous and pious. Ḥabîb ur-Raḥman received traditional learning on *Dars-e Niẓãmi* pattern. His teachers were Maulana Lutf-ullãh Aligarhi, Syed Ḥusain Khan Yamani Bhopali, Syed Muḥammad Shãh Muḥaddith Rampuri, Qãri 'Abd ur-Raḥman Pãnipati etc. Along with this, he studied English literature before Mr. Hoard.[14] He made the *bai'ah* at the hand of Maulana Shãh Faḍl ur-Raḥmãn Ganj Muradabadi.

14. Head Master of Muḥammadan College, Aligarh.

From 1883-84, he started writing articles which were published in several magazines and newspapers.[15] Later, his articles were compiled and published under the title ***Maqãlãt-e Sherwãni***, (مقالات شیروانی). He also composed poetry in Urdu and Persian under the poetical name *Hasrat*. He was editor of ***al-Nadvah*** monthly of Dãr ul-'Ulûm Nadvat ul-'Ulamã', Lucknow. Besides this, he had deep interest in the collection of books. In his personal library, there were more than 5000 books and rare manuscripts. Later, he donated his library to the Muslim University Aligarh. In 1941, he was awarded honorary degree of Doctorate of Theology by Aligarh Muslim University.

He did not take interest in politics and political movements, but he was always ready to take active part in educational movements. Earlier, he was trustee of Aligarh college and Later became the member of Muslim University Court and its Executive Council and Academic Council. He was a member of All India Muslim Educational Conference and later became its Joint Secretary and Secretary in 1890, 1917 and 1920 respectively. He was president of the managing committee of *Dãr ul-Muṣannefin*. He was member of All India Oriental Conference and in 1928, he became

---

15. Oudh Akhbãr-Lucknow, Âzad-Lucknow, Zamãnã-Kanpur, Makhzan-Lahor, Institute Ghazette-Delhi, Al-Bashir-Etawah, Aligarh Magazine-Aligarh, Urdue-Mu'alla-Aligarh, Al-Nadvah Lucknow, Ma'arif-Azamgarh etc.

Chairman of its Urdu-section. In 1918 he was appointed as *Ṣadr us- Ṣudûr* in the Asifiyyah State, Hyderabad and served there for 13 years. Due to his educational service, he was awarded by the title of *Nawãb Ṣadr-e Yãr Jang* in 1922/1341. Besides these, he was the first Vice-Chancellor of Jami'ah Usmaniyah Hyderabad. He was member of *Dã'irat ul-Ma'ãrif*, President of Asifiyyah library and secretary of *Anjuman-e Tarraqi Urdu*, Aurangabad.

He died at the ripe age of 86 on 11 August 1950, Friday morning, Aligarh.

Works :- ***Tadhkerah Bãbar*** (تذکرہ بابر), ***Dhikr-e Ḥabîb*** (ذکرحبیب), ***Dhikr-e Jamîl*** (ذکرِ جمیل), ***'Ulamã'-e Salaf*** (علمائے سلف), ***Nãbîna 'Ulamã'*** (نابینا علماء), ***Sîrat us-Ṣiddîq*** (سیرۃ الصدیق), ***Ustãdh ul-'Ulamã'*** (استاذ العلماء), ***Fiqh-e Ḥanafi*** (فقہ حنفی), ***'Ilm-e Ikhlãṣ*** (علم اخلاص), ***Dhikr-e Maḥboob*** (ذکرمحبوب), ***Musalmãnoṇ Kî T'ãlîm-e Qadîm*** (مسلمانوں کی تعلیمِ قدیم), ***T'ãlîm ul-Islãm Kã Athar 'Umar Aur Ṣeḥat per*** (تعلیم الاسلام کا اثر عمر اور صحت پر).

5. Maulana Shãh Sulaimãn Phulwãrwi :

He was a good teacher and preacher and an eloquent orator. He was born in 1859/1276 in Phulwãri, Patna. He received his education from Firangi Maḥal Lucknow, Saharanpur and Delhi. His teachers were Maulana 'Abd ul-Ḥai Firangi Maḥali,

Maulana Aḥmad 'Ali Sahãranpûri and Maulana Naẓîr Ḥusain Dehlawi. He studied *ṭib* in Lucknow.

He was present in the ceremony of convocation of *Madrasãh-e Faiḍ-e Âm* in 1892 where he lectured for the need of Nadvat ul-'Ulamã'. He wanted that Dãr ul-'Ulûm Nadvat ul-'Ulamã' be established at Lucknow instead of Delhi. In 1902, he became Dean of the Dãr ul-'Ulûm.

He was by nature very simple and pious. He was the follower of Qadiriya and Chishtiya order. A large number of people took *bai'ah* at his hand. Apart from this, he also composed poetry under the pen-name *Ḥãdhiq* (حاذق) in Urdu, Persian as well as in Arabic. He died at the age of 78 on Ist June, 1935/28the *Ṣafar*, 1354, Friday at 7 o' clock in the morning.

6. Munshi Iḥtishãm 'Ali Kakorwi :

He was very pious and generous. About him, Syed Sulaiman Nadvi writes that it should not be wrong to say that he was the last man of an Oudh's family as regards simplicity, humanity, piousness, generosity, hospitality and kindness to the poors.[16] He belonged to the village Kãkor of Oudh. His father Munshi Imtiaz 'Ali was a minister in the State of Bhopal. He joined Nadvat ul-'Ulamã' in April 1895 and served it whole heartedly as its treasurer till his death. He died on

16. Syed Sulaiman Nadvi, *Yãd-e Raftgãn*, Dãr ul-Muṣannefin, Azamgarh, 1986, P. 251.

22nd April, 1943. He left two sons behind him, viz. Munshi 'Inãm 'Ali and Munshi Iḥtirãm 'Ali. The latter too became the treasurer of Nadvat ul-'Ulamã'.

7. Maulana Masîḥ uz-Zamãn Khan :

He was born in 1836/1252 in Shãhjahãnpur. He was an Afghan. His ancestors came to Shãhjahãnpur and settled there permanently. He received education by his elder brother Maulana Muḥammad Zamãn Khan who was a teacher of Nawãb Mîr 'Ali Khan and Afzãl ud-Daulah of Hyderabad State. After the death of his brother, Maulana too became the teacher of Nawãb Mir 'Ali Khan (*Niẓãm-e Daccan*). Later, he became the *nãẓim* of the Department of *T'ãlîm-o Tarbîyat* of *Niẓãm* of Hyderabad. In 1883, he came to Shãhjahãnpur and stayed there till his death.

He attached himself from the very beginning with Nadvat ul-'Ulamã' and visited several places for its cause. In 1899, in the annual meeting of Nadvat ul-'Ulamã' at Shãhjahãnpur, he donated the half part of Ḥamzahpur (حمزہ پور) to Nadvat ul-'Ulamã'. In the 10th annual meeting of Nadvat ul-'Ulamã' at Madras on 3, 4, 5 January, 1904 he had been appointed as the acting *nãẓim* of Nadvat ul-'Ulamã'. ***Al-Nadvah***, monthly journal of Nadvat ul-'Ulamã', was started under his *niẓãmat*. On April, 12, 1905 he put his resignation from the *niẓãmat* due to his personal engagement.

He was the follower of Ḥanafi and Naqshbandi orders and made his *bai'ah* at the hand of Ḥãji Karãmat Khan Shãhjahãnpuri. He died on 17th December, 1910.

8. Nawab 'Ali Ḥasan Khan :

He was a man of dynamic personality. He played very influential role when Nadvah was passing through a crucial situation. He was president of the committee of reconciliation (مجلس اصلاح) in 1911-1913 that resolve the internal conflict of Nadvat ul-'Ulamã'. He also served Nadvah as its treasurer. After the death of Maulana 'Abd ul-Ḥai in 1923, he became *nãẓim* of Nadvat ul-'Ulamã'. Besides, he was a poet and composed poetry under the pen-name Salim in Urdu and Persian.

He was born on 16th August, 1886/4th *Rabi us-Thãni*, 1283, in Bhopal and received his primary education there. He learnt Persian and the grammar by Maulvi Aḥmad Ḥasan Belgrãmi.[17] Syed Sulaiman Nadvi writes about him,

> "By nature, he was very influential and very sensitive. He took active part in Sir Syed's educational movement and, then, in the religious movement of Nadvat ul-'Ulamã'. For a long time, he was honourary *nãẓim* of Nadvat ul-'Ulamã' and among the founder memebrs of *Dãr ul-Muṣannefin.*"[18]

Due to his illness and weakness, he resigned form

---

17. Author of ***Lughãt-e Shãhjahãni***(لغاتِ شاہ جہانی) and ***Artang Farhang*** (ارتنگ فرہنگ).

18. *Ma'arif*, vol. 38, No. 6, June. 1936, P. 204. Also in Syed Sulaiman Nadvi, *Yãd-e Raftgan*, Op. Cit. P. 175.

nizãmat in 1931. He died on 19th November, 1936/3rd *Ramadãn*, 1355 at his house Lal Bagh, Lucknow at the age of 72.

Works :- ***Fitrat ul-Islãm*** (فطرۃ الاسلام), ***Ma'ãthir Siddiquî*** (مآثر صدیقی) (4 volumes), ***Mardum-e Dîdah*** (مردمِ دیدہ), ***Tadhkerah-e Subh-e Gulshan*** (تذکرۂ صبحِ گلشن), ***al-Madanîyyah fi'l-Islãm*** (المدنیہ فی الاسلام), ***Bazm-e Sukhan*** (بزمِ سخن), ***Talãi' ul-Maqdûr Min Matale' uz-Dhahûr*** (طلائعِ المقدور من مطالع الذھور), ***Khirman-e Gul*** (خرمنِ گل), (Persian poetry), ***Nãlah-e Dil*** (نالۂ دل) (Urdu Poetry).

Along with these, he penned down several treatises such as ***Intizãm-e Khãnãdãri*** (انتظامِ خانہ داری), ***Shari'at ul-Islãm*** (شریعت الاسلام), ***Dîndãr Aur Duniyãdãr*** (دین دار اور دنیادار), ***Tã'lim-o Tarbîyat*** (تعلیم و تربیت) ect.

9. Khalîl ur-Rahmãn Sahãranpûri :-

He was the son of famous traditionist (*muhaddith*) of time Maulana Ahmad 'Ali Muhaddith Sahãranpûri (d. 16th April, 1879). He received his early education in *Mazãhir ul-'Ulûm* and studied *hadîth* by his father. After the death of his father, he started the business of timber merchant.

He was attached to Nadvah from the very beginning. In 1895, he became the member of managing committee. He was deputy *nãzim* during the *nizãmat* of Maulana Masîh uz-Zamãn Khan. After the latter's resignation in 1905, he became acting *nãẓim* and on 30 July 1913, he became *nãẓim* and served upto July 1915. He was against English learning and British culture and a staunch supporter of *Khilãfat* Movement. His son Maulvi 'Aqîl ur-Raḥman Nadvi was the secretary of *Khilãfat* Committee Saharanpur. He died on 4th February, 1936 in Saharanpur.

10. Maulana Lutf-ullãh Aligarhi :

He was known as 'Teacher of India' and 'Teacher of the teachers' (*Ustãdh ul-Hind* and *Ustãdh ul-Asãtidhãh*). He devoted his whole life to teaching. Almost all the Muslim scholars of his time had teacher-taught relation with him. Among them, Syed Muḥammad 'Ali Mongeri, Maulana 'Abd ul-Ḥaq Ḥaqqãni, Shibli No'mãni, Ẓahûr ul-Islãm Fatḥpûri, Maulana Noor Muḥammad Punjãbi etc. By nature, he was very simple and pious. He died in 1915/1334.

11. Maulana 'Abd ul-Ḥaq Ḥaqqãni :

He belonged to Ambala in Panjab but he received education by Maulana Lutf-ullãh Aligarhi in Kanpur. Later, he went Delhi and learnt *ḥadîth* under Maulvi Naẓîr Ḥusain Muḥaddith. He settled permanently in Delhi and engaged himself in teaching in the *Madrasãh Fatḥpûri.* He learnt sufistic teaching by Faḍl ur-Raḥman Ganj Murãdabãdi. He made untiring efforts for the propagation and development of Nadvat ul-'Ulamã'. He is best-known for his *tafsîr* of *Qur'ãn,* known as ***Tafsîr-e Ḥaqqãni*** (تفسیرِ حقّانی).

12. Maulana Ẓahûr ul-Islãm Fatḥpûri :

He was born in Rai Bareilly. For education, he went to Aligarh and learnt under Maulana Lutf-ullãh Aligarhi. Then he went to lucknow and completed study of *ḥadîth* under Maulana 'Abd ul-Ḥai Lucknowi. He made *bai'ah* at the hand of Faḍl ur-Raḥmãn Ganj Murãdabãdi. He founded a *Madrasãh Islãmiyah* at Fatḥpur in 1883/1301. He was very simple and generous. He died in 1920/1339 in Fatḥpur.

13. Munshi Aṭhar 'Ali Kãkorwi :

He was *ta'alluqahdãr* (تعلّقدار) of Kãkor, well-known advocate of his time and legal advisor of the department of *Ta'alluqahdãrãn-e Oudh*. He made *bai'ah* at the hand of Shãh Taqui 'Ali Qalandar Kãkorwi. He also learnt sufistical practice under Faḍl ur-Raḥmãn Ganj Murãdabãdi. He was famous for his generosity. He bore all the expenses of Nadvat ul-'Ulamã's meeting which was held at Lucknow. When Dãr ul-'Ulûm Nadvat ul-'Ulamã' was started at Golaganj, Lucknow, he was the first man who admitted his son, Anwar 'Ali.

Later, when the governor-general Lord Mac Donnel began to entertain certain misunderstandings against him, he migrated to Madinah and stayed there till his death. He was buried in *Jannat ul-Baqi*.

14. Maulvi Ghulam Muḥammad Shimlawi :

He was a lawyer by profession, an eloquent orator and also a man of dominating personality. In his youth, he left worldly life and its attractions and adopted sufistic way of life. He used to live alone, far from the society. But when he attended the meeting of Nadvat ul-'Ulamã', he left the life of seclusion and devoted the rest of his life for the cause of Nadvat ul-'Ulamã'. He journeyed to several places for its financial aid. He died on 29th March, 1934 at the age of 70.

15. Maulana Mushtaq 'Ali Naginawi :

He belonged to the town of Nagina in Bijnor district. He learnt *ḥadîth* by Maulana Y'ãqub Nãnautavi, Maulana Syed Aḥmad[19] and Maulana Aḥmad 'Ali Muḥaddith Sahãranpuri. After completing his education, he became teacher in *Madrasãh Islãmiya* in Faiḍabad. From the very beginning, he attached himself with Nadvat ul-'Ulamã' and worked for it as much as possible. He was the man who toured, with a letter of Maulana Mongeri, to Deoband, Jhansi, Patna, Aligarh, Etawah, Bhopal, Bombay, Makkah and Madinah to propagate the aims and objectives of Nadvat ul-'Ulamã'.

16. Maulana Shãh Muḥammad Ḥusain Allahabadi

He was a good scholar and an eloquent orator. He learnt *ḥadîth* at Makkah, during *ḥajj*, under Shaikh Aḥmad bin Zain Hallãn al-Shafa'i al-Makki. He spoke impressively in the first meeting of Nadvat ul-'Ulamã' in 1894 on its aims and objectives and highlighted the demerits of the prevalent system of education. He was a member of the committee which was formed in 1894 to analyse the prevalent courses of studies and to give useful advises. He compiled a treatise under tittle 'Systemization of Study and Teaching' and highlighted the *madrasãs* curriculum that it confined only to *mã'qulãt* and religious learnings were negligible.

19. Vice-Principal of Dãr ul-'Ulûm. Deoband.

CHAPTER-IV - B

SOME RENOWNED SCHOLARS OF NADVAT UL-'ULAMÃ

1. Maulana Syed Sulaiman Nadvi :

Syed Sulaiman Nadvi was born on 22nd November, 1884, Friday at Disna, near Patna, in an educated family. His real name was Abu Najîb Amîn ul-Ḥasan. His ancestral chain goes back to *Ḥaḍrat* Imãm Ḥusain. Syed Abu'l Ḥasan, a famous *ḥakîm*, was his father. Syed Sulaiman Nadvi obtained primary education particularly in Urdu and Persian in the *maktab* of a nearby village. For further study, he was admitted in several *madrasãs*, viz. *Khãnqãh Phulwãri* and *Madrasãh Imdãdiyah*, Darbhanga etc. Then in 1901, he took admission in Dãr ul-'Ulûm Nadvat ul-'Ulamã' where he got opportunity to learn under 'Allãmah Shibli and Maulana Fãrûq Chiryãkotî.

Soon after the completion of his study, he was appointed there as a teacher of *kalãm* and modern Arabic literature in 1907. At the same time, he also discharged the duty of the assistannt editor of

al-Nadvah, a monthly Urdu Journal. In May 1912 he joined the editorial staff of ***al-Hilãl***,[1] where he wrote several articles.[2] Later, he joined the Daccan college, Pune, as an Assistant Professor of Arabic and Persian.

After the death of his mentor Shibli No'mãni on 18th November, 1914 he came Azamgarh and founded *Dãr ul-Muṣannefin* and fulfilled the dreams of Shibli, i.e. completed the remaining volumes of ***Sîrat un-Nabî*** (سیرۃ النبی). Also, he started an Urdu monthly journal viz ***Ma'ãrif*** on July, 1916.[3]

In 1923, after the death of Maulana 'Abd ul-Ḥai, *nãẓim* of Nadvat ul-'Ulamã', he was appointed as the Dean of Nadvat ul-'Ulamã'. He took many steps[4] which stimulated the students to take interest in reading and writing of Arabic language and literature. Apart from Nadvat ul-'Ulamã', he visited several

---

1. Published from Calcutta, weekly, under the editorship of Maulana Abu'l Kalam Azad.
2. Some important articles are as follows : ***Al-Ḥurriyah fi'l-Islãm*** (الحریۃ فی الاسلام), ***Tadhkerah Nuzul-e Qur'ãn*** (تذکرہ نزول قرآن), ***Qaṣaṣ Bani Isrã'il*** (قصص بنی اسرائیل), ***Mashhad-e Akbar*** (مشہد اکبر).
3. In the first issue of ***Ma'ãrif***, Syed Sulaiman Nadvi wrote about the *Dãr ul-Muṣannefin* and ***Ma'ãrif***, i.e. rejuvenation and propagation of Islamic culture and also a criticism of modern scholastics and materialistic.
4. He introduced certain reforms in the curriculum, appointed qualified and able teachers, started an Arabic journal viz. ***Aḍ-Ḍiyã'***. Along with this, several Arabic journals and magazines were brought from Arab world for learning the modern Arabic and its usage.

madrasãs and institutions where he guided in the preparation of an up-to-date curriculum.[5] In 1946, he went to Bhopal-State and served there as Chief Justice (*Qãḍi ul-Quḍḍãt*). He was also appointed as the *nãẓim* of *Jami'ah Mashriqiah* of Bhopal.

Along with the literary activity, he also played an active role in the national and international politics. He journeyed through several European countries and lectured on the views of Indian Muslim regarding the issue of *Khilãfat*. His valuable suggestions and counsellings were also sought by Muslim Educational Conference, *Jami'at Ulamã'-e Hind, Anjuman-e Ḥimãyat-e Islãm,* Lahore, etc.

In June 1950 he migrated to Pakistan. After two years in August 1952 he became Chairman there of the *Idãrah T'ãlimãt-e Islãm*, an official body instituted to assist the new government in framing the constitution according to *shari'ah.*

During the last decade of his life, he was much influenced by Maulana Ashraf 'Ali Thãnvi and became his spiritual disciple and *Khalifãh-e Majãj* in 1942. He died on 22nd November, 1953.

Maulana Abu'l Ḥasan 'Ali ('Ali Miaṇ) sums up his contribution in the following words;

Maulanan Syed Sulaiman Nadvi

---

5. Such as King of Afghanistan Nadir Shãh Shahid in Oct. 1933, invited Syed Sulaiman Nadvi, 'Allãmah Iqbal and Sir Ross Mas'ûd for the preparation of courses of studies. Also, he played active role in the preparation of the curriculum of Muslim University-Aligarh, Jamia Millia Islamia-Delhi, *Madrasãh Shams ul-Huda*- Patna and the Departments of Education of Uttar Pradesh.

> (d.1953) hold the place of pride among Islamic scholars of the present times for the admirable contribution, he has made to literature, and to the study of the life of the Prophet of Islam, Islamic law and history. His works cover more than 7000 pages, besides the numerous articles, notes and reviews......Judged by his distinctions and achievements in the literary world, the Maulana was, without dispute, a great writer and a genuinely distinguished scholar of the East."[6]

Works :- ***Sîrat un-Nabî*** (سیرۃ النبی) (4 volumes), ***Arḍ ul-Qur'ãn*** (2 volumes) (ارض القرآن), ***Sîrat 'Âiysha*** (سیرۃ عائشہ) ***Khutbãt-e Madrãs*** (خطباتِ مدراس), ***Arab-o Hind ke Ta'lluqãt*** (عرب و ہند کے تعلقات), ***Nuqûsh-e Sulaimãn*** (نقوشِ سلیمان), ***Raḥmat-e 'Âlam*** (رحمتِ عالم), ***Ḥayãt-e Shibli*** (حیاتِ شبلی), ***Yãd-e Raftgãṇ*** (یادِ رفتگاں) ***Durûs ul-Adab*** (دروس الادب), ***Lughãt-e Jadîdah*** (لغاتِ جدیدہ), ***Ḥayãt-e Imãm Mãlik*** (حیات امام مالک), ***Maqãlãt-e Sulaimãn*** (مقالاتِ سلیمان) etc.

2. Maulana 'Abd us-Salãm Nadvi :

'Abd us-Salãm Nadvi was one of the celebrated personalities of Nadvat ul-'Ulamã'. He was the man to

---

6. Syed Abu'l Ḥasan 'Ali Nadvi, *Muslims in India*, Engl. tr. Muḥammad Asif Kidwai, Academy of Islamic Research and Publications, Nadvat ul-'Ulamã', Lucknow, 1960 P. 28.

whom 'Allãmah Shibli No'mãni had awarded Rs. 5/- on his first article *Tanãsukh* (تناسخ) in 1906. About him Shibli predicted.

> "We have a boy here in Nadvah called 'Abd us-Salãm, who is very brilliant and intelligent, shall perhaps deserve to chair the vacant position in Nadvah."[7]

He was born on 16th February, Friday, 1883 in the village 'Alã' ud-Dîn Patti in Azamgarh district. According to the tradition of that time, he learnt Persian and then studied Arabic literature. For further education, he journeyed to Kanpur, Agra, Ghazipur and then Lucknow. In 1906, he took admission in classV at Nadvat ul-'Ulamã'. After completing his education in 1909, he was appointed as a teacher of Arabic literature in Nadvah. He also worked as sub-editor of ***al-Nadvah*** (monthly magazine). 'Allãmah Shibli appointed him as an assistant for Arabic references in the *Sîrat un-Nabî* Project. Most of the material concernig the miracles,[8] moral excellencies and etiquettes[9] were collected by him. He also joined ***al-Hilãl*** in July 1914 as sub-editor with salary of Rs. 100/- (per month) and wrote many articles. After the death of Shibli, he joined *Dãr ul-Muṣannefîn* & remained there till his death.

7. Syed Sulaiman Nadvi (ed.), *Makãtib Shibli*, vol. II, Dãr ul-Muṣannefîn, Azamgarh, 1971, P. 208.
8. Sa'id Ansari, "Maulana Shibli Aur 'Ilm-e Kalãm",*Adîb*, (Shibli Number), Jamịʻah Urdu, Aligarh, September, 1960, P. 33.
9. Syed Sulaiman Nadvi, *Sirat un-Nabi* , vol. VI, Dar ul-Mıṣannefin, Azamgarh, 1966. P. 34.

'Abd us-Salãm was very simple and pious person with a high intellectual perception. He never cared about his name and salary. He never lived for worldly things. He considered this world as a *bãzicha-e aṭfãl* (Children's playground or garden). He was the man of independent nature. The ideas and thinking of 'Abd us-Salãm often went against the policy of *Dãr ul-Muṣannefîn*. So many of his books are still lying unpublished.[10]

He died at midnight of 4th October 1956. He was laid down to rest beside the grave of 'Allãmah Shibli in *Dãr ul-Muṣannefîn*, Azamgarh.

Works :- ***Uswã-e Ṣaḥãbah*** (2 volumes) (اسوۂ صحابہ), ***Uswã-e Ṣaḥãbiyãt*** (اسوۂ صحابیات), ***Ḥukamã-e Islam*** (2 vol.) (حکمائے اسلام), ***Sîrat 'Umar bin 'Abd ul-'Azîz*** (سیرت عمر بن عبدالعزیز), ***Imãm Rãzî*** (امام رازی), ***Tãrîkh-e Akhlãq-e Islãmî***, (Vol-I) (تاریخِ اخلاقِ اسلامی), ***Al-Qaḍã fi'l-Islãm*** (القضائی الاسلام), ***Fuqrã'-e Islãm*** (فقرائے اسلام), ***Tãrikh ul-Ḥaramayn us-Sharîfayn*** (تاریخِ الحرمین الشریفین), ***Shi'r ul-Hind*** (2 vol.) (شعر الہند), ***Iqbãl-e Kãmil*** (اقبال کامل), ***Tãrikh-e Fiqh-e Islami*** (تاریخ فقہ اسلامی) ***Inqilab ul-Umam***(انقلاب الامم), ***Ibe Khaldun***(ابن خلدون) ***Fiṭrat-e Niswãni*** (فطرتِ نسوانی), ***Ibn yamîn*** (ابنِ یمین), ***Al-Tarbiyat ul-Istaqlãliyah*** (التربیۃ الاستقلالیہ).

10. They are : ***Tãrikh-e Akhlãq-e Islãmi*** vol. II, (تاریخ اخلاق اسلامی), ***'Aijãz ul-Qur'ãn*** (اعجاز القران), ***Dalã'il ul-Qur'ãn***(دلائل القران), ***Tarikh ut-Tanqid***(تاریخ التنقید), ***Hindustan ki Tamadduni Tarikh***(ہندوستان کی تمدنی تاریخ), ***Shi'r ul-'Arab***(شعر العرب), ***Aik Karãmad Majmu'ah-e Ḥadith Ke Ḍarurat.*** (ایک کارآمد مجموعۂ حدیث کی ضرورت).

3. Maulana Abu'l Ḥasanãt Nadvi :

Abu'l Ḥasanãt Nadvi was born in 1890 in Ashrafpura, Patna, received his early education in his home town. In 1912, he met Syed Sulaiman Nadvi at Calcutta, in ***al-Hilãl***. The latter advised him to go to Nadvah. He joined Dãr ul-'Ulûm Nadvat ul-'Ulamã' and completed his studies there in 1918. Then he attached himself with *Dãr ul-Muṣannefîn* and served there till his death, where he authored several research articles which were published in ***Ma'ãrif***. He was a staunch supporter of *Khilãfat* Movement. In its support, he had written a series of articles under the tittle ***Turk-wa-Khilãfat*** (تُرک وخلافت) which was later compiled and published from *Dãr ul-Muṣannefîn*. After this, he wrote a reserach work on ***Hindustãn kî Qadîm Islãmî Darsgãheṇ*** (ہندستان کی قدیم اسلامی درس گاہیں), which was published in ***Wakîl***, Amritsar. Later, it was published in a book form from *Dãr ul-Muṣannefîn*. During his last days he started to compile the letters of Aurangzeb and collected the materials on Jamãl ud-Dîn Afghãni. But due to his illness, he could not give it the final shape. Besides he also composed poetry in Urdu as well as in Persian.[11] He died on 22nd November, 1924/12 *Rabi us-Thãni 1343*.

4. Ḥaji Mo'în ud-Dîn Nadvi :

He was famous for his cataloguing. He was invited by several libraries and institutions to prepare

11. *Ma'ãrif*, November, 1924, P. 323. Also in Syed Sulaiman Nadvi, *Yãd-e Raftgãn*, Dãr ul-Mւṣannefin, Azamgarh, 1986, P. 54.

catalogue of the books according to topic, authors and subject matters. He was born in 1891 in Asthiyãpûr village, Bihar. He received his early education at his home. For further studies, he was admitted in Dãr ul-'Ulûm Nadvat ul'-Ulamã'. During his education, he performed *ḥajj* so he was called *Ḥãjî* Mo'în ud-Dîn. After the completion of his studies in 1913 he helped Syed Sulaiman Nadvi in the establishment of *Dãr ul-Muṣannefîn*. During the time, he went Nadvat ul'-Ulamã' and made a catalogue of the library of the Dãr ul-'Ulûm. After that, he prepared an index of the manuscripts of the Bohar Imperial library Calcutta. From there, he joined Khuda Bakhsh library, Patna, and prepared a list of Arabic books in English, which was in several volumes and was later published by the Government. He also served in *Dãi'rat ul-Ma'ãrif,* Hyderabad, where he made an index of the important places of ancient India in Arabic language, which was also published by *Dãi'rat ul-Ma'ãrif.* After completing this work, he joined Government Library of Rampur. At last he became Principal of *Madrasãh Shams ul-Huda* and served there till his last breath in 1914/1360.

Works :- Besides the cataloguing, he wrote several books and treatises. Some important books are as follows :- ***Siyar us-Ṣaḥãbah*** (سیرالصحابہ), ***Khulafã'-e Rãshedîn*** (Part-1) (خلفائے راشدین), ***Muhãjerîn*** (Part-I) (مہاجرین), ***Mu'jam ul-Amkinah*** (معجم الامکنہ) etc.

5. Maulvi Abu Ẓafar Nadvi :

He was born in Disna, Patna, in 1889. He recieved his primary education from his father and local *madrasãs*. At the age of twelve, he was admitted in Nadvat ul-'Ulamã', where he completed his education. In 1933, he joined *Dãr ul-Muṣannefîn* and started working in the project of 'Compilation of Indian History'. There he authored several invaluable works such as ***Mukhtaṣar Tãrîkh-e Hind*** (مختصر تاریخ ہند), ***Tãrîkh-e Sind*** (تاریخ سند), ***Tãrîkh-e Khãndãn-e Ghazniyah*** (تاریخ خاندانِ غزنیہ), ***Tãrîkh-e Tamaddun-e Gujarãt*** (تاریخ تمدنِ گجرات), ***Safar Nãmah*** (سفرنامہ), ***Barmi Bol-Chãl*** (برمی بول چال), ***Mukhtaṣar Tãrîkh-e Gujrãt*** (مختصر تاریخ گجرات), ***Tãrîkh-e Auliyã-e Gujrãt*** (تاریخ اولیاء گجرات), ***Tadhkerah Muḥammad bin Ṭãhir Muḥaddith Paṭṭani*** (تذکرۂ محمد بن طاہر محدث پٹنی), ***Muntakhabãt-e Urdu*** (منتخباتِ اردو), ***Farhang-e-Iṣṭalãḥḥãt*** (فرہنگِ اصطلاحات), ***Jadîd T'ãlim Urdu*** (جدید تعلیم اردو) etc.

6. Dr. Syed 'Abd ul-'Ali :

Syed 'Abd ul-'Ali, scholar of modern sciences as well as traditional learnings, was born on Ist December, 1893 at Hinsuwa, Fatḥpur district, in a family of renowned scholars. His father Syed 'Abd ul-Ḥai was *nãẓim* of Dãr ul-'Ulûm Nadvat ul-'Ulamã' and the author of ***Nuzhat ul-Khawãṭir*** (نزھت الخواطر). Maulana Syed Fakhr ud-Dîn Khayãli, his grandfather was an eminent *ḥakîm*. His maternal grandfather was Maulvi Syed 'Abd ul-'Azîz and Maulvi Syed Abu'l Qãsim was his maternal uncle.

He started his primary education at his home town and learnt Persian and Arabic. Then he was admitted in Nadvat ul-'Ulamã' where he studied Arabic literature, *fiqh* and its principles, astronomy, mathematics. Later he was sent to Dãr ul-'Ulûm Deoband for the study of *ḥadîth*. After that he went to Delhi and studied *ṭibb* and modern medicine.[12] On returning to Lucknow, he enrolled himself in a missionary school and in 1915 passed the matric examination. He continued his modern education in Christian College and learnt English literature, biology, physics, chemistry and passed intermediate in 1917. From Canning College, he completed his B.Sc. in 1919.[13] Finally, he obtained from King George Medical College his M.B.B.S degree in 1925. And soon after started practise both *ṭibb* and modern medicine.

---

12. He was taught Persian prose and poetry by his grandfather Syed Fakhr ud-Dîn Khayãli, Arabic by Maulvi Muḥammad Aḥsan, Arabic literature by Maulana Syed 'Ali Zamini, *Fiqh* and its principles by Maulana Shibli Jairãjpuri, Astronomy by Maulana Sultan Muḥammad Kalbi, Mathematics by Maulana Shir 'Ali Hyderabadi, *Ḥadith* by Shaikh ul-Hind Maulana Maḥmud ul-Ḥasan and Maulana Anwar Shãh Kashmir and *Ṭibb* by Ḥakim Ajmal Khan and Modern Medicine by Dr. Mukhtar Aḥmad Anṣari.
13. He went first position, in B.Sc., in the college and second position in Allahabad University to which Canning College was affiliated.

In Nadvat ul-'Ulamã' :- After the death of his father, 1923, be became the member of managing committee of Nadvat ul-'Ulamã'. On 6th October, 1928, he was appointed as the deputy *nãẓim*. He also discharged the duty as Acting *nãẓim* form 20th September, 1930 to 9th June, 1931 and from 9th June, 1931 he became *nãẓim* of Nadvat ul-'Ulamã' and served till his death in 1961.

He laid more emphasis on Arabic literature. To develop the writing practice of the students, he started Arabic Journal ***aḍ-Ḍiyã'***[14] (الضیاء) in May, 1932 under the editorship of Maulana Mas'ûd 'Âlam and under the supervision of Syed Sulaiman Nadvi and Shaikh Taqi ud-Din Marãkashi. Later in 1955, a new monthly Arabic journal ***al-B'ãth ul-Islãmi*** (البعث الاسلامی) in place of ***aḍ-Ḍiyã'*** under the editorship of Maulana Muḥammad Miyãṇ,[15] was started. Due to its scholarly standard, this journal became famous even in the Arab world. In 1959 another fortnightly Arabic journal ***ar-Rãi'd*** (الرائد) was started under the editorship of Maulana Muḥammad Rãbeʿ Nadvi. Along with these journals, he had restarted the Urdu journal ***al-Nadvah*** in January,1940. But it was again closed in July, 1942.

---

14. *Aḍ-Ḍiyã'* was closed after four years in 1935.

15. He wrote editorials in ***al-B'ãth ul-Islãmi*** His writtings on 'support of true faith and refutation of falls thinking' (مسلک حق کی تائید اور باطل افکار ونظریات کی تردید) became so famous that it was compiled and published in a book-form under the title ***al-Islãm ul-Mumtaḥan*** (الاسلام الممتحن)

Apart from this, the foundation of mosque within the boundary of Nadvat ul-'Ulamã' was also laid. This construction was made under Maulana Mas'ûd 'Ali Nadvi's supervision. Department of *Ḥifẓ-e Qur'ãn* (حفظِ قرآن) and Raḥmani hostel were also built during his *niẓãmat.*

He also revised the curriculum of the Dãr ul-'Ulûm Nadvat ul-'Ulamã' and fulfilled its primary purpose, i.e. reforms in the syllabi. These courses of studies were free from philosophical and logical ambiguity and the books had been arranged in such a way that modesty and morality could develop among the students. More emphasis was laid on writing and speaking in Arabic as well as in Urdu language.

He was a patient of high blood preasure and on 7th May 1961 he died of heart-attack.

7. Maulana Syed Najîb Ashraf Nadvi :

He was scholar, historian, critic as well as a good teacher. In 1901, he was born at Disna, Patna, and received his education from Patna University and passed Intermediat in 1920. He participated actively in *Khilãfat* movement, where he met Syed Sulaiman Nadvi who invited the former in *Dãr ul-Muṣannefin.*

Syed Najîb Ashraf often used to write reviews, news-views and annotations for the journal ***Ma'ãrif.***[16]

---

16. He, during his studentship, started writing articles. His first article was ***'Pãn Kî Kahãni'***(پان کی کہانی) . He also translated a book of Mahatma Gandhi from English to Urdu under the title ***Swarãj*** (سوراج) which became very popular.

In *Dãr ul-Muṣannefin* he also completed the left-out work of Abu'l Ḥasanãt Nadvi, i.e. Compilation of Aurangzeb's letters under the tittle ***Muqaddimah Ruqa'ãt-e 'Âlamgirî*** (مقدمۂ رقعاتِ عالم گیری). Along with this, he had written several articles which were published in many journals viz. ***Ma'ãrif***-Azamgarh, ***Jãmi'ah***-Delhi, ***Nairang-e Khayãl***-Lahore, ***Zamindãr***-Lahore, ***Inqilãb***-Lahore, ***Ḥamdard***-Delhi, ***al-Nazîr***-Lucknow etc.

In 1930, he left *Dãr ul-Muṣannefin* and joined as Persian teacher in Gujrat College, Ahmadabad. After a year, he went to Bombay and joined as Urdu teacher in Isma'il College and served there till his retirement in 1955. After that, he became Director of *Anjuman-e Islãm Urdu*, Research Institute, where he edited ***Lughãt-e Gujrî*** (لغاتِ گجری). Along with this, he also served as an editor of a quartely journal ***Nawã'-e Adab***. He died in 1968, September, in Bombay.

Works :- ***Muqaddimah-e Ruqa'ãt-e 'Âlamgîrî*** (مقدمہ رقعات عالم گیری) ***Lughãt-e Gujrî*** (لغاتِ گجری), ***Swarãj*** (سُوراج), ***Barṭãnwi Hind Kã Niẓãm-e Asãsî*** (برطانوی ہند کا نظامِ اساسی) etc. The last two works are translated works.

8. Maulana Shãh Mo'in ud-Dîn Aḥmad Nadvi :

He was popularly known as *Shãh Ṣãḥab*, born in 1903 in Rudaul. His ancestors were the descendants of a famous *ṣufi* Shaikh Aḥmad 'Abd ul-Ḥaq Tauthiyah Rudaulvi.[17] His father Shãh Ḥasanãt was well acquainted with Arabic and Persian. He started his early education under his maternal grand father Shãh Sharf ud-Dîn. Later, he joined Nadvat ul-'Ulamã' and completed his studies. In 1924 *Madrasãh 'Âliyah*, Calcutta and *Jami'ah Millia Islamia* Delhi invited him as a teacher but he refused and joined *Dãr ul-Muṣannefîn* on the call of Syed Sulaiman Nadvi and served therefore more than fifty years. When the latter went to Pakistan, he became *nãẓim* of *Dãr ul-Muṣannefîn* and editor of ***Ma'ãrif***. Along with this, he was also life member of *Anjuman-e Taraqqi Urdu*, Hindustani Academy Allahabad and member of Urdu Academy Lucknow and *Jãmi'ah Urdu* Aligarh. He breathed his last in *Dãr ul-Muṣannefîn* on 13th December, 1947 and was buried at his home town Rudaul.

Works :- ***Tãrîkh-e Islãm*** (4 volumes.) (تاریخِ اسلام), ***Muhãjerîn*** (مہاجرین), ***Siyar us-Ṣaḥãbah*** (volume 6th & 7th) (سیر الصحابہ), ***Tãba'în*** (تابعین), ***Ḥayãt-e Sulaimãn*** (حیاتِ سلیمان), ***Dîn-e Raḥmat*** (دینِ رحمت), ***Adabi Nuqûsh*** (ادبی نقوش), ***'Arab ki Maujãdah Hukûmateṇ*** (عرب کی موجودہ حکومتیں) (translation) ***Islãm wa 'Arabi Tamaddun*** (اسلام و عربی تمدن). Apart form these works, he also translated the ***Malfuẓãt*** (ملفوظات), ***Anwãr ul-'Uyûn fi***

17. *Ṣufi* of Sãbri Chishtiya Order of 14th century.

Asrãr ul-Maknûn (انوارالعیون فی اسرارالمکنون) of Shaikh Aḥmad 'Abd ul-Ḥaq Tauthiyah Rudaulvi.

9. Maulana Syed Riyãsat 'Ali Nadvi :

He was born in 1904 in the village Âbgilah (آب گلیہ), Gaya and received primary education in nearby villages. Later, he took admission in Dãr ul-'Ulûm Nadvat ul-'Ulamã'. After completing his studies he joined *Dãr ul-Muṣannefîn*. He penned down several articles which were published in ***Ma'ãrif***. He was much interested in politics[18] because of which he had to resign from *Dãr ul-Muṣannefîn*. After some time, he became Principal of *Madrasãh Shams ul-Huda*, Patna. But he resigned from there also due to some internal conflicts and disturbances. Later, he worked on a project of U.G.C. in the Research Section of Arabic and Persian Department of Patna University. He died on 14th November, 1976, Sunday, at the age of 72.

Works :- ***Tãrîkh-e Ṣiqillîyah*** (تاریخِ صقلیہ) (2 volumes). ***Tãrîkh-e Andalus*** (تاریخ اندلس), ***A'immah-e Islãm*** (ائمہ اسلام), ***Sarguzasht-e Adab-e Turkî*** (سرگذشتِ ادبِ ترکی), ***Islãmi Niẓãm-e T'ãlîm*** (اسلامی نظامِ تعلیم) etc.

10. Maulana 'Abd us-Salãm Nadvi Kidwai :

He belonged to Thilandi in Rai Bareilly district. He was born in 1906. After completing his studies in 1930

18. His political interest made the *Dãr ul-Muṣannefîn* as a center of political discusssions, which was not liked by Syed Sulaiman Nadvi.

form Dãr ul-'Ulûm Nadvat ul-'Ulamã', he went to Jamia Millia Islamia, Delhi for further studies.[19] In 1934, he joined Dãr ul-'Ulûm Nadvat ul-'Ulamã' as a teacher of Islamic History and Arabic language and assisted Maulana Abu'l Ḥasan 'Ali Nadvi in the journal ***T'ãmir*** upto 1943. Then he became Director of the Department of Islamic Education, Lucknow and served there upto 1951. After that, he joined as a Professor of Theology in Jamia Millia, Delhi and served there for twenty one years till his retirement. He then again came to Nadvah and became honorary secretary of education. After the death of Shãh Mo'în ud-Dîn Aḥmad Nadvi in 1975, he joined *Dãr ul-Muṣannefîn* and worked there till his last breath.

Works :- ***Musalmãn Aur 'Aṣri Taqãḍe*** (مسلمان اور عصری تقاضے), ***Hamãrî Bãdshãhî*** (ہماری بادشاہی), ***Hindustãn kî Kahãnî*** (ہندوستان کی کہانی), ***Qur'ãn Majîd kî Pahlî Kitãb*** (قرآن مجید کی پہلی کتاب), ***Qur'ãn Majîd kî Dusrî Kitãb*** (قرآن مجید کی دوسری کتاب), ***'Arabi Zabãn ke Das Sabaq*** (عربی زبان کے دس سبق), ***Duniya Islãm se Pahle Aur Islãm ke Bãd*** (دنیائے اسلام سے پہلے اور اسلام کے بعد), ***Mithãlî Hukumrãṇ*** (مثالی حکمراں), ***Musalmãn Aur Waqt ke Taqãḍe*** (مسلمان اور وقت کے تقاضے).

19. In Jamia Millia, he worked for ***Khilãfat***, a daily paper, published from Bombay.

11. Maulana Muḥammad Imran Khan Nadvi :

He was by race an Afghani Pathan. His family lineage goes back to Noor Muḥammad, who dedicated himself to teaching *Qur'ãn* in Delhi. Later, after the Mutiny of 1857 he migrated and settled in Bhopal.[20]

Muḥammad Imran Khan was born on 13 August, 1913.He learnt *Qur'ãn* by heart and received his primary education under his father Muḥammad Ilyãs Khan. After matriculation from Alexendrya School, Bhopal, he was admitted in Dãr ul-'Ulûm Nadvat ul-'Ulamã' in 1925. In 1933, he completed *Faḍîlat* and became teacher of *ḥadîth* and *tafsîr* as well as section officer (منصرم) in Nadvat ul-'Ulamã'. After four years, he went to Jami'ah Aẓhar for *'Âlimîyat* and passed out with good marks in 1939.

He came back to Nadvah and engaged himself in teaching of *Qur'ãn* and *ḥadîth.* Along with this, he also served Nadvah as an assistant *muhtamim*. In 1941, he became acting *muhtamim* and after a year in January, 1942 he became *muhtamim*. He discharged his duty with sincerity and characteristic boldness.[21]

---

20. For detail see Mas'ûd ur-Raḥmãn Khan Nadvi, *Ḥayãt-e Imrãn*, vol. I, Bhopal, 1995 P. 44.
21. Ibid., PP. 127-128. (When he took the charge of *muhtamim*, the condition of Dãr ul-'Ulûm was very bad. Students had become disrespectful and they often used to disregard and even dishonour the teachers in their speeches. Imran Khan Nadvi through his gifted administrative quality, successfully brought under control the irresponsible behaviour and almost all the irregularities. Syed Sulaiman Nadvi, who was *mu'tamid* at that time, appreciated his literary ability and administrative quality.)

Due to internal conflicts among the teachers in 1947, he resigned from the post of *muhtamim* and went to Bhopal. But his absence from Nadvah was deeply felt, so on 7th January, 1949 a resolution was passed that Imran Khan Nadvi should be the *muhtamim*. He took the charge for the second time on 6, February, 1949 and served till 1958.

For the development of Nadvat ul-'Ulamã', his untiring efforts and selfless services cannot be forgotten-particularly he improved the financial condition of Nadvah. He visited several cities such as Hyderabad, Madras, Banglore, Calcutta, Nagpur, Bhopal, Burma etc. He removed to a large extent the irregularities in the functioning of the Dãr ul-'Ulûm and endeavoured for harmonious relation among the students and between the students and teachers. He was very simple and pious and never cared about financial gain or post or power or for respect and honour.[22]

12. Maulana Abu Laith Iṣlãḥi Nadvi :

He was a powerful writer, eloquent speaker and a moderate thinker, born in the village of Chand Patti in Azamgarh on 15 February, 1913. He started his education at home then *Madrasãt ul-Iṣlãḥ*, Azamgarh and then proceeded to Dãr ul-'Ulûm Nadvat ul-'Ulamã' and completed *Faḍîlat*. He studied under several teachers including Syed Sulaiman Nadvi and Manãẓir Aḥsan Gilãni etc.

22. For detail see Ibid., PP. 194-205.

After completing his studies, he worked for a Urdu paper ***Madînah*** of Bijnor. He was also the member of *Jam'ãt-e Islãmi Hind* and in April, 1948 he became its President and served upto 1972. He again, for the second time, became its President form October, 1981 to March, 1990. He was also among the founders of *All India Muslim Majlis-e Mashawara* and the 'All India Muslim Personal Law Board.' Besides this, he was also associated with *Jami'at ul-Falãh* Azamgarh, *Dãr ul-Muṣannefîn* Azamgarh and Dãr ul-'Ulûm Nadvat ul-'Ulamã'.

Works :- ***Bhãrat kî T'ãmîr-e Nau Aur Hum*** (بھارت کی تعمیر نو اور ہم), ***D'ãwat-e Islãmi Hindustãn Mein*** (دعوتِ اسلامی ہندوستان میں), ***Tashkîl-e Jam'ãt-e Islãm : Kyoṇ Aur Kaise*** (تشکیلِ جماعت اسلام کیوں اور کیسے) etc.

13. Maulana Syed Abu'l Ḥasan 'Ali Nadvi ('Ali Miaṇ) :

He was famed by the name of 'Ali Miãṇ, a prolific writer and eloquent speaker, born in Takia Kalaṇ, Rai Bareilly, on 6 *Muḥarram* 1333/24 November 1914. He was brougt up by his father Maulana Syed 'Abd ul-Ḥai, a bibliophile scholar and *nãẓim* of Nadvat ul-'Ulamã' and elder brother of Dr. Syed 'Abd ul- 'Ali, Physician and *nãẓim* of Nadvat ul-'Ulamã'.

He learnt *Qur'ãn, ḥadîth, tafsîr, fiqh, tajvîd, 'ulûm ul-Qur'ãn*, Arabic language and literature.[23] Along with these subjects, he also learnt English in order to keep himself well-aware of English writings relating to Islam and Arab culture. After the completion of his education, he became teacher of *ḥadîth, tafsîr*, Arabic literature, Arabic History as well as Logic in Dãr ul-'Ulûm Nadvat ul-'Ulamã' in 1934. In 1945 he became Dean and in 1961 the *nãẓim* in Nadvat ul-'Ulamã' and served on this post till his last breath.

He had earlier attached himself with *Jam'ãt-e Islãmi* but later in 1939 he was influenced by the thinking and works of Maulana Muḥammad Ilyãs Kãndhalwi. Abu'l Ḥasan 'Ali had a burning missionary spirit which took him to several lands and places for the propagation of Islam. In 1951, he established *Payãm-e Insãniyat* (پیامِ انسانیت) movement and preached the Islamic teachings of love, equality, morals and modesty. In 1959, he also founded the 'Acadmy of Islamic Research and Publications' in Nadvat ul-'Ulamã' for publishing the books on Islamic literature and Sciences. Besides these, he always took keen interest in the Community problems and its unity. Apart from these, during his whole life, he remained

---

23. He studied *Qur'ãn* under Maulana Syed 'Abd ul-Ḥai (father), Arabic language and literature from 'Allamah Khalil bin Muḥammad Yamani, *ḥadîth* from *Muḥaddith* Ḥaider Ḥasan Khan at Lahore. He revised it under Maulana Ḥusain Aḥmad Madani, *tafsîr* and *'ulûm ul-Qur'ãn* under Maulana Ḥusain Aḥmad Madani, *fiqh* from Shaikh. 'Ali, *tajvid* from Qãḍi Aṣghar 'Ali.

attached with several magazines and journals as a member of their Advisory Committee and Editorial Boards.

Achievements and Awards :

He took active interest always in the promotion of Muslim organisations and institutions and served them in various capacities which were widely acknowledged.

☆ Director of the Managing Committee of *Dãr ul-Muṣannefin*, Azamgarh.

☆ President of *Dînî T'ãlim* Council, U.P.

☆ Founder of the Constituent Council of the *Rabita al-Alam al-Islami*, Makkah.

☆ Member of Academy of Arts and Letters, Demoscus.

☆ Member of Higher Council of the Madinah University.

☆ Member of Executive Committee of the Federation of Islamic University Ribat.

☆ Member of *Majlis-e Shûra* of Dãr ul-'Ulûm, Deoband.

☆ Member of Advisory Council of the World Islamic University, Islamabad.

☆ Member of Arabic Academy of Demoscus, Cairo, Urdun.

☆ Chairman of the Islamic Studies of Oxford University in 1983.

☆ Founder-Member of *Jamia'h Islãmiyah* Madinah Munawwarah.

- ☆ In 1984, the Islamic literature Association was founded under his charimanship.
- ☆ In 1979, he was awarded King Faisal Award by Saudi Arabia.
- ☆ In 1981, Kashmir University awarded him the degree of Doctorate (Ph.D).
- ☆ On 7 January 1999, the Government of Dubai selected him the 'Muslim Personality of the year 1998'.
- ☆ In 1996, the Government of Turkey organised a seminar on Maulana Syed Abu'l Ḥasan 'Ali Nadvi.

Works :- Equipped with a religious bent of mind, creative thinking, keen observation and deep insight, he wrote books on almost every aspect of life. He was the author of neerly 170 books. Most of his works have been translated into English, Turkish, Persian, Tamil and some other languages. Some of his famous books are as follow:

The Four Pillars of Islam, Glory of Iqbal, Islamic concept of Prophethood, Muḥammad Rasûl-Allãh; The life of Prophet Muḥammad, Saviour of Islamic spirit (3 Volumes). ***Purãne Chirãgh*** (2 Volumes) (پرانے چراغ), ***Kãrwãn-e Zindagi*** (6 Volumes) (کاروانِ زندگی), ***Dayãr-e Kãbul se Dayãr-e Yarmûk Tak*** (دیارِ کابل سے دیارِ یرموک تک) ***Ḥaḍrat Maulana Muḥammad Iliyãs Aur Unkî Dînî Dã'wat*** (حضرت مولانا

محمد الیاس اور ان کی دینی دعوت), ***Ḥayãt-e 'Abd ul-Hai*** (حیاتِ عبدالحیٔ) ***Sîrat Syed Aḥmad Shahîd*** (سیرت سید احمد شہید), ***Musalmãn Momãlik Mein Islãmiyat Aur Maghrabîyat ki Kashmakash*** (مسلمان ممالک میں اسلامیت اور مغربیت کی کشمکش) etc.

14. Maulana Mujîb-ullãh Nadvi :

He was born in village Kusmi (کُسمی), Ghazipur, in 1921. His father Shaikh Ḥabib-ullah was an Assistant Sub-Inspector in Police department, posted in Azamgarh. Mujib-ullah received his primary education from Azamgarh. From there, he proceeded to *Maẓhar ul-'Ulûm*, Varanasi,[24] and from there he was admitted in Dãr ul-'Ulûm Nadvat ul-'Ulamã'.[25] After completing *Faḍilat,* he joined *Dãr ul-Muṣannefin*[26] on a salary of Rs. 40/- and served there for 22 years, since 1944 to 1966. For journal ***Ma'ãrif,*** he wrote several articles

24. *In Mazhar ul-'Ulûm* he studied ***Sharḥ Waqayah*** (شرح وقایہ) in 1939.

25. At Dãr ul-'Ulûm Nadvat ul-'Ulamã' he studied under *'ulamã'* including Maulana Shãh Ḥalim 'Aṭã, Maulana Shibli *Faqih*, Maulana Mưḥammad Nãẓim Nadvi and Maulana Syed Abu'l Hasan 'Ali Nadvi. He learnt ***Ḥujjat-ullah ul-Bãlighah***(حجۃ اللہ البالغۃ) and ***ul-Fauz al-Kabîr***(الفوز الکبیر) under Syed Sulaiman Nadvi.

26. He preferred and was more interested in reading and writing than in holding any post or authority. So he refused the offer of principalship and its salary of Rs. 100/- and joined *Dãr ul-Muṣannefin* for only Rs. 40/-

which were spread over more than 1500 pages. Later his articles were compiled and published in a book form.[27]

He worked in the Project of ***Siyar us-Ṣa ḥãbah wa'l-Tãba'în*** (سیر الصحابہ والتابعین) and authored a book entitled ***Ahl-e Kitãb Ṣaḥãbah wa Tãba'în*** (اہلِ کتاب صحابہ تابعین).[28] He further extended the area of the project by writing one more volume ***Tabã' Tãba'în*** (تبع تابعین) Part-I.[29]

In 1962, he opened a religious institution called *Jãmi'at ur-Rashãd* in Azamgarh. There were mainly two objectives behind its establishment i.e. (i) to develop religious atmosphere in Azamgarh (ii) to unite all the *madãris* of Azamgarh under one head. Students got education upto *Faḍilat* level. There is also a separate arrangement of education for girls known as *Jami'at ut-Ta'libat*. He stressed more on the primary

---

27. ***Fatãwã-e 'Alamgiri Aur Uske Muallefîn***(فتاوی عالمگیری اور اس کے مؤلفین), ***Khidmat-e Ḥadîth Mein Khwatîn Kã Ḥiṣṣah*** (خدمت حدیث میں خواتین کا حصہ), ***Islam ke Bain ul- Aqwami Uṣul wa Taṣawwurãt*** (اسلام کی بین الاقوامی اصول وتصورات) ***Thubût-e Rajm*** (ثبوت رجم), ***Islam Mein Qanun-e Ujrat*** (اسلام میں قانون اجرت), ***Ijtihãd wa Tabdili Aḥkãm*** (اجتہاد و تبدیلی احکام), ***Fiqh-e Islami Aur Daur-e Jadîd ke Masã'il***(فقہ اسلامی اور دورِ جدید کے مسائل), ***Islami Fiqh***(اسلامی فقہ) (3 volumes).
28. It was published in 1951 from Dãr ul-Muṣannefîn. The book comprises the biographies and works of 93 such *ṣa ḥãbah, ṣa ḥãbiyãt, tãba'in* and *tãbe'ãt* who were earlier either Christian or Jews.
29. ***Taba' Tãba'în***(تبع تابعین), Part Ist , was published in 1959.

education. For this, he started 'Rashad Junior High School' where the students used to learn religious culture and training. Along with this he established the department of ***Nadvat ut-Talif wa Tarãjum*** (ندوة التاليف وتراجم) within the boundary of *Jãmi'at ur-Rashãd*. In 1981, he started a monthly journal ***ar-Rashãd*** (الرشاد) under his editorship. He also started an Arabic Journal viz ***Majallat ur-Rashãd*** (مجلۃ الرشاد) but due to lack of fund, it was closed down.

Besides literary activities, he also took interest in the political activities. He played dominant role in the Shah Bano case and the case of Babari Masque. He went to Ayodhya and managed for the settlement of those Muslims who had migrated form Ayodhya. He opened a school for religious education which is looked after by his son Dr. 'Abd-ullãh 'Ammar.

He was among the founder members of the Milli Council.[30] He is also the member of Islami *Fiqh* Academy.[31] He often travelled in India as well as abroad and attended the political and religious conferences and meetings. He visited Egypt, Malaysia, Dubai, South Africa, apart from Ḥijaz.

15. Maulana Mas'ûd 'Ali Nadvi :

"There were three pillars of *Dãr ul-Muṣannefin*,

30. Milli Council is a platform on which the common problems of the Muslims are discussed and proper steps are proposed to be taken for their remedies.

31. *Islami Fiqh Academy* was founded by Maulana Mujahid ul-Islam Qasmi. This academy issues *fatvãs* (legal verdicts) for the emerging problems of Islamic Law (*Shari'ah*).

viz. Syed Sulaiman Nadvi, 'Abd us-Salãm Nadvi and Mas'ûd 'Ali Nadvi",[32] as pointed out by Shãh Mo'în ud-Dîn Aḥmad Nadvi. He is famous for his architectural (building) work and managing quality. He was the man of good taste, good tongue and good manners.

He belonged to the village Bhayãrah (بھیارہ), district Barabanki. After getting primary education form his home town, he took admission in Dãr ul-'Ulûm Nadvat ul-'Ulamã' in 1904 and completed it in 1913. After the death of his mentor 'Allãmah Shibli, he stayed at Azamgarh and prepared an outline of *Dãr ul-Muṣannefin* and became its *muhtamim*. Almost all the buildings of *Dãr ul-Muṣannefin*, Shibli College and the mosque and the hostels of Nadvat ul-'Ulamã' had been constructed under his supervision. Along with this, he took interest in the national and religious movements of the country. He was a staunch supporter of *Khilãfat* Movement.

He died on 27 August 1967 in *Dãr ul-Muṣannefin*, Azamgarh and was burried by the side of Shibli's grave.

Apart from these Nadvi scholars, there are many other writers of Nadvat ul-'Ulamã' who got repute from their literary work. Such as Prof. M. Sãlim Kidwai, Prof. Mas'ûd ur-Raḥman Khan Nadvi, Prof. Syed Ijtiba Nadvi, Prof. Syed Ḍia ul-Ḥasan Nadvi,

32. *Ma'arif,* vol. 100. No. 3, September, 1967, P. 162.

Prof. Muḥammad Sheeis Islma'il, Prof. Iḥtisham Aḥmad Nadvi, Maulana Syed Rābi' Ḥasani Nadvi, Maulana 'Abd-ullāh Abbās Nadvi, Maulana Khalîl Nadvi, Maulana Waḍeh Rashîd Nadvi, Maulana Muḥ ammad Fārûq Nadvi, Maulana Syed Maḥmud Ḥasan Ḥasani Nadvi, Dr. M. Akram Nadvi, M. Yaḥyā Sallo Nadvi, Qāri 'Abd ul-Bāri Nadvi, Maulvi Shamsh ul-Ḥ aq Nadvi, Maulana Taqi ud-Dîn 'Uthmāni Nadvi, Maulana Muḥammad al-Ḥasani Nadvi, Maulana Ra'îs Aḥmad Jā'fri Nadvi, Maulana Syed Salman Nadvi, Maulana Shafeeq Aḥmad Nadvi, Maulana Moḥsin Usmani Nadvi, Maulana Muḥammad Ja'far Shāh Phulwārwi Nadvi, Maulana Muḥammad Ilyās Moḥi ud-Dîn Nadvi, Maulana Muḥammad Raḍi ul-Islām Nadvi, Maulana 'Abd ul-Ḥalîm Nadvi. etc.

CONCLUSION

To bring about reforms in the prevalent educational system and in the courses of studies of the *madãris-e islãmiyah* (religious seminaries) in accordance with changing needs and also to eliminate the conflict of warring Muslim groups on religious issues were the two main objectives behind the establishment of Nadvat ul-'Ulamã'.

With regard to the reforms and updating the syllabi of *madãris-e islãmiyah*, the founders members of Nadvat ul-'Ulamlã' were in favour of the inclusion of modern subjects, viz. history, geography, economics, mathematics, Arabic language and literature. In *Musavvidãh-e Niṣãb-e 'Arabi* (draft syllabi) Maulana Muḥammad 'Ali Mongeri, along with other subjects, advised for the inclusion of six new subjects in the curriculum, namely-history, grammar, phonetics, prosody, *taṣawwuf* and ethics. He emphasized that unnecessary portion of old philosophy and logic should be excluded from the curriculum so that the Islamic sciences concerning *Qur'ãn*, *ḥadîth*, *tafsir*, *fiqh*, may find greater share in the syllabi.

Moreover, 'Allãmah Shibli along with these subjects introduced, English, Hindi, Sanskrit, modern Arabic, *'Ilm-e Kalãm* in the curriculum so that the students might be able to face the challenges of the time.

In the syllabi of Nadvat ul-'Ulamã' more emphasis was laid on the education of Urdu and Arabic language and literature so as to enable the students, to acquire greater expertise and proficiency in these languages. There is no denying of the fact that the graduates of Nadvat ul-'Ulamã' can not compare with the students of modern institutions in so far as government services and jobs are concerned. But they are certainly well-aware of the modern-day developments and competent enough in their own field-whether it's the teaching and preaching of Islam or defending it on intellectual grounds against its critics. In this way, the Nadvi graduates have been fulfilling the dreams of the founders-members through there awareness of the modern thought and the emerging problems by the virtue of their reformed syllabi and intelligent training.

The courses of studies of Nadvat ut-'Ulamã' in the course of time have been welcomed by the Muslim world and these have been introduced in the *madrasâs* of India and several other countries such as Nepal, Bengladesh, Malaysia, Thailand etc. Approximately, more than two hundred *madrasãs* introduced the syllabi of Nadvah in their institutions and established the pattern of training of Dãr ul-'Ulûm Nadvat ul-'Ulamã'. Many of these *madrasãs* have been founded by the graduates of Nadvat ul-'Ulamã itself. There are twenty such *madrasãs* in Lucknow itself and one hundred forty others are functioning in various parts of India and abroad.

Dãr ul-Ulûm Nadvat ul-'Ulamã' has produced hundreds of scholars, reformers, writers and leaders who are well- known for their contribution in the Islamic fields, not only in India but also in foreign countries. Similarly, students from all corners of India and other countries, viz. Australia, Holland, Canada, Nepal, Bangladesh etc. come to Nadvat ul-'Ulamã' to quench their thirst of Islamic learning.

For sharpening the pens and minds of the teachers and students, Dãr ul-Ulûm Nadvat ul-'Ulamã' publishes academic journals in Urdu, Arabic as well as English. These journals are either fortnightly, monthly or quarterly. There are or have been Urdu journals like ***al-Nadvah*** (monthly, started from 1904-1916, again in 1940-1945), ***Tã'mîr-e Ḥayãt*** (fortnightly, since 1964). Arabic journals ***aḍ-Ḍiyã'*** (from 1932-1935), ***al-Bã'th ul-Islamî*** (monthly, since 1959), ***ar-Rã'id*** (fortnightly, since 1959) and the English journal ***The Fragrance of East*** (quarterly) which help the teachers and students get acuainted with latest trends and issues and provide guidance for the dissemination of Islamic faith and learning.

In Dãr ul-Ulûm Nadvat ul-'Ulamã', there is a printing press as well as publishing arm in addition to the Nadvah's Academy of Islamic Research and publications (established in 1959). From here, the books on different topics and subjects have been published in various languages, viz., Urdu, Arabic and English. Along with these, Nadvah has a big library with thousands of books including six hundred fifty rare books and three thousands manuscripts.

The graduates of Nadvat ul-'Ulamã' rendered remarkable and admirable services in imparting and propagating the Islamic learning and religious sciences. Hundreds of works have been authored by them which hold important place in the intellectual circles. Their works contain invaluable research materials on *Qur'ãn, ḥadith, tafsir, fiqh,* Islamic history, philosophy, *sîrah, taṣawwuf,* education, Urdu and Arabic literature and other fields such as ethics, politics, economics *'ibãdãt* and *mu'ãmalãt*. Many of these works have been translated into English, Turkish, Persian and Indian languages e.g. Bengali, Tamil, Telgu etc. The Nadvi scholars took endless pains in collecting the historical data and test their accuracy. They have written in elegant and modernistic style and above all with fare and impartial criticism.

Books of Nadvi graduates related to *Sîrah* of Prophet Muḥammad (S.A.W.) and the biographies of *ṣaḥãbah, tãba'in* and *taba' tãba'in* and the heroes of Muslim world inspire the Islamic ideals and desire to act and live in society accordingly. In these biographical writings, it is clearly seen that a true believer should nurture such ideal qualities as gentle disposition, tenderness of heart and susceptibility to goodness, courage, steadfastness, toleration, abstinence, sincerity, trust in Allãh, patience, contentedness etc.

The historical writings of the graduates of Nadvat ul-'Ulamã' are also very rich and informative. A number of books have been written by them almost on all aspects of Islamic history. While some of these books provide a vivid account of the history of Muslim monarchs and their nobles and courtiers and some others deal with the history of pre-Islamic Arabs, Prophet Muḥammad's (S.A.W.) period, *Khulafa-e Rãshedîn,* Umayyads, Abbasids, Ottomans, Mughals etc. providing rich information about many of areas of Europe, Africa and Asia and Muslim lands situated there. Their books are a store-house of research and precious information not only about political and religious conditions but also social and economic life of different Muslim periods and lands such as Arabia, Egypt, Syria, Iraq, Iran, India, Turkey, Afghanistan,

Spain etc.

In philosophical writings, the scholars of Nadvat ul-'Ulamā' tried to remove the misconception that the Muslim philosophers were not true believers or they were weak in their faith. On the other hand, they also highlighted the latter's effort and contributions to bring about a harmonization between philosophy and Islamic faith. Religion itself is a kind of philosophy because it deals with the same broad questions, and therefore, it can also be explained through the philosophy. So a harmonization of the two is only desirable. The Nadvi scholars introduced the Muslim philosophers in the light of their philosophical contributions.

The writers of Nadvah have also contributed in the field of literature and other writings of literary significance, such as letters and *safarnāmas.* They also compiled dictionaries and thereby enriched the Arabic Urdu literature.

They highlighted the importance of Arabic language because for Islamic learning it is fundamental. One cannot study the original sources of Islamic Sciences without acquiring proficiency in Arabic language and literature. The scholars who do not know Arabic are prone to commit blunders while writing on *Qur'ān, ḥadîth. tafsîr, fiqh* and other branches of Islamic learnings. Besides these, their other works on *taṣawwuf,* education or contemporary issues are also not insignificant.

This is amply clear from the writings of the graduates of Nadvat ul-'Ulamã' that they have versatile interests. Their perspective is wide-ranging and covers almost every aspect of Islam. They also made worth while contributions in Islamic arts and sciences through their translations.

The second objective of Nadvat al-'Ulamã' is to lessen the differences among Muslim groups on different religious issues. Let us see how much success Nadvah achieved in this objective. In the first meeting of Nadvat ul-'Ulamã, in April 1894, in *Madrasah-e Faiḍ-e Âm*, Kanpur, almost all the Muslim sects and groups, having kept their differences aside, participated in the meeting. But unfortunately, this could not be continued for longer time due to the differences in their sectarian views or other considerations. The followers of Shi'ah sect withdrew themselves because they found it difficult to stand shoulder to shoulder with *Ahl us-Sunnah wa'l Jama'at* in theological field. A group of Muslims became aloof from Nadvah when they saw the involvement of British government, particularly at the time of foundation ceremony. No doubt, Shibli tried to unite them by pointing out in his lectures that the pulpit of the Prophet's mosque was constructed by a Christian. Some well-wishers of Nadvah left it when Shibli forcefully introduced English, Hindi and Sanskrit in the curriculum.

The followers of Barelvi group played a leading role in defaming the Nadvah. Aḥmad Raḍã Khan Barelvi, 'Abd ul-Qãdir Badãuni and Nãẓir Aḥmad Rampuri opposed Nadvat ul-'Ulamã' openly and published more than 40 books, letters and pamphlets in Nadvah's criticism. Among them ***Khadwah*** (خدوہ), ***Jazwah*** (جذوہ), ***Siṭwah*** (سطوہ), ***Jathwah*** (جثوہ), were the magazines which were brought out against Nadvah. Not content with this, they even tried to get *fatvãs* against them from Arab world. They used to vilify and slander the Nadvah in relation with the name of the place and its situation. For example they propagated among the traders of Surat that the members of Nadvat ul-'Ulamã were Wahhabi and had no faith in *peer-mureed* system. Among the teachers and students of *Madrasah-e 'Aliyã,* Calcutta, they used to preach that Nadvi's were naturist and had no faith in real religious education. They used to say among moderate Muslims that the Nadvah's members were conservative and opposed to the education of modern arts and sciences.

In the reply to the Barelvi group, the supporters and well-wishers of Nadvat ul-'Ulamã' wrote several books and treaties and refuted their charges and blames. Such as the book ***Irshãd ul-Kumlã*** (ارشادالکملا)

of Maulana Hafiẓ-ullãh, ***Itmãm ul-Ḥujjat 'Alã Mukhãlifi al-Nadvah*** (اتمام الحجۃ علی مخالفی الندوہ) of Maulana 'Abd ul-Ḥai, ***Maqãṣid Nadvat ul-'Ulamã' Aur Uski Mukhalifat*** (مقاصد ندوۃ العلماء اور اس کی مخالفت) of Mirza Hairat 'Ali, ***Hidãyat ul-Albab*** (ہدایت الالباب) of Muḥammad 'Ali Mongeri had been written in refutation of Barelvi's blames. Furthermore, Maulana 'Abd ul-Ḥai wrote that they did not spare any one and often used to defame our senior respected *'ulamã'* even, like Shãh 'Abd ul-'Azîz, Shãh Wali-ullãh, Shaikh Aḥmad Sirhindi, Muḥammad Qãsim Nãnautavi, Rashîd Aḥmad Gangohi etc, then how could Nadvah be saved by their pens and tongues.

No doubt, the attacks of Barelvi group could not damage the image and the status of Nadvat ul-'Ulamã' in the Muslim Community. But they failed in uniting the different Muslim groups under one flag. In the wake of this objective, however, the members of Nadvat ul-'Ulamã' continued an endeavour to make the people to realize the advantages of cooperation and disadvantages of non-cooperation.

GLOSSARY

Âdhãn **:** The call or announcement to Prayer. A technical term for the call to the divine service of Friday and the five daily *salãt*.

Adîb- (Pl-*Udaba*) **:** Writer, literature.

Ahl ul-ḥadîth **:** A group emerged in 19th century in India during the time of Shãh Isma'îl Shahîd who rejected the *taqlîd* of all the schools of *fiqh* and upheld the cause of literal and consistent reference to and rigid and faithful conformity with the Prophetic (S.A.W.) tradition, known as *Ahl-e Ḥadîth*. With the influence of Nawãb Ṣiddîq Ḥasan and Syed Naẓir Ḥusain, this became an original school. The inspiration of this rather literalist school in *ḥadîth* and *fiqh* comes after Imam Aḥmad ibn Hanabal from Shaikh ibn Taymiyyah who are known in Islamic history for their uncompromising adherence to *ḥadîth*.

Ahl-e Kitãb **:** The People of the revealed book. The term initially was applicable to the Jews and Christians only but in later years, its scope was widened to practically include some other communities also.

Ahl-e Sunnat wa'l Jam'ãt (*Sunnî*) **:** Majority of Muslims which accept the authority of the whole first generation of Muslims and the validity of the historical community in contrast to the *Khãrijîs* and the *Shia'h.*

Akhlãq **:** Good qualities, virtues, moral dispositions.

As-Ṣirãṭ al-Mustaqîm **:** The 'straight path' which defines the life of Islam in general and the spiritual life in particular.

Anjuman **:** Association, assembly, organisation.

Aqã'id (PL of *Aqîdah*) **:** Faith, belief, creed.

Arûḍ **:** Prosody.

Asharah Mubashshrah' **:** The companions to whom the Prophet (S.A.W.) foretold they would enter Paradise. They are :- Abu Bakr, 'Umar, 'Uthmãn, 'Ali, Ṭalaḥa, Zubair, 'Abd ur-Raḥmãn, Sa'd bin Abi Waqqãs, Sa'id bin Zaid, Abu Ubaydah ibn ul-Jarrãh (R.A.A.).

Auqãf **(PL of *waqf*) :** Charitable, endowments, trusts: A plain endowment of certain incomes, commonly rents or land revenues, for the upkeep of mosques, a hospital etc. In Muslim legal terminology, it means primarily to protect a thing to prevent it from becoming the property of a third person. A term which in the language of the law signifies the appropriation or dedication of perpetual nature; such property cannot be sold or transferred.

Balãghat : Rhetoric, eloquence.

Barakãh: Blessing, auspiciousness, prosperity, spiritual power inherent in a saint; conveyed in *tabarruk*, sacred reliecs or blessings.

Bãtin : The inward, esoteric, hidden aspect of being doctrine, or religion. A term used in the theology so that which is in its meaning in particular, denotes esoteric knowledge. One of the 99 special names of Allãh.

Bay'ah : Pact made between the head of the Islamic community and leaders within the community as well as the initiatic pact made between the spiritual master and the disciple. Both of these practices go back to the Prophet.(ﷺ)

Bida't : The introduction of something new is *bida't* only when it contradicts the spirit of Islam. A practice or a belief which was not present in Islam as it was revealed in the *Qur'ãn,* and established by the *sunnah*.

Chishti : A *ṣufi* path of those initiated into the chain of succession that begin with Mu'in ud-Dîn of Ajmer (R.A.).

Dãirah : *A 'dhikr'* circle.

Dãr ul-'Ulûm : A place of advanced religious learning.

Dãr ul-Ifta' : Department of legal opinion, juridicial verdict.

Darjãh-e Â'lã : Higher Classes.

Darjãh-e Faḍîlat : Graduate level.

Darjãh-e Ibtida : Primary Classes.

Dars wa Tadrîs : Study and Teaching.

Dars-e Niẓãmi : A syllabus for religious institutions had been prepared by Mulla Niẓãm ud-Dîn Sihãlwi in which more emphasis was put on the study of *m'ãqûlãt* rather than the study of *Qur'ãn, ḥadîth, tafsîr and fiqh*.

Darvesh : Persian word for a religious mendicant. Broadly through Islam, it is used in the sense of a member of religious fraternity.

Dastãrbandi : Convocation function for honouring student, learned man by tying turban round his head.

Dastûr ul- 'Amal : Rules of procedure, modus operandi, rules & regulations.

Dhimmî : *Dhimmî* is from *'dhimmãh'* meaning covenant or obligation, a Person belonging to the category of "protected people" in the Islamic state. They were granted, security of life and property, complete religious freedom & defence against others. In return they were required to pay *jizyah* (head tax) and *kharãj* (exemption tax).

Diwãn : Originally a Persian word meaning a "many-leaved book", and hence an account-book, record, collection of poems and, by extension, a government department containing such records.

Fãḍil : Accomplished person, scholar.

Faqîh : (Pl. *Fuqaha*) Jurist, doctor of the Islamic law (*shari'ah*).

Farã'iḍ : The name given to the Muslim laws of inheritance. The jurists of Islam attached great importance to them in view of social justice.

Farmãn : Charter, Command.

Fatwa : (Pl. *Fatãwã*) - It is a formal legal opinion given by a *muftî* (Canon lawyer), in answer to question submitted to him either by a private individual or an organisation.

Fiqh : Literally the word means "knowledge", "understanding", "comprehension". It is, however, the name given to the jurisprudence in Islam which covers all the aspects of the Muslims' life : collective and individual. The law that regulated the public & private life of the Muslims were based on relgion; the science of these laws come to be known as *'fiqh'*.

Ḥadîth : (Pl. *A ḥadîth*) It means speech, report, account. Specifically, traditions relating to the deeds and utterances of the Prophet (S.A.W.) as recounted by his companions. In *shi'ism* the term is used also for the sayings of one of the twelve *Imãms*, but a close distinction is made between the syaings of the Prophet (S.A.W.) and those of the *Imãms*.

Ḥaḍrat : Dignity, a title applied to any great person.

Ḥãfiẓ : Guardian or protector. One of the name of *Allãh 'al-Ḥãfiẓ'*; One who has memorised the *Qur'ãn*.

Ḥajj : The pilgrimage to Makkah performed in the month of *Dhul-Ḥijjah*. One of the five pillars of Islam. It is incumbent upon those whose health and means permit it.

Ḥanbali : Referring to *sunni* legal *madhhab* ascribed to Aḥmad Ibn Ḥanbal (780-855).

Ḥanafi : Referring to the *sunni* legal *madhhab* ascribed to Abu Ḥanîfa (699-767).

Ḥaram : Restricted, forbidden, sacred. The sacred areas around Makkah, Madinah are called *ḥaram*. It was also the apartments of woman in Muslim aristocratic households.

Ḥakîm : Wise person, doctor of medicine. One of the 99 attributes of Allãh.

Hijrah : The migration of the Prophet Muḥammad (S.A.W.) from Makkah to Madinah in 622 A.D. which marks the beginning of the Islamic calendar.

'Ibãdat Khãna : Place of worship.

'Ibãdat : Worship, religious obligations; particularly those of the canonically prescribed rituals, owed by man to Allãh.

***'Îd ul-Aḍḥã* :** "The feast of sacrifice". It is celebrated on the 10th *Dhul-Ḥijjah*, and is a part of the rites of the Makkan pilgrimage. The feast is a commemoration of *Ḥaḍrat* Ibrãhim's (A.S.) sacrifice of the ram as a Divine dispensation, releasing him from the intended sacrifice of his son. Also known as *'Id ul-Kabîr*.

***'Îd ul-Fiṭr* :**"The feast of breaking fast". It commences as soon as the month's fast in *Ramaḍãn* is over, and consequently on the first day of the month of *Shawwãl*. It is especially a feast of alms-giving. Also known as *'Id us-Ṣaghîr*.

***Ijtihãd* :** The word means "exerting oneself to the utmost degree to attain an object", but technically its meaning is the utmost effort to understand the spirit and points of law and form an opinion. It is applied to those questions which are not covered by *Qur'ãn* and *sunnah*.

***Ikhlãṣ* :** Sincerity, Purity. That sincerity which is surrendered to Allãh "with all one's heart, and all one's mind, and all one's soul". In Islam, this is the true affirmation of the Divine Unity.

***Ikhwãn* :** Brotherhood or brathren, usually used by members of a *ṣûfi* order when referring to the other members.

'Ilm : Knowledge, Science.

'Ilm ul-Kalãm : Literally 'word', 'speech;. Applied to Islamic theology which is the "study of Divine Speech". It seeks to defend the tenets of the faith through the use of rational arguments. It is the science whereby we are able to bring forward proofs of our religious belief. It includes the discussion of the nature of the existence and the attributes of Allãh.

Imãm : Leader of the canonical prayer in Muslim community. A pre-eminent scholar of any discipline or field. Among the *shi'ah*, 'Ali (R.A) and his descendants as proper leaders of the Islamic community, held to have a spiritual function as successors to Prophet Muḥammad (S.A.W.).

Imãn : Faith, *Imãn* is defined as faith in Allãh, His Angels, His Books, His Prophets and the Day of Judgement. Muḥammad (S.A.W.) said, "Faith (*imãn*) is a confession with the tongue, verification with the heart, and an act with the members".

Insãn : Human, implying the start of the human being with the possibility of its full perfection rather than its earthly and imperfect condition.

Irshãdãt : Instructions, commands, or guidance showing the path of righteousness.

Ishrãq : Illumination.

Islãm : Surrender to the Will of Allãh.

Istighfãr : Seeking pardon.

Jãgîr : The right of the revenue of a piece of land given by government as a reward for services.

Jãhîlî (Period) : Period of ignorance before the rise of Islam in Arabia.

Jihãd : Literally 'effort' or 'exertion' but usually translated as 'holy war'. Jihãd in the widest sense means all actions performed to establish equilibrium in life according to the norms of Islam.

Kãfir : (Ingrateful) The word is generally used in Islamic law to define one who is an unbeliever.

Khãnqãh : A *ṣûfi* center for disciples where *dhikr* is observed under the guidance of a spiritual mentor.

Khilãfat : Successorship to a spiritual mentor, giving permission to initiate the desciples.

Kufr : Unbelief in Allãh or Islam.

Mã'qûlãt : Rational subjects.

Madãris-e Islãmiya : The traditional schools of higher study.

Madhhab : In *sunni* Islam, one of the four equally legitimate schools of law: Ḥanafi, Ḥanbali, Maliki and Shãfa'i.

Maghrib : Evening or sunset, the fourth time specified for the performance of the daily prayers.

Majlis : Gathering, used in sufism in a technical sense as the gathering of the *ṣûfis*.

Majlis-e Shûra : Legislative, advisory body.

Maktab : A writing or primary school.

Malfûẓãt : Sayings of saints.

Mãliki : Referring to the *sunni* legal *madhhab* ascribed to Mãlik bin Anas (R.A.) (715-795).

Manqûlãt :The 'copied' subjects, *Qur'ãn* and *ḥadîth* as distinguished from *ma'qulãt*, which are the products of the man's reasoning.

Maulana : A title given to a person respected for religious learning: our master.

Maulavi : A learned man in Islamic law.

Moḥkamãt : Those verses of *Qur'ãn* which have a clear precise meaning.

Mu'ãmalãt : (Pl. of *Mã'malãh*) - Dealings, affairs.

Mufassir : Writer of Quranic exegesis.

Mufti : An expert in the *shari'ah*, who gives opinions in cases of law and conscience.

Muḥaddith : A scholar of *ḥadîth*.

Muḥarram : The first month of the Islamic lunar year during which *Ḥaḍrat* Ḥussain (R.A.) was martyred in Karbala.

Muḥtamim : A manager. A Rector or Principal.

Mujtahid : An authority in Islamic legal system who can give independent opinion in the *shari'ah*, that is, practice *ijtihad*. Among the *shias,* this term is used almost exclusively for religious authorities who constitute a distinct class and wield greater power.

Mumin : The person of faith, the Muslim who not only has surrendered his will to Allãh to follow the injunctions of Islam and has ardent faith in Allãh in his heart.

Murîd : A disciple of spiritual mentor or order.

Mutashãbehãt : Those verses of *Qur'ãn* which have no definite and clear meaning.

Nabî : Prophet, he who is appointed by Allãh to bring His message to men. If this message is a book or new dispensation from heaven, than *nabî* is called *rasûl.*

Nafs : The self, the soul.

Naḥv: Syntax; the Arabic grammar.

Naqashbandi : The *ṣûfi* path of those initiated into the sufistic order of Shaikh Bahã ud-Dîn Naqshband (d. 1389).

Nãẓim : Administrator, Rector.

Nûr : Light

Pandit : One well-versed in Hindu religious lore, Brahman teacher.

Pãṭḥhshãla : Primary school.

Pîr : Spiritual master, *shaikh.*

Pûrab : East

Qãḍi ul-Quḍḍãt **:** The chief justice.

Qãdri **:** The *ṣûfi* path of those initiated into the order of Shaikh 'Abd ul-Qãdir Jilãni (R.A.) (d. 1166).

Qiblah **:** The direction determined by the location of the *Kã'bãh* which Muslims must face while offering their prayers.

Ra'îs **:** The head or chief, a person of authority.

Ramaḍãn **:** The ninth month of Islamic calender during which all Muslims who have the capability are obliged to fast from dawn to sunset, is one of the five pillars of Islam.

Ribãt **:** Camp, Cantonment.

Rûh **:** The spirit including both the Supreme Spirit and the spirit within men.

Ṣadr us-Ṣudûr **:** The chief judge.

Ṣaḥãbah **:** Companions of the Prophet Muḥammad (S.A.W.).

Salãt **:** The canonical daily prayers which are obligatory for all Muslims to perform five times ạ day.

Shafa'î **:** Referrig to the *sunni* legal *madhhab* ascribed to al-Shafa'î (767-819).

Shaikh **:** Elder, revered person, a learned man or a teacher more specifically a spiritual master.

Shari'ah **:** The Divine Law, which is rooted in the *Qur'ãn* and *ḥadîth*, and thereafter in *ijma* and *qiyãs*.

Shuhada : (Pl. of Shahîd) martyrs.

Sipãsnãamh : Address of welcome.

Sirãh : Biography, used especially in reference to the life of the Prophet Muḥammad (S.A.W.).

Ṣuffah : Platform in the *Masjid-e Nabavi* which served as the first centre of Islamic education.

Ṣûfi : One who practices Sufism; a common term for that aspect of Islam which cultivates spiritual development. The Arabic *faqîr* and the Persian *darvesh,* both meaning 'poor' are often applied for *ṣûfis*.

Sunnah : The tradition of the Prophet (S.A.W.) embracing his manners and ways of doing and acting in different circumstances in life.

Sûrah : A chapter of the *Qur'ãn*.

Tãba'in : Followers of the companions of the Prophet (S.A.W.).

Tabã' Tãba'în : Followers of successors of the companions of the Prophet (S.A.W.).

Tafsîr : Exegesis of the Holy *Qur'ãn*.

Tajvîd : Phonetics, declamation, recitation of the Qur'ãn. The recital of *Qur'ãn* is governed by the science of *tajvîd*, which determines the full, smooth and balanced pronunciation, in context of each letter and syllable.

Tanãsukh : Transmigration of soul.

Tarîqat : The mystical way; especially the way of a *ṣufi* order.

Taṣawwuf : Sufism, Islamic esoterism and mysticism. It is the science of the direct knowledge of Allãh; its doctrines and methods are derived from the *Qur'ãn* and *sunnah*.

Ṭib : The classical Muslim system of Medicines practiced by a *ḥakîm* or *ṭabîb*.

'Ulamã' : (Pl of *'Alim*) - Class of learned men in Islamic society.

Ummah : The community, usually identified with the Islamic people but also applied to the followers of other Prophets and therefore other religious communities.

Vidyalaya : School for higher education.

Vyãkarana : Grammar.

Wahhãbi : A follower of 18th century Arabian reformer Muḥammad bin 'Abd ul-Wahhab who taught an anti-*ṣufi*, Ḥanbali Islam.

Wãjib : That act which is obligatory for a Muslim according to the injunctions of the religion. The term is used mostly but not exclusively in the domain of law.

Zãhid : (Pl. *Zuhhãd*) - Ascetic, hermit. The one who renunciates the ease and comfort for the sake of relgious enlightment in order to detach the soul from the material world.

Ẓãhir : (Pl. Ẓawãhir) - The outward or manifest, also a name of Allãh who is as manifest as hidden.

Zakãt : Religious tax which is obligatory and constitutes one of the pillars of Islam.

BIBLIOGRAPHY

Books : (A) English :

'Abd ul-Hai, Syed :

India During Muslim Rule, Eng. tr. by Moḥi ud-Din Aḥmad, Lucknow, 1997.

Aḥmad, 'Aziz :

An Intellectual History of Islam in India, Edenburg, 1969.

Islamic Modernism in India and Pakistan (1857-1964), London, 1967,

Studies in Islamic Culture in the Indian Environment, London 1964.

Ahmad 'Aziz and G.E. Von Grunebaum :

Muslim Self-statement in India and Pakistan, (1857-1968), Wiesbaden, 1970.

Aḥmad, Muḥammad Akhlaq :

Traditional Education among Muslims, Delhi, 1985.

Aḥmad, Moḥi ud-Din :

Syed Aḥmad Shahid : His Life and Mission, Lucknow, 1975.

'Alam, Zafar :

Education in Early Islamic Period, Delhi, 1991.

'Ali, A Yusuf :

Making of India, London, 1925.

Alvi, Shariq :

Fiasco in Nadva : As viewed by National Press, Lucknow, 1995.

Amir 'Ali, Syed :

The Spirit of Islam, Calcutta, 1902.

Andrews, C.F. :

Zaka-Ullah of Delhi : With an Introductory Memoir by the Late Maulvi Naẓir Aḥmad, Cambridge, 1929.

Ashraf, K.M. :

Muslim Revivalists and the Revolt of 1857, Delhi, 1957.

Ashraf, Mujeeb :

Muslim Attitude Towards British Rule and Western Culture, Delhi, 1982.

Baljon, J.M.S. :

The Reforms and Religious Ideas of Sir Syed Ahmad Khan (2nd Edition), Lahore, 1896.

Barthrop, Micheal :

Indian Mutiny (1857-59), London, 1994.

Bosworth, C.E. and others (ed) :

The Encyclopaedia of Islam vol. VII (New Edition), New York, 1993.

Daud, Abu :

Sunan-e Abu Daud, vol. III Eng. tr. Aḥmad Ḥasan, New Delhi, 1985.

Desai, Zia al-Din. A :

Centres of Islamic Learning in India, Govt. of India, 1978.

Dutt, R.C. :

The Economic History of India in the Victorian Age, London, 1908.

Elliot and Dowson :

History of India : As told by its own Historians, vol. III, Allahabad, 1964.

Embree, Ainslie. T. :

Imagining India : Essays on Indian History, New Delhi, 1989.

Espisito, John.I. (ed) :

The Oxford Encyclopaedia of the Modern Islamic World, vol. III, New York 1995.

Faḍl, Mirza Abu'l :

Sayings of The Propeht Muḥammad, Allahabad, 1924.

Faruqi, Zia al-Ḥasan :

The Deoband School and the Demand for Pakistan, Bombay, 1963.

Farquhar, J.N. :

Modern Religious Movement in India, New York, 1915.

Gibb, H.A.R. and J.H. Kramers (ed) :

The Shorter Encyclopaedia of Islam,. Leiden, 1961.

Gopal, Ram :

The Indian Muslim, Bombay, 1959

Ḥali, Altaf Ḥusain :

Ḥayãt-e Javed (Eng. Translation), Delhi, 1979.

Hardy, Peter :

The Muslims of British India, Cambridge, 1972.

Hashmi, Syed Masroor 'Ali Akhtar :

Muslim Responses to Western Education, New Delhi, 1989.

Ḥasan Qamar :

Muslim in India, New Delhi, 1987.

Holt, P.M. and others :

The Cambridge History of Islam, vol. II, Cambridge,1970.

Hunter, W.W. :

Report of the Indian Education Commission, Calcutta, 1982.

The Indian Musalmans, Lahore, 1964.

Husain, Syed 'Abid :

The Destiny of Indian Muslims, Bombay 1965.

Ḥusain, Syed Sajjad and 'Ali Ashraf :

Crisis in Muslim Education, Hodder and Stonghton and King 'Abd ul-'Aziz University, 1979.

Ḥusain, Yusuf :

Glimpses of Medieval Indian Culture, Bombay, 1959.

Jaffar, S.M :

Education in Muslim India (1000-1800 AC), Delhi, 1936.

Jalbani, G.N. :

Teachings of Shah Waliyallah of Delhi, Lahore, 1967.

Kashyap, Subhash C. (ed) :

Maulana Abul Kalam Azad : A Centenary Volume, New Delhi. 1989.

Khan, M. Sharif :

Traditional Muslim Education and its Relevance, Aligarh, n.d.

Khan, Syed Ahmad :

An Essay on the Causes of the Indian Revolt, London, 1860.

Law, N.N :

Promotion of Learning in India, Delhi, 1973.

Lelyveld, David. S :

Aligarh's First Generation : Muslim Solidarity in British India, Princeton, 1978.

Mahmood, Syed :

A History of English Education in India (1781-1893). Aligarh, 1895.

Malik, Hafeez :

Moslem Nationalism in India and Pakistan, Washington. D.C. 1963.

Sir Syed Ahmad Khan and Muslim Modernisation in India and Pakistan, New York, 1980.

Mallick, 'Aziz al-Rahman :

British Policy and the Muslims in Bengal (1757-1856), Decca, 1961.

May. Lini :

The Evolution of Indo-Muslim Thought after 1857, Lahore, 1970.

Metcalf, Barbara Daly :

Islamic Revival in British India : Deoband (1860-1900), New Jersey, 1982.

Mujeeb, Muhammad :

The Indian Muslims, London, 1967.

Nadvat ul-'Ulamã' :

Nadvat ul-'Ulamã' : Its Genesis and Growth 1902, Lahore, n.d.

Nadvi, 'Abd us-Salam Kidwai :

85 Years of Nadvat ul-'Ulamã', Lucknow, 1975.

Nadvi, Syed Abu'l Hasan 'Ali :

Muhammad Rasul-Allãh, Lucknow, 1979.

Western Civilization : Islam and Muslim, Eng. tr. by Muhammad Asif Kidwai, Lucknow, 1969.

Qureshi, Ishtiaq Husain :

'Ulama in Politics, Delhi, 1985.

Rahman, M.F. :

The Bengali Muslim and English Education (1765-1835), Decca, 1973.

Ray, Krishnalal :

Education in Medieval India, Delhi, 1984.

Rizvi. Syed Mahboob :

History of the Dar ul-'Ulûm Deoband, (2 volumes) Eng. tr. Murtaz Husain F. Qureshi, Deoband, 1980, 1981 (Respectively).

Sharma, Kamlesh :

Role of Muslims in Indian Politics (1857-1947), Delhi, 1985

Sharma, S. R. :

The Crescent in India, Bombay, 1966.

Smith, W. Cantwell :

Modern Islam in India, London, 1946.

Tahir, Muhammad :

Encyclopaedic Survey of Islamic Culture, vol. III, New Delhi, 1997.

Umar, Muhammad :

Islam in Northern India During the Eighteenth Century, Delhi, 1993.

Vakil, K.S. :

Education in Indian Modern Period (1540-1940), Kolhapur, 1940.

ul-Wasey, Akhtar :

Education of Indian Muslims : A Study of the All India Muslim Educational Conference (1886-1947), New Delhi, 1977.

Wasti, Syed Razi :

The Political Triangle in India (1858-1924). Lahore, 1976.

Zakariya, Rafiq :

Rise of Muslims in Indian Politics, Bombay, 1970.

B : Urdu

'Abd ul-Bar, Ibn :

Al-'Ilm wa'l 'Ulamã', Urdu tr. 'Abd ur-Razzaq *Malihabadi,* Delhi, 1953.

'Abd ul-Ḥai, Syed :

Delhi Aur Uske Aṭrãf : Aik Safarnãmah Aur Roznãmah Unnîswi Ṣadî Ke Âkhir Meiṇ, Lucknow, 1958.

Islãmi 'Ulûm-o Funûn Hindustãn Meiṇ, Azamgarh, 1970.

Nuzhat ul-Khawãtir, Urdu, tr. Abu Yahyã Imran Khan Naushaharawi, Lahore, 1965.

Rudãd-e Jalsah (Majlis-e Nadvat ul-'Ulamã'), Lucknow, n.d.

'Abd ul-Ḥaq, Maulvi :

Marhûm Delhi Kãlej, Delhi, 1945.

'Abd ur-Raḥman, Syed Ṣabãh ud-Din:

Bazm-e Mamlûkiyah, Azamgarh, 1934.

Maulana Syed Sulaiman Nadvi Ki Taṣãnif, Azamgarh, 1988.

Aḥmad, Munshi Nehal :

Mukhtaṣar Kaifiyãt (Jalsah-e Panjum Nadvat ul-'Ulamã' 8-9 March 1998), Lucknow, n.d.

Aḥmad, Shãh Mo'in ud-Dîn :

Ḥayãt-e Sulaimãn, Azamgarh, 1973.

'Ali, Raḥman :

Tadhkerah-e 'Ulamã'-e Hind, Karachi, 1964.

All Inida Muslim Educational Conference :

Pachãs Sãlah Tãrikh, Badayun, 1937.

Anjum, Khaliq (comp) :

Syed Sulaiman Nadvi, Delhi, 1986.

Ansari, Muhammad Inayat-ullãh :

Tadhkerah-e 'Ulamã'-e Firangi Maḥal, Lucknow. n.d.

Badauni, Munshi Niẓãm ud-Din Ḥusian Niẓãmi :

Mukhtaṣar Kaifiyat Jalsah-e Shasham (26-28 March 1899) Kanpur, n.d.

Dairat ul-Ma'arif Islamiya, vol IX, Lahore, 1972.

Dairat ul-Ma'arif Islamiya, vol XI, Lahore, 1972.

al-Darimi, 'Abd-ullah bin 'Abd ur-Raḥman :

Sunan Darimi, Urdu tr. Muhammad Sa'id, Karachi, n.d.

Dasnuwi, 'Abd ul-Kawi :

Yãdgãr-e Sulaiman, Patna. 1984.

Dehlavi, Syed Abu Zafar :

Tablîgh, Calcutta, n.d.

al-Ghazali, Imam Abu Ḥamid :

Iḥyã 'Ulûm ud-Dîn, vol. I Eng. tr. Maulana Fazlul Karim, New Delhi, 1982.

Gilani, Manãzir Aḥsan :

Hindustãn Mein Musalmanoṇ Ka Niẓãm-e T'ãlim-o Tarbîyat (2 volumes), Delhi, 1944.

Swãneḥ Qãsimi, (3 volumes) Delhi, 1955-56.

al-Ḥasani, Syed Muḥammad :

Payãm-e Nadvat ul-'Ulamã', Dafter Ijlas Nadvat ul-'Ulamã', 1975.

Rudãd-e Chaman, Lucknow, 1976.

Sîrat Syed Muḥammad 'Ali Mongeri : Bãny-e Nadvat ul-'Ulamã', Lucknow, 1964.

Hashim, Syed :

Syed Sulaiman Nadvi : Ḥayãt Aur 'Ilmi Kãrnãme, Aligarh, 1995.

Ḥusain, Syed 'Âbid :

Musalmãnoṇ Ki T'alim Aur Jamiah, Delhi, 1925.

Ibn Mãjah, Muḥammad bin Yazîd :

Sunan-e Ibn Mãjãh, vol. I Urdu tr. 'Abd ul-Ḥakîm Khan Akhtar Shãhjahanpuri, New Delhi, 2nd ed. 1990.

Ibrahim, Maulvi Abu Muḥammad :

Maḍãmîm-e Araba', Lucknow, n.d.

Ikram, Shaikh Muhammad :

Mauj-e Kauthar, Delhi, 1998.

Rud-e Kauthar, Lahore, 1968.

Shibli Nãmah, Lahore, n.d.

Yãdgãr-e Shibli, Lahore, 1971.

Khalil ur-Raḥmãn Syed :

Khair Andeshî Nadvat ul-'Ulamã', Calcutta, n.d.

Khan, Iqtidar Muḥammad :

1947 Ke Bãd Hindustãn Mein Islãmi Tahrikeṇ, Delhi, 1995.

Khan, Shams Tabrez :

Sadre Yãr Jang, Lucknow, 1972.

Tãrikh-e Nadvat ul-'Ulamã', vol. II, Lucknow, 1983.

Khan Syed Ahmad :

Asãr us-Ṣanãdîd, Delhi, 1965.

Asbãb-e Baghãwat-e Hind, Karachi, 1957.

Kidwai, Muḥammad Sãlim :

Hindustãni Mufasserîn Aur Unkî Tafsîreṇ, New Delhi, 1973.

'Ilm-e Ḥadîth Aur Chand Aham Muḥaddethîn, New Delhi, 1981.

'Ulûm-e Islãmiyah Aur Hindustãni Musalmãn, Aligarh, 1990.

Miyan, Syed Muḥammad :

'Ulamã'-e Hind Ka Shãndar Mãḍi, vol. IV, Delhi, 1960.

Muḥammad Ghulãm :

Tadhkerah-e Sulaiman, Karachi, 1960.

Nadvat ul-'Ulamã', :

Dar ul-'Ulûm Nadvat ul-'Ulamã': Uskã Paighãm aur T'ãlimi Niẓãm 1982-83, Lucknow. n.d.

Dastûr ul-'Âmãl, Lucknow, n.d.

Dastûr ul-'Âmãl, (Majlis-e 'Ashã'at ul-Islãm),

Shahjahanpur, n.d.

Dastûr ul-'Âmãl, (Majlis-e Dãr ul-'Ulûm), Lucknow, 1919.

Dastûr ul-'Âmãl, Nadvat ul-'Ulamã' (Approved in the meeting of Managing Committee 1982), Lucknow, n.d

Karwãi Arkãn-e Nadvat ul-'Ulamã' (3 Rabi ul-Awwal 1312), Lucknow, n.d.

Karwãi Jalsãh-e Intiẓãmiyah Nadvat ul-'Ulamã' (August 1958), Lucknow, n.d.

Karwãi Jalsãh-e Intiẓãmiyah Nadvat ul-'Ulamã' (22 October 1984), Lucknow, n.d.

Karwãi Jalsãh-e Intiẓãmiyah Nadvat ul-'Ulamã' (19 September 1985), Lucknow, n.d.

Karwãi Jalsãh-e Intiẓãmiyah Nadvat ul-'Ulamã' (12 August 1992), Lucknow, n.d.

Maqãṣid Nadvat-ul 'Ulamã', Kanpur, n.d.

Maqãṣid Nadvat-ul 'Ulamã', Lucknow, n.d.

Niṣãb-e T'ãlîm Dãr ul-'Ulûm Nadvat ul-'Ulamã', 1952, Bhopal, n.d.

Nisãb-e T'ãlîm Ibtida, Mutawassit, Thãnvi, Lucknow, 1980.

Rudãd Nadvat ul-'Ulamã', 1894, Kanpur, n.d.

Rudãd Nadvat ul-'Ulamã', 1895, Kanpur, n.d.

Rudãd Nadvat ul-'Ulamã', 1896, Kanpur, n.d.

Rudãd Nadvat ul-'Ulamã', 1897, Kanpur, n.d.

Rudãd Nadvat ul-'Ulamã', 1910, Kanpur, n.d.

Rudãd Nadvat ul-'Ulamã', 1914, Lucknow, n.d.

Rudãd Nadvat ul-'Ulamã', 1915, Lucknow, n.d.

Rudãd Nadvat ul-'Ulamã', 1925, (held at Ambala) Lucknow, n.d.

Rudãd Nadvat ul-'Ulamã', 1926, Lucknow, n.d.

Rudãd Nadvat ul-'Ulamã', 1927, (held at Amritsar) Lucknow, n.d.

Sipãsnãmah -Arkãn-e Nadvat ul-'Ulamã', Lucknow, 1995.

Tajwîz Dãr ul-'Ulûm Nadvat ul-'Ulamã', (meeting held at Bareilly in 1895), Kanpur, n.d.

Nadvi, 'Abd ul-Bãri :

Barkley Aur Uskã Falsafah, Azamgarh, 1924.

Madhhab Aur 'Aqlîyyat, Aligarh, 1919.

Madhhab Aur Science, Lucknow, 1971.

Niẓãm-e Ṣalãh wa Iṣlãḥ, Karachi, 1962.

Tajdîd Taṣawwuf wa Sulûk, Lucknow, 1949.

Nadvi, 'Abd us-Salãm :

Al-Qaḍã fi'l-Islãm, Azamgarh, 1929.

Fiṭrat-e Niswãni, Pakistan, 1987.

Fuqarã'-e Islãm, Lahore, n.d.

Ḥukamã-e Islãm (2 volumes), Azamgarh, 1953-1956.

Ibn Khaldûn, Azamgarh, 1940.

Ibn Yamîn, Lahore, n.d.

Iqbãl-e Kãmil, Azamgarh, 1948.

Imãm Rãzi, Azamgarh, 1950.

Inqilãb ul-Umam, Azamgarh, 1917.

Sîrat 'Umar bin 'Abd ul-'Azîz, Azamgarh, 1920.

Shi'r ul-Hind (2 volumes), Azamgarh, 1926.

Tãrîkh-e Akhlãq-e Islãmî, (Vol. I), Azamgarh, 1939.

Tãrîkh-e Fiqh-e Islãmî, Azamgarh, 1927.

Tãrîkh ul-Haramayn us-Sharîfayn, Lahore, 1923.

Uswã-e Ṣaḥãbah, (2 Volumes), Azamgarh, 1922.

Uswã-e Ṣaḥãbiyãt, Azamgarh, 1922.

Nadvi, 'Abd us-Salãm. Kidwai :

Duniyã Islãm ke Pahle Aur Islãm Ke B'ãd, New Delhi, 1972.

Hamãri Bãdshãhi, Azamgarh, 1942.

Mithãli Hukûmrãṇ, Lucknow, 1955.

Muslim Aur Waqt Ke Taqãḍe, New Delhi, 1974.

Nadvat ul-'Ulamã' Ka Takhayyul Aur Paighãm, Lucknow, 1975.

Qur'ãn Majîd Ki Pahli Kitãb, Lucknow, n.d.

Qur'ãn Majîd Ki Dûsrî Kitãb, Lucknow, 1952.

T'ãlimãt-e Qur'ãn (2-volumes) New Delhi, 1960, 1961 (Respectively).

Nadvi, 'Abd ul-Qayyûm :

Tãrîkh-e Millat (3 volumes), Lahore, 1960.

Nadvi, 'Abu'l Ḥasanãt :

Hindustãn Kî Qãdîm Islãmî Darsgãheṇ, Azamgarh, 1936.

Nadvi, 'Abu Mas'ûd :

Aḥadîth-e Qudsiyah, New Delhi, 1994.

Nadvi, Ashfaq Aḥmad :

Jibrãn Khalîl Jibrãn, Lucknow, 1980.

Nadvi, Ḥãji Mo'în ud-Dîn :

Muhãjerîn, vol. I, Azamgarh, 1928.

Khulafa-e Rãshedîn, vol. I, Azamgarh, 1946.

Nadvi, Syed Muḥammad Ijtiba :

Tãrîkh-e Fikr-e Islãmi, New Delhi, 1998.

Nadvi, Muḥammad Iṣḥãq Jalis :

Tãrîkh Nadvat ul- 'Ulamã', vol I, Lucknow, 1983.

Nadvi, Jalîl Aḥsan :

Zãd-e Rah, Delhi, 1980.

Nadvi, Mas'ûd 'Alãm :

Dayãr-e Arab Meiṇ Chand Mãh, Karachi, 1950.

Makãtîb Syed Sulaiman Nadvi, Lahore, 1954.

Hindustãn Ki Pahli Islãmi Taḥrik, Delhi, 1977.

Muḥammad bin 'Abd ul-Wahãb : Eik Maẓlûm Aur Badnãm Muṣleḥ, Hyderabad, 1947.

Maulana Sindh Aur Unke Afkãr-o Khyãlãt Par Eik Naẓar, Patna, 1943.

Nadvi, Mas'ûd ur-Raḥman Khan :

Ḥayãt-e Imran, New Delhi, 1995.

Nadvi, Mati ur-Raḥman 'Auf :

Ashã'at-e Islãm Aur Tahrîk-e Nadvat ul-'Ulamã', Lucknow, 1997.

Nadvi, Muḥammad Ikram-ullãh Khan :

Viqãr-e Ḥayãt, Aligarh, 1925.

Nadvi, Muḥammad Ilyãs Moḥi ud-Dîn :

Muslim Duniyã : Mãḍí Aur Ḥal, Delhi, 1994.

Nadvi, Muḥammad Na'îm Siddiqui :

'Allãmah Syed Sulaimãn Nadvi, Lucknow, 1985.

Nadvi, Muḥammad Owais Nigrãmi :

T'ãlim ul-Qur'ãn, Lucknow, 1955.

Nadvi, Muḥammad 'Umair Siddiqui Daryabadi :

Tadhkerat ul-Fuqahã, Azamgarh, 1997.

Nadvi, Mujib-ullãh :

Ahl-e Kitãb Ṣaḥãbah wa Tãba'în, Azamgarh, 1951.

Fiqh-e Islãmi Aur Daur-e Jadîd Ke Masã'il, New Delhi, 1977.

Islãmi Fiqh, Delhi, 1957.

Khidmat-e Ḥadîth Mein Khwãtîn Kã Ḥiṣṣah, Azamgarh, 1994.

Taba' Tãba'în, vol. I, Azamgarh, 1959.

Thabût-e Rajm, Azamgarh, 1994.

Nadvi, Shah Mo'în ud-Din Aḥmad :

'Arab Kî Maujûdah Ḥukûmateṇ, Azamgarh, 1934.

Ḥayãt-e Sulaimãn, Azamgarh, 1973.

Islãm Aur 'Arabî Tamaddun, Azamgarh, 1952.

Muhãjerîn, (vol. II), Azamgarh, 1952.

Siyar us-Ṣaḥãbah, (vol. 6 & 7), Azamgarh, 1932

Taba'în, Azamgarh, 1937.

Tãrîkh-e Islãm (4 volumes), Azamgarh, 1939, 1949 (2nd ed.), 1944, 1945 (Respectively).

Nadvi, Muḥammad Jã'far Shãh Phulwãrwi :

Commercial Interest Kî Fiqhî Ḥaithîyat, Lahore, 1959.

Gulistãn-e Ḥadîth, Lahore, 1959.

Ijtihãd-e Masã'il, Lahore, 1956.

Izdiwãji Zindagî Ke Lîye Aham Qãnûni Tajãwiz, Lahore, 1955.

Islãm Aur Mausiqi, Lahore, 1934.

Mas'alah T'addud-e Izdîwãj, Lahore, 1959.

Maqãm-e Sunnat, Lahore, 1952.

Riyãḍ us-Sunnah, Lahore, 1954.

Nadvi, Syed Abu'l Ḥasan 'Ali :

Arkãn-e Araba', Lucknow, 1969.

'Aṣr-e Ḥãḍir Mein Dîn Kî Tafhîm Wa Tashrîh, Lucknow, 1978.

Dãr ul-'Ulûm Nadvat ul-' Ulamã'-1992, Lucknow, n.d.

Dastûr-e Ḥayãt, Lucknow, 1983.

Dayãr-e Kãbul Se Dãyar-e Yarmûk Tak, Lucknow, 1974.

Faith verses Materialism, Lucknow, 1970.

Ḥaḍrat Maulana 'Faḍl ur-Raḥmãn Ganj Murãdãbãdi, Lucknow, 1958.

Ḥaḍrat Maulana Ilyãs Aur Unkî Dînî D'ãwat, Delhi, n.d.

Ḥayãt-e 'Abd ul-Ḥai, Delhi, 1970.

Hindustãni Musalmãn, Lucknow, 1972.

Islam and the World, Lucknow, 1961.

Islamic Concept of Prophethood, Lucknow, 1979.

Khutbãt-e Istiqbãliya, Lucknow, 1975.

Muslim in India, Lucknow, 1960.

Muṭãl'ah Qur'ân Kî Uṣûl wa Mabãdi, Lucknow, 1981.

Nadvat ul-'Ulamã' : Eik Dabistãn-e Fikr Eik Rahnumã T'ãlimî Taḥrîk, Lucknow, 1975.

Nuqûsh-e Iqbãl, Lucknow, 1976.

Purãn-e Chirãgh (2 volumes), Lucknow, 1975, 1980 (Respectively).

Qadianism : A Critical Study, Lucknow, 1974.

Sharq Awsaṭ Kî Dãiry, Lucknow, 1971.

Sirãt Syed Aḥmad Shahîd, Lucknow, 1939.

Sohbat-e Bã Ahl-e Dil, Lucknow, 1977.

Swãneḥ Ḥaḍrat Maulana 'Abd ul-Qãdir Rãipuri, Lucknow, 1963.

Tãrikh-e D'ãwat-o 'Azîmat (5 volumes) Lucknow, 1954, 1957, 1962, 1980, 1984 (Respectively).

Nadvi, Syed Abu Zafar :

Gujrat Ki Tamadduni Tãrîkh Musalmanoṇ Ke 'Ahad Meiṇ, Azamgarh, 1962.

Mukhtaṣar Tãrîkh-e Hind, Azamgarh, 1936.

Tadhkerah 'Allãmah Shaikh Muḥammad bin Ṭãhir Paṭṭani, Delhi, 1954.

Tãrîkh-e Gujrãt, Delhi, 1976.

Tãrîkh-e Sindh, Azamgarh, 1947.

Nadvi, Syed Ḍiyã ul-Ḥasan :

'Arabi Adab Dayãr-e Ghair Meiṇ, Hyderabad, 1981.

Nadvi, Syed Iḥtishãm Aḥmad :

'Aṣr-e Ḥãḍir Ki Islãmi Tahrîkeṇ, Aligarh, 1998.

Nadvi, Syed Najîb Ashraf :

Lughãt-e Gujrî, Bombay, 1962.

Muqaddimah Ruq'ãt-e 'Alamgiri, Azamgarh, n.d.

Nadvi, Syed Riyãsat 'Ali :

'Ahd-e Islãmî Kã Hindustãn, Patna, 1950.

Islãmî Niẓãm-e T'ãlim, Azamgarh, 1984.

Tãrîkh-e Andalus, (4 volumes), Azamgarh, 1950.

Tãrikh-e Ṣiqilliyah, (2 volumes), Azamgarh, 1933, 1935 (Respectively)

Nadvi, Syed Sulaiman :

'Arab-o Hind Ke Ta'lluqãt, Hyderabad, 1962.

'Araboṇ Kî Jahãzrani, Azamgarh, 1935.

Bahãdur Khwãtin-e Islãm, Azamgarh, 1986.

Barîd-e Farhang, Azamgarh, 1986.

Ḥayãt-e Mãlik, Karachi, 1920.

Ḥayãt-e Shibli, Azamgarh, 1943.

Khayyãm, Azamgarh, 1933.

Khutbãt-e Madras, Azamgarh, 1937.

Lughãt-e Jadidah, Azamgarh, 1936.

Makãtib Shibli (2 volumes), Azamgarh, 1916, 1917

(Respectivly).

Maqãlãt-e Shibli (3rd volume), Azamgarh, 1955.

Raḥmat-e 'Âlam, Azamgarh, 1972.

Sair-e Afghãnistãn, Hyderabad, 1945.

Sîrat-e 'Âishah, Azamgarh, 1920.

Sîrat un-Nabî (vol. 3-7), Azamgarh, 1924, 1932, 1935, 1938, 1980.

Tãrikh-e Arḍ ul-Qur'ãn (2 volumes), Azamgarh, 1915, 1918 (Respectively).

Yãd-e Raftgãn, Azamgarh, 1986.

Nadvi, Taqi ud-Dîn Maẓahari :

Fann-e Asmã' ur-Rijãl, Gujrat, 1969.

Muḥaddethîn-e Uẓẓãm Aur Unke 'Ilmî Kãrnãme, Lucknow, 1966.

Nãnauvtavi, Muḥammad Qãsim and Sir Syed Aḥmad Khan :

Tasfiyat ul-'Aqã'id, Deoband, n.d.

No'mãni, Shibli :

Khutbãt-e Shibli, Azamgarh, 1941.

Safarnãmah Rome wa Miṣr Wa Shãm, Azamgarh, 1940.

Qãsimi, Muḥammad Ṭayyab :

Âzãd Hind Kã Khãmosh Rahnuma, Deoband, 1957.

Dãr ul-'Ulûm Deoband Kî Ṣad Sãlah zindagi, Deoband, 1968.

Rizvi, Syed Maḥbub :

Dãr ul -'ulum Deoband ki T'ãlîmi Khuṣuṣiyãt, Deoband, 1950.

Tãrikh-e Deoband, Deoband,1952.

Sherwãni, Ḥabîb ur-Raḥman Khan :

Nadvat ul-'Ulamã' : Is 'Ahd-e Inqilãb Meiṇ Uskã Kãm Aur Uskã Paighãm, Lucknow, 1955.

Ustãz ul-'Ulamã', Aligarh, 1937.

Siddiqui, Afaq (comp) :

Aurang-e Sulaimãn, Karachi, 1985.

Siddiqui, Atiq Aḥmad :

Sir Syed Aḥmad Khan : Ek Siyãsî Muṭãla'h, New Delhi, 1977.

(e.d) : *Syed Sulaimãn Nadvi*, Aligarh, 1985.

al-Tirmidhî, Abu 'Isa Muḥammad bin 'Isa :

Jãme' Tirmidhî, vol. 2, Urdu tr, Badî' uz-Zaman, Delhi, 1983.

BIBLIOGRAPHY

Articles : (A) English :

'Abd al-Subhan :

"Nawab Abd al-Latif (1824-1893) : Pioneer of Muslim Awakening in the Bengal", *Majallah ut-Tarikh ul-Islami,* 1:1, New Delhi, 1995.

'Alam, M. Shafiqui :

"Nawab Abd al-Latif's Contribution to the Education of the Muslims of Bengal", *Journal of Asiatic Society of Bengaladesh,* Dhaka, 39 : 1, 1994.

Ashraf, Syed 'Ali :

"Education, Society and Culture in Muslim Bengal (1857-1947)", *al-Islam,* Dhaka, 7:3, 1991.

'Azmi, Niyaz Ahmad :

"Shibli on Muslim Education and Politics", *Islam and the Modern Age,* 25:3, August, New Delhi, 1994.

Burke, Jaffery. C :

"A Critique of the Aligarh and Deoband Movement", *Islam and the Modern Age,* 25:2, New Delhi, 1994.

Greaves, R.A :

"India 1857 : A Mutiny or a War of Independence? The Muslim Perspective", *Islamic Studies,* 35:1, Pakistan, 1996.

Kaur, Kuldeep :

"Relevance of Madrasa Education in the Modern Age", *Islam and the Modern Age, 25:2,* New Delhi, 1994.

Khan, A. Sattar :

"A Critical Appraisal of Dar al-'Ulum Deoband and its leadership" *Journal of the Research Society of Pakistan,* 31:4, Lahore, Pakistan, 1994.

"Indian Police Raid on Nadvat al-'Ulama', Lucknow (Centre of Islamic Studies in India)" *The Muslim World League Journal,* 22:7, Saudi Arabia, 1994.

Khan A. Sattar and Anwar Zulfiqar :

"The Movement of Shah Waliullah and its Political Impact", *Journal of Research Society of Pakistan*, 32:4, Lahore, Pakistan, 1995.

Khan, Zafar al-Islam :

"Syed Ahmad Shahid (d. 1246/183) and the Mujahedin Movement in Modern India", *Majallah ut-Tarikh ul-Islami,* 1:1, New Delhi, 1995.

Mohi al-Din, Syed Ghulam :

"Modern Education and the Educational Problems of

the Indian Muslims", *Muslim Education Quarterly 2:, Islamic Academy,* Cambridge, U.K. 1985.

Al-Nadvi, S.M. Wazeh Rashid :

"Traditional Muslim Education in India; Origin, Curriculur, Revision and the Present Day Condition", *Muslim Education Quartely*, 2:4, Islamic Academy Cambridge, U.K. 1985.

Pickthal, M :

"Muslim Education", *Islamic Culture*, 1:1 Hyderabad, 1927.

Rawlinson, H.G. :

"Sir Syed Ahmad Khan", *Islamic Culture,* 4:3 Hyderabad, 1930.

Robb, P.G. :

"Muslim Identity and Separatism in India", *Bulletin of the School of Oriental and African Studies,* 54:1, London, 1991.

Al-Taftazani, Abu'l Wafa Al-Ghuneimi :

"Islamic Education : Its Principles and Aims", *Muslim Education Quartely,* 4:1, Islamic Academy Cambridge, U.K. 1986.

Troll, Christion. W. :

"Muhammad Shibli No'mani (1857-1914) and the Reform of Muslim Religious Education", *Islam and the Modern Age,* 24:1, New Delhi, 1993.

B - URDU

Aḥmad, Maftûn :

"Shibli Aur Nadvat ul-'Ulamã'", *Nigãr,* 63:3, Lucknow, 1953.

Ansari, Muḥammad Iqbal :

"Nadvat ul-'Ulamã' : Ek Dînî Wa T'ãlîmî Taḥhrîk", (3-Parts), *Islãm Aur 'Aṣr-e Jadîd,* April, July, New Delhi, 1975.

Ansari, Muḥammad Raḍa :

"Jashn-*e* Nadvah", *Âjkal,* 2:6, January, New Delhi, 1976.

Ansari, Sa'îd. :

"Maulana Shibli Aur Iṣlãḥ-*e* T'ãlîm", *Jamia*, 5:1, Delhi, 1965.

Ḥashim, Syed Muḥammad :

"Allãmah Shibli", *Fikr-o Naẓar* (Nãmvãrãn-*e* Aligarh) (Pahla Karwaṇ), 22:1, 2, 3, 1985.

Al-Islãm, Khurshîd :

"Allãmah Shibli", *Fikr-o Naẓar* (Nãmvãrãn-e Aligarh (Pahla Karwaṇ), 22:1, 2, 3, 1985.

Jaisi, Kabir Aḥmad :

"Dãr ul-Muṣannefin Ke Bihãri Rufaqa", *T'ãmîr-e Insãniyat,* 4: 6, 7, Lahore, 1958.

Nadvi, 'Abd ul-Halim :

"Rudãd 85 Sãlãh Jashn-*e* T'ãlîmî Nadvat ul-Ulamã'", *Islãm Aur 'Aṣr-e Jadîd,* 8 : January, New Delhi, 1976.

Nadvi, Muḥammad Na'îm Siddiqui :

"Pachãsi Sãlãh Jashn-*e* T'ãlîmî "Nadvat ul-'Ulamã'" *Ma'ãrif,* 116:5, November, Azamgarh, 1975.

Rizvi, Syed Maḥbub :

"Maulana Nãnautavi : Sir Syed Ki Naẓar Mein", *Burhãn,* 17:2, 1946.

JOURNALS

Adîb, **:** 'Abd us-Salãm Number, Aligarh, 1961.

Adîb, **:** Shibli Number, Aligarh, 1960.

Fikr-o Naẓar, **:** Shibli Number, Aligarh, 1960.

Fikr-o Naẓar, **:** Sir Syed Number, Aligarh, 1966.

Mãhanãmah Rafiq-*e *Manzil :

T'ãlîmî Taḥrîkãt wa Shakhṣîyãt (special Number), May June, 1997, Delhi,

T'ãlîmî Rahnumã (Special Number), December, 1994, Delhi-

Ma'ãrif, :

Special issue on Syed Sulaiman Nadvi, May, 1955.

Azamgarh,

Ar-Riyãḍ **:**

Special issue on Syed Sulaiman Nadvi, March, 1954.

Karachi.

Al-Nadvah :	**vol.**	**No.**	**Year**
	1	1, 2, 3, 4	1905
	2	1, 5, 11	1906
	3	1, 2, 8, 10, 11	1907
	5	7, 9	1908
	6	1, 3, 5, 12	1909
	7	1	1910
	9	1	1912

Al-Hilal	16, 21, 28	January,	1914
	4, 11	February,	1914
	4, 11, 18, 25	March,	1914
	18, 15, 22, 29	April,	1914
	6, 13, 20, 27	May,	1914
	2, 4	June	1914
	1. 22, 29	July	1914
	5, 12, 19,	August	1914
	9, 30	September	1914

Tahdhib ul-Akhlãq, Sir Syed Number, Aligarh, 1998.

T'ãmîr-e-Ḥayãt :

10 December	vo. 12,	No. 3.	1974
25 May-10 June	vol. 12.	No. 14, 15	1975
10-25 October	vol. 12,	No. 23, 24	1975
10-25 November}	vol. 13.	No. 1, 2, 3, 4,	1975
10-25 December}	vol. 13.	No. 1, 2, 3, 4,	1975
10 January	vol. 13,	No. 5.	1976
10 March	vol. 21,	No. 9.	1984
25 March}	vol. 21,	No. 10, 11, 12,	1984
10 April}	vol. 21,	No. 10, 11, 12,	1984
25 April}	vol. 21,	No. 10, 11, 12,	1984
10 June	vol.21,	No. 15,	1984
25 June	vol.21,	No. 16,	1984

10 July } Special No. on Maulana Syed Abu'l

25 August} Hasan 'Ali Nadvi — 2001

INDEX

A

B

E

H

I

N

T

U